Anton
    The Politics of State
Expenditure in Illinois

THE POLITICS
OF STATE
EXPENDITURE
IN ILLINOIS

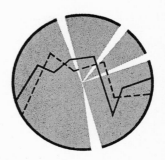

The Politics
of State
Expenditure
in Illinois

THOMAS J. ANTON

University of Illinois Press, Urbana and London, 1966

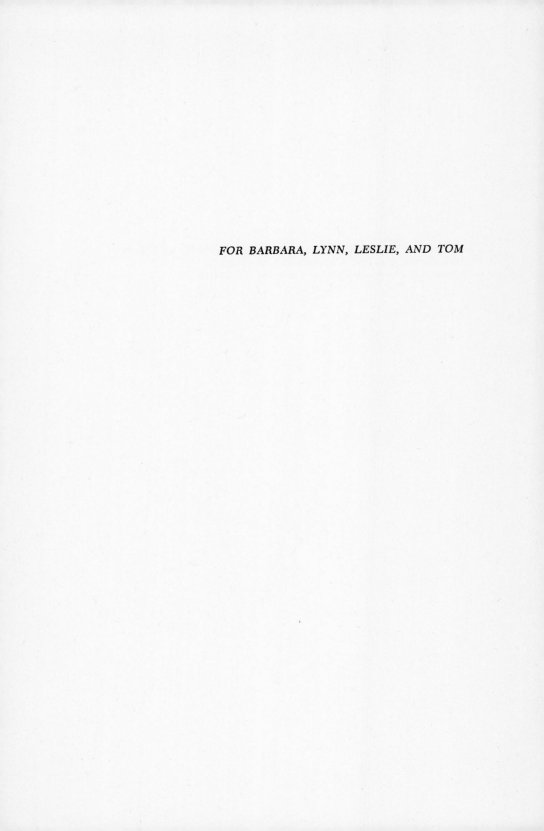

FOR BARBARA, LYNN, LESLIE, AND TOM

ACKNOWLEDGMENTS

Readers of this study will have little difficulty in recognizing the large debt I owe to the work of Talcott Parsons, Edward A. Shils, Richard C. Snyder, Robert K. Merton, and the late C. Wright Mills. Both the organization and the analysis of the material presented here are based primarily upon ideas developed by these men. I am pleased, therefore, to record my gratitude for the stimulation provided me by their work.

My debt to various officials of the State of Illinois is at least as large. Despite a heavy schedule, Governor Otto Kerner graciously found time to discuss state finances with me, as did former Governor William G. Stratton and officials of eighteen state agencies. Director of Finance James A. Ronan and Assistant to the Director T. R. Leth not only discussed their activities with me on numerous occasions, but also made it possible for me to obtain data that would not otherwise have been available.

I am particularly indebted to five officials whose knowledge, patience, and cooperativeness helped to shape my thinking about Illinois state finance. Mr. Edward F. Merten, Deputy Director for Administrative Services in the Department of Mental Health, discussed his work with me on several occasions, tolerated my presence during departmental budget hearings, and gave me the benefit of his critique of many of my ideas. Former Assistant Secretary of State Robert G. Cronson also tolerated my presence during budget hearings for the Office of Secretary of State, argued with me about my conclusions, and generally helped to keep my thinking in line with ascertainable fact. The significance of many of the activities discussed in the following pages would not have been apparent to me were it not for the unfailing good nature and cooperation of Mr. Vernon L. Shontz, Jr., of the Department of Finance and Mr. Francis A. Whitney, Executive Director of the Illinois Budgetary Commission, both of whom served as teachers and critics for a period of several years. Finally, State Representative John C. Parkhurst gave generously of his time and knowledge before, during, and after two legislative sessions. Since, with one exception, these men have been kind enough to comment upon all or portions of an earlier draft of this study, I know that they disagree more or less strongly with many of my interpretations. Nevertheless, I am extremely grateful to all of them for helping me to order what seemed initially to be an extraordinarily confusing set of facts.

The Institute of Government and Public Affairs of the University of Illinois provided the environment within which the study was conceived and the resources for carrying it out. My colleagues Gilbert Y. Steiner, Director of the Institute, and Samuel K. Gove, sometime Acting Director, were helpful in countless ways at every stage of the project, but were especially helpful as critics of both my writing and, what is more important, my thinking. My other colleagues Glenn W. Fisher, Tom Page, and James H. Andrews took the trouble to read the entire manuscript and offered valuable suggestions for improvement. Similarly valuable comments on the entire manuscript were offered by Phillip Monypenny, Clyde F. Snider, James G. Coke, Herbert Gamberg, Everett G. Smith, Jr., and Aaron Wildavsky, while Denis G. Sullivan and Joseph M. Heikoff criticized smaller portions of the manuscript. Kathleen Harris struggled through a jungle of state documents to produce the table which appears as an appendix to the book and performed a variety of other chores during the course of a summer's work. Mrs. Jean Baker, Miss Loretta Ward, and Miss Doris Falk translated my handwriting into a series of drafts with high efficiency. All of these people helped, in one fashion or another, to save me from errors of fact or of logic; I am indebted to each of them.

None of these people, however, should be held responsible for the use made of their respective contributions. I alone am responsible for the statements of fact and the interpretations of fact presented in the following pages.

CONTENTS

INTRODUCTION

On April 19, 1961, Governor Otto Kerner told members of the Illinois legislature that the state had run out of cash. The state government, he said, "has substantially no general revenue funds to pay the day-to-day bills of the state. We must borrow money to replenish the working balance," he continued, "and, in addition, we will have to make up a projected cash deficit of $12 million." To deal with these problems and to provide sufficient funds to operate the state during the 1961-63 fiscal period, the Governor proposed tax measures designed to produce additional revenues in the amount of $378 million. Characteristically, the legislature did not begin to deal seriously with either the budget or the tax proposals until the last month (June) of the biennial legislative session. Not so characteristically, legislative action on these matters was marked by all-night filibusters, fist fights, and other forms of physical violence leading ultimately to the use of state troopers to maintain order within legislative halls. When the session had ended, appropriations finally approved by the legislature were shown to have exceeded approved revenues by some $90 million—a situation which forced Governor Kerner to veto many of these appropriations and to take other steps during the latter half of 1961 to reduce the outflow of state funds. These measures were only partially effective and by the end of the year it began to appear that available revenues might not be sufficient to meet daily expenses, let alone finance a full two-year biennium. The crisis in state finance, Illinois version, had arrived.

By 1961, of course, fiscal crises in state governments were becoming commonplace; indeed, the well-publicized troubles of one state had added a new word to the vocabulary of state finance— "Michiganized." But if few competent observers of Illinois politics were surprised at the advent of crisis in 1961, many were nevertheless distressed by the actions which had produced this result. Veteran newspaper reporters were generally agreed that the 1961 legislative session was the most unruly session in memory, while one participant-observer described the procedures which led to tax and expenditure decisions as chaotic. "As far as I could tell," this participant reported, "final decisions were made by two men in the Governor's private bathroom on the night before the legislative session ended." Surely these kinds of actions were not normal. Of what, then, did normal actions consist? What persons are typically involved in decisions to spend state money? What procedures are followed? What kinds of criteria are applied in making decisions, and with what effects? In short, just how are decisions to spend state money made? Answers to these kinds of questions were not available in 1961, despite their obvious political importance and despite their relevance to the crisis which now confronted the state. This study, begun in the fall of 1961, represents a response to such questions.

The inquiry was organized around two predominant goals. First, I wanted to describe the behavior of persons involved in the determination of state expenditures in as much detail and with as much accuracy as possible, within the always-present limits of time, money, and physical possibility. Pursuit of this goal led to a decision to invest much of my research effort in the observation of actions which occurred in the period October, 1962, through June, 1963, when expenditure determinations were made for the 1963-65 fiscal period. Though an initial round of interviews with various state officials, conducted largely during the spring of 1962, had produced valuable information, there was nothing available to provide a check on that information. Records of hearings conducted by state or legislative agencies do not exist in Illinois, while official legislative journals present little more than tabulations of roll call votes. Beginning in October, 1962, therefore, I observed hearings conducted by two of the larger state agencies, and I attended most of the hearings conducted by the Illinois Budgetary Commission and many of the hearings scheduled by the House and Senate Appropriations committees. Finally, I spent a good many days in the House and Senate galleries observing action centering on appropriation bills. Not the least of the advantages derived from spending so much time in the state capital was the opportunity to engage in innumerable conversations with the persons involved in decision-making. In many cases such conversations were off the record and, for that reason, have not been reported in the body of this work. Nevertheless, such discussions have contributed a great deal to my understanding and are reflected, if not acknowledged, in the pages that follow.

My second major goal was to present the data in such a way that its relevance to larger bodies of social theory would be apparent, particularly to my social science colleagues. I have attempted to do this in terms of three central concepts: decision-making, role, and social system.

Use of the decision-making concept[1] is designed to focus attention upon the processes by which choices to spend state money are determined. Operationally, the statements and figures found in such documents as budget estimates, the budget book, appropriation bills, and gubernatorial veto messages are taken here to represent a certain class of decisions (or outcomes), namely, those that deal with the allocation of financial resources. A major purpose of the study will be to elucidate the patterns of action according to which such decisions are produced. In describing the relationship between actions and decisions, I assume the existence of such a relationship but I assume nothing about the content of a decision, or series of decisions. Instead, for each case, or series of cases, I seek to show the meaning of the thing decided for each of the persons or groups involved. Nor do I assume anything about the quality of the actions which produce decisional outcomes. Actions leading to decisions may be planned or accidental, calculated or mechanical, conscious or unthinking. The quality of the actions taken is determined on the bases of evidence available from interviews and from observation.

Conceptually, my presentation of this evidence will focus on decision-making *roles*, rather than decision-making individuals, with the various roles viewed as constituent parts of a larger *social system*.[2] Empirically, the concept "role" refers to actions

[1] My understanding and use of this concept is based, in most respects, on the work of Professor Richard C. Snyder. For a good introduction to this work, see his "A Decision-Making Approach to the Study of Political Phenomena," in Roland Young, ed., *Approaches to the Study of Politics* (Evanston, Ill.: Northwestern University Press, 1958), pp. 3-38.

[2] Though the literature on roles and social systems grows larger every day, I remain most indebted here to Talcott Parsons and Edward Shils, eds., *Toward a General Theory of Action* (New York: Harper Torchbook Edition, 1962), pp. 3-27, 53-109, and 190-233.

taken by individuals which are patterned (i.e., occur repeatedly) according to the expectations of both the role-player and others with whom he interacts. Since actions define roles, the personality characteristics of individual role-players may vary greatly without altering the content of the role in any significant way. In analyzing a system of roles, therefore, it is not necessary to probe into the personality characteristics of role-players. One can understand the role of the policeman on the corner, for example, whether or not one understands the psychology of the individual wearing the uniform. Such an analysis would explicate the expectations of both the policeman and those with whom he interacts concerning the proper boundaries of the policeman's role, and the actions resulting from such expectations. Mutual anticipation of legitimate action provides the basis for patterned behavior which, in turn, serves as the focus of the analyst's research. Though it is always individuals who are observed in action, it is the action, and not the individual, which is subjected to analysis.[3]

Note that roles are specified in terms of actions that can or cannot be taken by role-incumbents and that such specifications are mutually anticipated. Because roles are specified in terms of legitimate actions (i.e., "right" as opposed to "wrong" actions), their content is based ultimately on value propositions concerning what is "good" or "bad." And, because roles are built upon shared expectations, these value propositions also must be widely shared. According to this approach, then, roles cannot be examined without simultaneously examining the shared values upon which roles are structured. Where shared values and role expectations exist among a number of individuals, a social system is said to exist. The pages that follow will describe and analyze the social system which has developed around the problem of allocating the financial resources of the State of Illinois.

---

[3] In emphasizing actions here, I do not mean to slur over the useful distinction between role expectations and role behavior. Indeed, it was the possibility of conflict between expectation and behavior, among other things, which led me to an extended period of observation after gathering information concerning role expectation. The following chapters incorporate both perspectives in analyzing roles. For a useful analysis of role, see Daniel J. Levinson, "Role, Personality, and Social Structure in the Organizational Setting," reprinted in Neil J. Smelser and William T. Smelser, eds., *Personality and Social Systems* (New York: John Wiley and Sons, Inc., 1963), pp. 428-441.

From the preceding discussion it should be apparent that my principal purpose here is to produce a work of scholarship. That is, I will be seeking to describe, as fully and as objectively as I can, the operations of an identified social system as it deals with a stated range of problems. However, the reader should not on that account infer that my work is in any sense "value free." As an American, most of whose professional training has been in the field of political science, I am committed to the belief that democratic government is the best form of government. Connected to this general sentiment is a commitment to two subsidiary values which have particular relevance to this study: reason and responsibility. By reason I mean that quality of an official action which renders it comprehensible, by whatever standard, to both the official and the citizen. Lest I be misunderstood, I do not believe that every public official can or should act with the wisdom of Solomon, nor do I believe that public acts should accord with my own preferences in order to be described as reasonable. I mean only to state my belief that, in a democracy, public officials should have some minimal idea of what it is they are doing and why and that they should be able to give public expression to such ideas.

By responsibility I mean that quality of a political system which renders it amenable to change by the citizenry or by representatives of the citizenry. Clearly this implies some minimal level of public knowledge of what is going on within the system, as well as some evaluative standards by which to judge political acts. More significantly as far as this work is concerned, it implies the existence of some mechanism or mechanisms, within the political system itself, for generating and disseminating public knowledge of official acts. Where such mechanisms do not exist, or where they are faulty, neither the political system nor the officials within it can hope to act in a responsible manner.

The reader is forewarned, then, that my commitment to these values will affect the judgments I make in the following pages. Many of the issues raised, particularly in the latter portions of the book, would not have occurred to me without this commitment and many of my interpretations of fact would have been different in its absence. On the other hand, I have tried very hard to present a relatively comprehensive description of events, according to a reasonably self-conscious scheme of analysis. At the very least, therefore, the reader should be in a position to fully appreciate the bases for my conclusions. Indeed, I am hopeful that readers who feel compelled to discount some or many of my conclusions will be able to find evidence to support their particular points of view within these very pages. Should that occur, it would demonstrate that I have succeeded in being objective, even though I have not attempted to be completely "neutral."

One final word. By the time this material appears in print almost three years will have elapsed from the end of the period (July, 1963) in which the actions described here took place. In the meantime another General Assembly, this one with House members elected on an at-large basis, has met, and another series of expenditure decisions have been made for the State of Illinois. Have any changes which have taken place since 1963 affected the conclusions offered here? During the period January through June, 1965, I spent a number of days in Springfield, talking to and observing participants in the system in an effort to determine an answer to this question. In that time I neither saw nor heard anything which would lead me to introduce any major modifications in the conclusions set forth in these pages, although some adjustments in the distribution of power seem to have occurred. I am satisfied that the system continues to operate according to rules which are essentially the same as those described here.

CHAPTER ONE

THE SYSTEM
AND ITS
ENVIRONMENT

Governmental decisions are never made in a vacuum; they are made by people working in and for organizations. Within the organizational environment people pursue goals they would not otherwise pursue, according to rules of behavior they would not otherwise follow. Indeed, an organization may be defined as a group of people pursuing the same goal, or similar goals, according to a common set of rules. Precisely because both goals and rules are held in common by the organizational membership, behavior patterns become standardized and therefore predictable. Individuals may accept goals with more or less intensity, or they may interpret rules more or less strictly, but insofar as their organizational behavior is concerned, there tends to be little variation from standard patterns. To the extent that governmental decisions are organizational decisions, therefore, we are likely to understand them best by searching out the goals and rules which structure decision-making behavior in governmental organizations.

To say that this behavior is structured by goals and rules is to say very little, for people in most organizations—including governments—make a great many different kinds of decisions. This is particularly the case if the organization is both large and complex, as is the Illinois state government. Well over 70,000 people are employed by the State of Illinois to conduct a great variety of activities, ranging from the regulation of horse races to the operation of large universities. Such varied activities suggest that people in the state organization pursue a number of goals, rather than a single goal, according to many sets of rules, rather than a uniform set of rules. From a systematic point of view this means that this large and complex organization, like others of its kind, is composed of a great many decision-making systems, organized around particular purposes and operating according to differentiated sets of procedures. The pages that follow will be concerned primarily with just one of these systems, namely, the system organized around the problem of making decisions, on behalf of the entire state organization, to allocate state financial resources.

Note that this formulation provides two distinct levels of analysis. At one level we will be talking about the actions of a *system* which produce decisions to spend state money. At a higher level we will also be talking about the state *organization,* which is made up of a great number of decision-making systems in addition to the expenditure system that will be our principal focus. Decisions produced by the expenditure system are extremely important to the organization, for without them the organization could not continue to carry on its many activities. Moreover, the problem around which this system of action is organized—i.e., resource allocation—is a problem common to all organizations. To the extent that we can understand the manner in which the state organization meets this particular problem through the actions of the expenditure system, therefore, we will have provided a foundation for useful comparisons between this and other organizations, as well as between this and other decision-making systems. The importance of the system to the organization and the potential significance of comparisons with other organizations and systems both require that a clear distinction between these two levels of analysis be kept in mind.

Our first job, then, is to identify the participants in the system. Fortunately, this is a relatively easy task, for the Illinois state government, in addition to being large and complex, is also a formal organization, which is to say that most of its activities are conducted according to procedures which are prescribed in written documents. Since decisions to spend money are among the most important decisions made in the state organization, it is not surprising that instructions for making such decisions are written out in considerable detail. Thus the state Constitution establishes the biennium as the basic fiscal period, states the conditions under which money can be drawn from the state treasury, and assigns responsibility for meeting those conditions to certain officials. Each of these provisions is amplified by statutory rules which assign further responsibilities and specify permissible procedures. These written directives do not reveal anything about how officials perform their duties, nor do they necessarily provide an exhaustive list of participants in the system. But they do indicate the officials who *must* be involved in expenditure decisions, the kinds of forms which are utilized in making such decisions, and what officials are supposed to do with these forms. All of these provisions must be understood before we can hope to understand the operations of the system.

CONSTITUTIONAL LIMITS

By Constitutional directive, no money can be drawn from the state treasury "except in pursuance of an appropriation made by law . . ." (Art. IV, Sec. 17). The *appropriation* is thereby established as the basic form in which decisions to allocate resources are to be cast. This form has several important qualities. To begin with, an appropriation is *not* a grant of money; it is a grant of *authority to expend* up to a given sum of money for specified purposes. Agencies granted authority to expend a stated sum are not required to do so. If the appropriation exceeds their needs, or if organizational superiors (such as a governor) order a cutback in spending, agencies may simply use up less money than is authorized by appropriation. Indeed, precisely because the appropriation deals with authority rather than money, an absence of funds from which to draw appropriations effectively prohibits any expenditure. Thus, even a grant of authority to spend is meaningless unless funds are available.

The authority granted in appropriations does not continue indefinitely, however. Each General Assembly is directed by the Constitution to provide all appropriations necessary to support the expenses of the government "until the expiration of the first fiscal quarter after the adjournment of the next regular session . . ." (Art. IV, Sec. 18), at which time all appropriations from state funds "shall end." Again, this does not mean that unspent money from existing appropriations must be returned to the treasury, for money never leaves the treasury unless and until an authorized expenditure is made. It means only that all authority to spend from existing appropriations ceases to exist, or lapses, at that time. Funds that remain available as a result of "lapsed" appropriations are simply carried over as assets available for expenditure during the next biennium.[1]

In setting forth these provisions to regulate the expenditure of state funds, the Constitution also assigns responsibilities to specific agencies and officials. As already noted, the General Assembly is obligated to provide the appropriations necessary to support state activities, appropriations which can only be "made by law." But the General Assembly need not work in the dark in this matter, for the Governor is directed to "present estimates of the amount of money required to be raised by taxation for all purposes" (Art. V, Sec. 7). Moreover, all state officers, officers of the Executive Department, and officers of all state institutions must submit annual or semiannual reports to the Governor (Art. V, Secs. 20, 21). Should these reports prove insufficient, the Governor is further authorized to require information from officers of the Executive Department "upon any subject relating to the condition, management and expenses of their respective offices" (Art. V, Sec. 21). Within the relatively brief confines of the Constitution, then, four different officials or agencies are established as participants in the appropriations process: the General Assembly, the Governor, departmental officers, and state officers.[2]

FROM "APPROPRIATING" TO "BUDGETING"

Although these provisions were adopted in the Constitution of 1870 (which is still in effect), no attempt to follow them very

---

[1] These provisions have been interpreted to mean that charges against appropriations can be incurred through the end of June of the second year of the biennium. Payment of charges against biennial appropriations, however, can be made through the end of September of the second year of the biennium. The period July 1 to September 30 is known as the "lapse period," during which no new charges against old appropriations can be incurred, and all charges made through the preceding June 30 must be paid in full. Funds remaining after these payments are the funds which are said to "lapse."

[2] The Constitution also assigns special responsibility to the Auditor and the Treasurer for the issuance of warrants pursuant to appropriations. Since these responsibilities have to do with methods of expenditure rather than decisions to spend, they will be ignored here.

closely appears to have been made, perhaps because they were far too general to be of any use. Thus, it was not until 1915 that the Governor presented the first executive estimate of the taxes required to support state operations. In the meantime, individual state agencies negotiated their appropriations through the good offices of individual legislators or, sometimes, legislative committees. Unspecified lump-sum appropriation acts were the characteristic result of such negotiations, conducted on a piecemeal, agency-by-agency basis. Since little attention was paid to revenue, it was frequently necessary for the Governor to intervene by exercising his item veto (granted by Constitutional amendment in 1884) to bring the total appropriated into line with expected state revenues.[3] But considerations of revenue, like the activities of the Governor, appear to have been largely an afterthought in a decision-making system dominated by the General Assembly and representatives of state agencies.[4]

The inadequacies attributed to this system increasingly became the object of public and official concern as state expenditures mounted. A legislative Efficiency and Economy Committee, created in 1913, recommended a wholesale reorganization of the state government in the following year, but its proposals for reducing the number of state agencies and centralizing administrative control in the Governor were not adopted. Some improvement, however, was brought about by the creation, also in 1913, of a Legislative Reference Bureau, which was assigned the task of collecting and summarizing all requests for appropriations for the 49th biennium, beginning in 1915. The activities of these agencies added fuel to the public fire by exposing considerable duplication of programs and lack of coordination among state governmental units, which continued to increase in both number and cost.[5] Reacting to these exposures, Colonel Frank Lowden emphasized the extravagance and disorganization of state gov-

---

[3] Article IV, paragraph 18 of the Illinois Constitution prohibits biennial appropriations which "exceed the amount of revenue authorized by law to be raised in such time."

[4] The best review of this system is provided by Finley F. Bell, "The Illinois Budget," *The Annals*, 62 (November, 1915), 73-84.

[5] Between 1909 and 1913, thirty-four new state agencies were created and biennial appropriations rose from $19.8 million to $37.9 million.

ernment in his campaign for governor in 1916 and promised reform if elected at the head of the Republican ticket.[6]

Lowden's subsequent election led to a four-year period of reform which, by statutory elaboration of the Constitutional system of appropriation, created the financial framework under which the state has operated for the past half-century. The framework was constructed in two parts. During the 1917 session of the General Assembly, Lowden was able to secure passage of the Civil Administrative Code, which represented a modified version of the reorganization plan put forward earlier by the Efficiency and Economy Committee. Literally scores of agencies and offices were abolished by the code and replaced by just nine code departments, each controlled by a director, appointed by and responsible to the Governor. By far the most important of these new departments was the Department of Finance, which was given broad powers over state revenue and expenditures. The department was authorized "To prescribe and require the installation of a uniform system of bookkeeping, accounting and reporting for the several departments," to maintain "summary and controlling accounts" as a check on spending by all state agencies, to investigate and examine all accounts, expenditures, and activities of state-supported agencies with a view toward recommending plans for improving their efficiency, and to undertake a number of other activities whose cumulative effect was to centralize control over the method and substance of state spending in the offices of this single department. The capstone to this centralization was the power, assigned to the Finance Department, "To prepare and submit to the Governor biennially, not later than the first day of January preceding the convening of the General Assembly, a State budget."[7]

---

[6] For a summary of the rapid-fire activities which were taking place during this period, written by a participant observer, see J. E. Fairlie, "Budget Methods in Illinois," *The Annals*, 62 (November, 1915), 85-87. William T. Hutchinson's *Lowden of Illinois* (Chicago: University of Chicago Press, 1957) is an excellent biography of this "reform" governor, containing useful summaries of both Lowden's campaign (Ch. 12) and the reforms he initiated (Ch. 13).

[7] This summary of the Civil Administrative Code is taken from the *Illinois Annotated Statutes*, Ch. 127. All quotations are taken from *Illinois Annotated Statutes*, Ch. 127, Sec. 36.

Although a number of changes have been made in the code since 1917, particularly in connection with the Hodge scandal of 1956,[8] the powers available to the Department of Finance have remained essentially the same. Structurally, they are now exercised through three divisions: Accounting, Administrative Services, and Budgets. The responsibilities of the latter are stated as follows:

[Section] **35.5 Duties of department—Division of Budgets.**] The Department, through its Division of Budgets, shall be responsible for assisting the Governor in submitting a recommended budget, including estimated receipts and revenue, to the General Assembly. In performing this responsibility the Department shall have the power and duty to:
(a) Require information from state agencies in conformance with Section 37 of this Act.
(b) Prepare biennial, annual and periodic estimates of state income and revenue.
(c) Do such preparation and compilation of budgetary material and information as the Governor may require.

Section 37, to which the above paragraph refers, goes on to specify the timing and mechanics of the budget process in greater detail. Not later than September 15 of the year preceding the meeting of the legislature, the Director of Finance is required to distribute blank budget forms to all state agencies. The minimum information to be reported on these forms is specified, but the director is empowered to prescribe forms for the development of such other information as he may think necessary. Each state agency, in turn, is ordered to file its estimate of receipts and expenditures for the coming biennium with the Director of Finance by November 15 of the same year. If these estimates are not satisfactory to the director, he can make further investigations, and, in any case, "He may approve, disapprove or alter the estimates." The director's estimates of revenues and appropriations necessary for the next biennium must be submitted to the Governor, in writing, on or before January 1. As soon as possible thereafter, and "not later than April 1 after the organization of the General Assembly," the Governor, according to Section 38,

[8] See Gilbert Y. Steiner and Samuel K. Gove, *Legislative Politics in Illinois* (Urbana: University of Illinois Press, 1960), pp. 134-163.

must submit a state budget containing his recommendations for the amounts "to be appropriated to the respective departments . . . and for all other public purposes, the estimated revenues from taxation, the estimated revenues from sources other than taxation, and an estimate of the amount required to be raised by taxation."

One other series of provisions contained in these sections is worth noting here. While the Constitution requires that appropriation bills specify the "objects and purposes" for which appropriations are made (Art. V, Sec. 16), it remained for the Civil Administrative Code to give meaning to this provision. Accordingly, the code laid it down that all expenditure estimates were to be formulated in terms of an object classification whose principal categories were Personal Services, Contractual Services, Travel, Commodities, Equipment, Permanent Improvements, and Land. In 1961, however, the General Assembly added the requirement that expenditure estimates as well as the Governor's budget recommendations be formulated "according to the various functions and activities for which the respective department . . . is responsible." Moreover, ". . . comparative performance data formulated according to the various functions and activities, and . . . according to the work units, for which the respective departments . . . are responsible" were now to be included in the budget. Beginning with the 1963-65 biennium, then, budget estimates were to be formulated according to both major objects of expenditure *and* major functions or activities.[9]

CLARIFICATION OF "BUDGETING"

The effect of these provisions of the Civil Administrative Code was to centralize both the state organization and the responsibility for determining the appropriations to support it. In addition, the duties of officials involved in making such determinations were given a somewhat more precise definition, in terms of both timing and the nature of the information required for appropriations purposes. But a great deal of ambiguity remained evident in the code, particularly with regard to the appropriations proc-

---

[9] State of Illinois, *Laws 1961*, p. 3894. See Chapter 8, below, for a detailed discussion of these provisions.

ess. To clarify this uncertainty, a second major reform measure
was enacted in 1919: "An Act in Relation to State Finance." [10]

This act accomplished a number of related purposes. It clarified the meaning of the "fiscal year" concept, it defined in some
detail the procedures for and restrictions upon the disbursement
of state money, and it attempted to specify the meaning of the
"major-object" categories set forth in the code. Its principal
thrust, however, was aimed at clarification of the status of state
funds and the appropriations which could be made from them.
Much of the revenue flowing into the state treasury was available
for specifically defined uses only, while other revenue was usable
for any legitimate purpose whatever. In order to avoid further
confusion over what moneys were usable for what purposes, the
1919 legislation stated that "All money, belonging to or for the
use of the State, paid into the treasury thereof, not belonging
to any special fund in the State Treasury, shall constitute the general revenue fund." [11] Immediately thereafter, the act provided a
list of the special funds in the state treasury, that is, funds set
aside for particular purposes only. This list, which has varied
considerably from biennium to biennium, included thirty-eight
special funds at the beginning of the 73rd biennium in 1963. [12]

The significance of these special funds, from the point of view
of the appropriations process, can hardly be exaggerated. Section
7 of the act makes it clear that, unless otherwise provided by
law, all appropriations "shall be paid from the general revenue
fund." Section 8 then goes on to indicate in some detail the purposes for which the various special funds can be expended. Thus,
appropriations for state aid to local school districts, county superintendents' salaries, and the teachers' pension fund "are payable
from the common school fund." Or, to use another example

----

[10] *Illinois Revised Statutes 1963*, Ch. 127, Secs. 137-167.

[11] *Illinois Revised Statutes 1963*, Ch. 127, Sec. 140.

[12] The least confusing (for the layman) place to learn the current number
of special funds is the biennial compilation of state appropriations issued
by the Department of Finance. The figure cited here is taken from State
of Illinois, Department of Finance, *Appropriations, Regular Session, 72nd
General Assembly* (Springfield, 1961), pp. 403-404. The current text of
"An Act in Relation to State Finance" is reproduced as an appendix to each
of these compilations. A useful discussion of the historical origins of the
most important special funds is contained in a memorandum prepared by
the Illinois Legislative Council, "Selected Earmarked Funds in Illinois State
Finance" (File 4-394, Mimeo., July 2, 1962).

which begins with the fund rather than the activity, "Appropriations from the State Parks Fund shall be made only to the Department of Conservation, and shall be used only for the maintenance, development, operation, control and acquisition of State parks." The state's largest fund—the Road Fund—is subject to an even more detailed statement of its legitimate expenditure purposes by this same section. Certain activities and departments are, by this means, granted a special status which, so long as this law is unchanged, encourages automatic and predetermined appropriations.[13]

Whether or not appropriations from these special funds are in fact "automatic" and "predetermined" is a question that will be explored below. The *tendency* of these grants of special status to remove certain activities from the purview of decision-makers, however, seems clear enough, particularly in the context of other provisions of the same act which reach the same end by more explicit means. Thus, each of the three university systems operated by the state is, by separate and specific provision, authorized to retain endowment funds, gifts, trust funds, and federal aid funds in its own treasury.[14] These funds, in other words, are not considered to be any part of the state treasury and are not, therefore, subject to appropriation by the state. Such complete freedom from the appropriation authority of the state is an extreme case, at least for a state agency. But it does emphasize the tendency of any grant of special fund status—to an activity or an agency—to limit the alternatives open to those charged with responsibility for determining appropriations. From an agency point of view, of course, this form of limitation may well be something to be strongly desired.

THE ILLINOIS BUDGETARY COMMISSION

With the enactment of these twin measures of reform, the decision-making structure for the state organization became highly centralized and much more well defined than had formerly been the case. And, though a number of changes have been made in these statutes from time to time, the decisional structure has re-

---

[13] Quotations in this paragraph taken from the *Appropriations* book for the 72nd biennium, *op. cit.,* pp. 415, 417.

[14] *Ibid.,* pp. 405-413.

mained centered on the department official, the Department of Finance, the Governor, and the legislature. The only major change in this structure since 1917 occurred in 1937, when the Illinois Budgetary Commission was established by law.[15] As the first member of this new body, the statute named the Governor, albeit in an ex officio capacity. He was to be joined by the chairmen of the House and Senate Appropriations committees, respectively, and by two other members of each chamber. Four of the seven members constituted a quorum, empowered to do the commission's business, which was defined quite broadly. The chief duty assigned the commission was "to make a thorough study and investigation of all State expenditures and income from any source," but recommendations for salary classification and license fee improvements were also placed within the commission's scope of authority. All state agencies were ordered to assist the commission in its work and a report to the Governor and General Assembly was to be submitted "not later than the first day of September prior to the convening of the next regular session of the General Assembly. . . ."

Here, then, was yet another agency, with predominantly legislative membership, which was assigned virtually complete powers of investigation and recommendation in the area of state expenditures. By 1957, as an aftermath to the financial scandal of the preceding year, these powers were given further amplification. Membership was enlarged from seven to fifteen by adding four additional members from each house. Commission authority was expanded to apply specifically to budget procedures and recommendations, including a mandate that the commission present its budget recommendations to both the Governor and the General Assembly. Moreover, the commission was now directed to publish its recommendations by March 1 of the year in which the General Assembly began its meeting. Finally, the commission was for the first time authorized to hire a professional staff: an executive director, experienced in "government and in management and fiscal analysis," was provided by the amendments and specifically authorized to perform cost studies and management analyses, to investigate agency performance under appropriation bills, and to assist House and Senate Appropriations committees

---

[15] *Illinois Revised Statutes 1963*, Ch. 127, Secs. 193-200.

(and any other legislative committees) in their deliberations during sessions of the General Assembly.

CENTRALIZATION AND ENVIRONMENTAL CHANGE

According to the Constitutional and statutory provisions summarized briefly above, then, expenditure decisions for the state organization are to be made by a system comprised of five principal participants—agency (or department) officials, the Department of Finance, the Budgetary Commission, the Governor, and the legislature—each of whom is authorized or required to take some action before state funds can be spent. From beginning to end, the nature and timing of the actions to be taken by these officials are elaborated in considerable detail. Thus the bulk of all moneys received by state agencies is required by law[16] to be quickly deposited in the state treasury, from which it can be removed only by appropriation.[17] Appropriations, in turn, are to be based on requests submitted by state agencies to the Department of Finance. There, a special administrative staff reporting directly to the Governor and fully authorized to gather whatever information it requires[18] must compile these requests in the form of a total budget and submit this budget to the Governor by a specified date. The Budgetary Commission can review the budget before and after the Governor submits it to the legislature, which can approve or modify the budget as it sees fit. The Governor's signature on (or veto over) appropriation bills passed by the legislature completes the decision-making process.

The most noteworthy characteristic of this system, of course, is the extent to which it centralized decision-making authority in

---

[16] *Illinois Revised Statutes 1963*, Ch. 127, Secs. 170-176a.

[17] In addition to the funds maintained separately by the universities, there are a number of state and federal trust funds which are not subject to appropriation by the state. Moreover, expenditures from federal funds can exceed appropriated amounts, since segregated federal funds are not subject to the state Constitution's prohibition of expenditures unless by appropriation. An excellent summary of the fund system can be found in the *Fortieth Annual Report* of the Department of Finance (Springfield, 1958), pp. 11-14.

[18] Even the elected state officers are required to complete the budget forms issued by the Department of Finance and to return them by November 15 of the year prior to the convening of the General Assembly. *Illinois Revised Statutes 1963*, Ch. 127, Sec. 37.

the hands of the Governor. Introduction of the "budget" idea into Illinois state finance gave the Governor both the authority and the tools (i.e., the Department of Finance) to develop comprehensive information about agency expenditures and to use that information in preparing a budget to reflect *his* choices, whether or not other agencies agreed with those choices. Moreover, this change was part of an over-all reorganization of state government which reduced the number of agencies and created code departments controlled by gubernatorial appointees. Centralization of authority resulting from "budgeting," in other words, was accompanied by considerable organizational centralization. The later creation of the Budgetary Commission—a potential challenger to the Governor's authority—did not affect this centralized structure of budgeting. The Governor retained sole authority to formulate his budget and, while this budget could be closely reviewed by the commission, the Governor himself was a commission member. Thus the budgetary system created by law was one in which decision-making authority was highly centralized and which remained highly centralized during the period of this study.

On the other hand, the existence of written requirements does not guarantee their fulfillment, nor do grants of authority necessarily determine that authority will be exercised, or the manner in which it will be used, if it is exercised. These admonitions, always applicable to formally defined systems, are especially relevant here because of relatively rapid changes in the organizational environment within which the expenditure system has operated. Two environmental conditions have been particularly noticeable since 1949: growth and decentralization.

One convenient measure of growth is provided in Table 1, which summarizes total appropriations made for each biennium since 1949. The steady and persistent increases revealed in Table 1 are suggestive of the degree to which the state government has expanded its activities, particularly in the period since 1955, when biennial appropriation increases in excess of one-half billion dollars have occurred. It is also of more than passing interest to note that the consistent increases recorded above have occurred under one Republican and two Democratic governors, which implies that factors other than the partisanship of the Governor may be at work to guarantee appropriation increases. What some of

THE POLITICS OF STATE EXPENDITURE IN ILLINOIS

Table 1. BIENNIAL STATE APPROPRIATIONS:
66TH THROUGH 72ND BIENNIA

Biennium		Total Appropriated [a]
66th:	1949-51	$1,342,985,383
67th:	1951-53	1,474,123,043
68th:	1953-55	1,601,845,049
69th:	1955-57	1,857,216,978
70th:	1957-59	2,361,357,411
71st:	1959-61	2,864,222,206
72nd:	1961-63	3,647,363,855

[a] The figures in this column include supplemental appropriations made by the succeeding General Assembly to complete the previous spending program.
Source: *Illinois Blue Book 1963-64*, p. 339.

these "other factors" may be, and why their effects should so consistently produce increases, are questions which will receive considerable attention in the following pages.

As the state organization has grown, the power to control its activities has become increasingly decentralized. Power, of course, refers to the *ability* to decide, which is not the same as authority, or the *right* to decide. To assert that organizational power has become decentralized, therefore, is to assert that the ability to determine what the organization shall do (as distinguished from the ability to determine what the organization shall spend) has become lodged within the various subunits of the organization. This appears to be true in spite of the continued existence of the Civil Administrative Code, which centralized administrative authority in the hands of the Governor. The Governor still has much of that authority, but his ability to use it has been hampered by several factors.

For one thing, Constitutional provisions have prohibited complete administrative centralization, with or without the code, by providing for the election of six state officers in addition to the Governor. Two of these officers have few administrative responsibilities, but the other four perform important duties with relatively large staffs. Indeed, the Secretary of State is among the largest employers in the entire state organization. The political independence of these officers, of course, means that their activities are relatively immune from gubernatorial control. But even code departments become difficult to control if their numbers increase. When originally enacted, the code provided for nine departments; by 1963 eight more had been added, along with a great variety of other noncode agencies such as boards or commissions. A thorough reorganization of the executive branch was the target of the Illinois "Little Hoover" commission (known in the state as the Schaefer Commission) in 1950, but the bulk of its recommendations failed of implementation. Thereafter, the tempo of organizational proliferation increased. Two major commissions were created in 1955; three departments, two of them under the code, were created in 1957; two major boards came into existence in 1961; and more additions were planned for 1963 and after. Like warts on a toad, separate additions to the basic state organization are now so numerous that they have themselves become the chief characteristics of the structure.

While numbers alone render centralized control difficult to achieve, the problem is further complicated by the arrangement of activities within departments. The Department of Public Works and Buildings, for example, houses the state architect, a Division of Waterways, and the mammoth Division of Highways under the same departmental roof. The Department of Registration and Education combines professional licensing functions with the predominantly research activities of the state surveys (water, natural history, and geological), and until recently included the administration of the universities under the jurisdiction of the Teachers College Board. And note that, within the terms of this two-agency comparison alone, there are units concerned with water problems in each department. Presumably the factors which account for this situation also account for the use of two agencies to administer the inheritance tax, or the use of different agencies to operate the state office building in Chicago on the one hand, and the state building complex in Springfield on the other. Thus it is not uncommon for a single department to pursue a variety of unrelated goals or, alternatively, for a single goal to be pursued by several agencies insulated from one another by departmental lines.

It would be a serious mistake to view such apparent anomalies as products of minds insufficiently schooled in the principles of public administration. Participants in the work of the Schaefer Commission recall that efforts to "rationalize" such relationships were frequently opposed by the most highly trained professionals employed by the state. The bases for such opposition are not difficult to see. It is obvious, to begin with, that inclusion of agencies with widely different goals within the same department hinders the exercise of departmental authority. Unless the department head is a specialist in each of the activities carried on under his administration, he is unlikely to possess sufficient knowledge of these activities to be able to control them. Where the activities are particularly specialized or complex—e.g., highway construction or the operation of universities—the chief officer of the department may even lack the ability to find out what his subordinates are doing, i.e., he may not know what questions to ask. Under these conditions any attempt to gather similar agencies together in a single-purpose department would amount to little more than the imposition of departmental control where it does not now exist. And if departmental control is weak, gubernatorial control must be weaker still, for appointment of the department head by the Governor is the chief mechanism of control available to the Governor under the code. In this sense the existence of so many multipurpose and overlapping agencies is simply a reflection of the considerable decentralization of organizational power which has developed, despite what appears to be a high level of formal centralization of authority in the code departments.

What, then, can be the meaning of a highly centralized system for determining expenditures in an organizational environment marked by rapid growth and decentralization of power? To answer this question we need to know more than which officials are authorized to take what actions with regard to expenditure decisions. We must know how these officials interpret their responsibilities, what actions they take, according to what criteria, and with what kinds of effects. We must, in short, come to some understanding of the roles that are played in making decisions to spend state money.

CHAPTER TWO

THE DEPARTMENT OF FINANCE: BOOKKEEPER FOR BILLIONS

The Department of Finance is the communications crossroads of all activities related to expenditure of state moneys. Expenditures from code department appropriations must be approved by this department before they are made, and spending from all agency appropriations (except the General Assembly and the courts) is recorded here by the Accounting Division. Centralized state purchasing, printing, and control of property is also administered by Finance, through its Division of Administrative Services.[1] These responsibilities place the Department of Finance in a position of considerable strategic importance. Every time a voucher is processed, or a warrant for payment made out, a record of the transaction is made by Finance. Of necessity, then, departmental officials have more contact with Finance than with any other sister department, and because they do, Finance is in a position to know a great deal about departmental activities. This knowledge, it is important to note, exists quite apart from the knowledge which may or may not be generated by the department's Budget Division in the process of putting together the biennial spending program.

The department is thus in a position to utilize two distinct channels of information in carrying out its financial activities. On the one hand the process of controlling and recording expenditures, supervised by divisional administrators responsible

---

[1] A good brief description of the responsibilities of Finance is contained in the department's *Fortieth Annual Report, op. cit.,* pp. 6-10.

to the director, enables the department to keep track of expenditures on a day-by-day basis. And on the other hand the preparation of the biennial budget, guided by a Superintendent of Budgets also responsible to the director, gives the department an alternative source of financial knowledge. Because both channels of information are nominally controlled by the Director of Finance, this position is one of great significance. But directors come and go with each change of administration. Moreover, in recent years directors have been chosen on the basis of political, rather than financial, competence.[2] In order to do their jobs, therefore, directors have had to rely heavily on the advice available from more experienced subordinates.

Since 1943, the principal source of this advice has been Mr. T. R. Leth, a former official of the village of Oak Park, Illinois, and a Finance Officer for two decades under Democratic and Republican governors alike. For most of this time Leth has held two official positions simultaneously: Assistant to the Director and Superintendent of Budgets. As the director's assistant, Leth has served as second-in-command for all departmental operations, including each of the three divisions. In practice, of course, Leth has frequently operated as chief executive officer whenever his knowledge and experience were required in order to make day-to-day decisions. As Budget Superintendent, Leth has performed the additional task of directing the preparation of each biennial budget since 1943, translating the budget into appropriation bills, and seeing to it that expenditures from appropriations are properly made.

By holding both positions at once, Leth has been able to exercise considerable control over *both* systems of communication. Indeed, he himself has played some part in shaping the present communications network by initiating a number of changes in it during the long period of his incumbency. If the Department of Finance occupies a strategic position within the state organization, then, Leth occupies the most strategic position within the department itself, acting to centralize the flow of all forms of financial information and to provide administrative

---

[2] Governors Stratton and Kerner both selected the chairman of their respective state party organizations to fill the position.

continuity to departmental activities. To understand the impact of Finance on the allocation of state resources, therefore, we must understand the manner in which Leth interprets his dual role.

THE SUPERINTENDENT OF BUDGETS: PRACTICAL WISDOM

"Common sense" is the term most frequently used by Mr. Leth to describe the requirements of his job. "Most people," he once told a class in state administration, "think that budgeting is a very complicated thing that is very hard to understand. I've been doing the job for twenty years," he continued, "and there's nothing very hard or complicated about it at all. All you really need is common sense and the courage to stick by your common sense when you have to." Common sense, of course, is not something that can be taught or learned in universities, according to Mr. Leth. Indeed, he frequently expresses considerable disdain for the recommendations of the college professors who, from time to time, have suggested reforms in the state's system of budgeting. The chief defect of such recommendations, as far as Mr. Leth is concerned, is that the people who make them have little or no understanding of how the system really operates, because they never take enough time to find out. His own approach to the problem presents a marked contrast. "Why when I first got here," he told an interviewer, "I did nothing for six months except to go from department to department to meet people and find out what they were doing. Before I could change anything around here I had to know what was going on and I had to establish some lines of communication." Common sense, in short, is something that can only be learned through experience.

The learning process centers principally on the acquisition of judgment. Government, in this view, is only partially conducted according to written rules and regulations. In reminiscing about his activities as a financial official both in Oak Park and in Springfield, Mr. Leth makes it clear that no government (i.e., none in his experience) can operate completely "by the book." Again and again, problems arise that cannot be resolved by existing rules or that are just not covered by existing rules. In such situations somebody has to be willing to make the decisions necessary to maintain governmental operations, and that somebody frequently is the Assistant to the Director.

Suppose you pick up the telephone at midnight some night and the guy on the other end is the superintendent of one of our state hospitals. He tells you his boiler has just exploded and 500 patients will be freezing in two or three hours unless he can get it repaired, but he doesn't have an appropriation to repair his heating plant. What do you do? Do you tell him to wait fifteen months until the legislature comes back and votes him an appropriation? Of course not. You tell him to go ahead and hire somebody to fix the thing right away and we'll find the money somewhere to pay for it.

The judgment necessary to make such decisions depends less on a knowledge of the rules than the ability to know when and how the rules can be broken, or avoided completely. This is a very special talent, and one in which Mr. Leth takes considerable pride. "When people call me, they know they'll get an answer, yes or no, because I'm not afraid to give it to them—and I'm usually right." [3]

In applying his common sense judgment to budgeting, Mr. Leth is aided immeasurably by his concentration on the monetary aspects of the state budget. The chief problem, for him, is to see to it that requests for appropriations do not exceed the total amount of money which the state will have available for expenditure. Although a man of strong political and programmatic opinions, he is careful to separate his opinions from his official budgetary responsibilities. The policies and programs carried out by the various state agencies are matters to be decided by the Governor and the General Assembly; his responsibility is to see to it that requests for money do not exceed what the state can afford, and to present such requests in an accurate manner to those who determine policy. Accordingly, he pays little or no attention to what the various agencies and departments do, concentrating instead on how much money they request. "This [the Department of Finance] is the only place in state government," he told an interviewer, "that gets the whole picture. We get all requests for appropriations in here and we can put them all to-

---

[3] The propriety of making such emergency calls to Leth, rather than the Governor or the department head, is taken for granted by all who are concerned.

gether and match them against the money we have and then make sure the departments don't go hog wild in what they ask for." Every state agency, in this view, is naturally interested in expanding its activities and expenditure as far and as fast as possible. Leth's job is to act as a sort of "watchdog," to keep requests within what he conceives to be reasonable financial limits.

Officially, the role of watchdog is performed by Leth for the Governor. As a state officer, Mr. Leth is an appointee of the Governor, whose appointment must receive Senate confirmation for each biennium of service. This aspect of his job is viewed by Mr. Leth in terms of almost classic professional neutrality. "I work for the Governor," he says, "and I do whatever the Governor tells me to do." And, since Mr. Leth has served two Republican and two Democratic governors during the course of his state tenure, it would seem fair to conclude that he defines his relationship more to the office of governor than to the partisan quality of its occupant. But if Mr. Leth does not appear to be a strong partisan, he is nevertheless an extremely political man, whose sensitivity to the nuances of power—including his own—within the environment of state government is finely tuned. Because his utility to a director or a governor depends principally on his ability to exercise judgment in cases where his official superiors lack this skill, his presence in an administration is thought to be not only convenient, but indispensable. As one high-ranking official in the present administration remarked, "Ted Leth has run this state almost single-handedly for the past twenty years." [4] Mr. Leth, of course, is fully aware of this estimate of his own importance and the considerable degree of independence which it bestows upon him. Thus, despite his official interpretation of his subordinate relationship to the Governor, occasionally he has openly opposed policies put forward by the state's chief executive.[5] Retention of his position for twenty years in the face of

[4] Interview, Mr. Theodore Isaacs, February 21, 1963. Less exaggerated, though similar, estimates of Leth's importance were frequently encountered in interviews with other administration officials and with legislators. Some officials, however, recalled that Leth was seldom consulted by Republican Governor Stratton, who was vastly more experienced than his successor. It seems likely, therefore, that Leth's actual significance, as well as estimates of his significance, are in some measure a product of the expertise otherwise available to the administration in power.

[5] See Chapter 8 for a discussion of Mr. Leth's opposition to Governor Kerner's "program budget" proposals.

such occasional conflicts must be taken as a sign of considerable political, as well as technical, skill.

COMMUNICATIONS CATEGORIES AND POLICIES

The Department of Finance, then, is both bookkeeper and budgeter for the state organization, and Mr. Leth stands at the center of both processes, directing a system of information which in some respects is a product of his own design. It is pertinent, therefore, to examine this informational system with some care to determine where and how Mr. Leth's impact has been felt and also to reveal something of the quality and characteristics of the information which forms the backbone of Illinois state finance. Much of this discussion will be drawn from the budget instructions prepared by the Department of Finance and distributed to all state agencies in July of every even-numbered year for their use in the preparation of budget estimates. The instructions distributed in July, 1962, for use in preparing estimates for the 1963-65 biennial budget will be particularly valuable. Legislation requiring budget preparation in terms of "functions and activities" was enacted in 1961, and, to minimize the possibility of departmental confusion over these new requirements, the Department of Finance expanded its instructions to include much detail that had previously been thought unnecessary. While this additional information will be extremely useful here, it should be pointed out that the bases for agency budget estimation were not changed by these expanded instructions. Instead, the instructions made clear that "all agency requests will be in the major object, by agency format which has been used for the past several biennial periods." Continuing, the instructions explained why: "This will allow the initial decisions . . . to be made from data directly comparable to the current appropriation structure." [6]

As the above statement suggests, the heart of the informational system is the appropriations structure, and the accounting categories which record its use. Regular operating appropriations

---

[6] State of Illinois, Department of Finance, "Instructions for 1963-65 Budget Estimates" (Mimeo., Springfield, July, 1962), p. 2. This, and the instructions dated July, 1960, will hereafter be cited as "Instructions 1962" or "Instructions 1960."

are made to agencies in terms of sums of money allocated to major objects such as Personal Services, Contractual Services, Travel, Commodities, Equipment, etc. When such appropriations are approved they are immediately recorded by the Accounting Division in its centrally maintained books. Checks and warrants payable from such appropriations are subtracted from the proper major-object sum, and the resulting information is summarized and made available to each agency on a quarterly basis. Thus, for any given quarter, records maintained by the Finance Department enable an agency to see at a glance its appropriation (by object and by total), the amount obligated against each object during the preceding quarter, the accumulated total of obligations against each object account, and the sum that remains available for expenditure. "Line-item" type appropriations (e.g., capital items or contingencies) are accounted for in the same manner.[7]

It is these periodic summaries of expenditures from major-object accounts which provide the informational foundation for the budget forms distributed to state agencies along with the instructional material. Separate work sheets are included for each of seven major objects, plus line items, agency revenue estimates, and, for the first time in July, 1962, workload data. In each case the format is designed to produce information that can be summarized on the budget recapitulation sheet which, as far as budget review is concerned, is the single most important form (see illustration). This form contains nine columns, beginning with a vertical listing of the major expenditure objects, followed by the current appropriation for each object. The next three columns summarize the obligations incurred against each object account for the first year of the current biennium. Note that it is possible to take these figures directly from Finance reports. As the 1962 instructions make clear, "These columns account for the first year expenditures of the 72nd [1961-63] Biennium and should be actual amounts which are in agreement with charges shown on the June 30, 1962, Statement of the Accounting Division of the Department of Finance." [8]

To this point, the budget recapitulation form asks only for

---

[7] See Department of Finance, *Fortieth Annual Report, op. cit.,* pp. 11-14, for a good description of the department's accounting system.

[8] "Instructions 1962," p. 5.

THE POLITICS OF STATE EXPENDITURE IN ILLINOIS

DEPARTMENTAL BUDGET RECAPITULATION   FUND.............................

BY DIVISION OR ACTIVITY, AND BY OBJECT

State of Illinois—Department of Finance

BUDGET ESTIMATE FOR THE BIENNIUM BEGINNING JULY 1, 1963

(Please read Instructions carefully before filling out this form. Do not use Columns 9 and 10.)

	Col. 1	Col. 2	Col. 3	Col. 4
			OPERATIONS OF BIENNIUM	
	Expenditure Object	Total Appropriation	Vouchers Issued 1961-1962	Outstanding Encumbrances June 30, 1962
PERSONAL SERVICES—TOTAL				
PERSONAL SERVICES—Regular Positions (From Form FB-2A)				
PERSONAL SERVICES—Other than Regular Positions (From Form FB-2B)				
CONTRACTUAL SERVICES (From Form FB-3)				
TRAVEL				
COMMODITIES (From Form FB-4)				
STATIONERY, PRINTING AND OFFICE SUPPLIES				
EQUIPMENT (From Form FB-5)				
LINE ITEMS—OPERATIONS (From Form FB-6)				
REFUNDS				
CONTINGENCIES				
TOTAL DIRECT				
STATE OFFICERS' SALARIES (INDIRECT) (From Form FB-2B)				
TOTAL—OPERATIONS				
LINE ITEMS—GRANTS-IN-AID (From Form FB-6)				
GRAND TOTAL (Excluding Capital)				

THE DEPARTMENT OF FINANCE

SHOW AMOUNTS IN DOLLARS ONLY

Form FB-1

.... Department:... Page.................of

Division (or activity):.. ....pages.

Col. 5	Col. 6	Col. 7	Col. 8	Col. 9	Col. 10
1961-1963			Estimated Needs Biennium 1963-1965	Budget Recommendation Biennium 1963-1965	COMMENTS
Total Charges 1961-1962	Estimated Expenditures 1962-1963	Total Estimated Expenditures			

Approved ....

Division Head (or other title)..

Approved ....

Department Head

information that is known: the first year of the biennium has been completed by the time agencies begin working on their budget estimates and total charges against appropriations are easily available from agency records or from the central accounts maintained by Finance. What is *not* known is the level of expenditure which will be reached in the second year of the biennium. This level must be estimated by each agency and the amount inserted on the appropriate "object" lines provided by the next, or sixth, column on the recapitulation form. An obvious method of developing such estimates, of course, is to simply subtract first year expenditures from the total appropriation. In an effort to discourage this practice, the 1962 instructions warned that "The practice of estimating the expenditure of all remaining appropriations during the second year of the biennium is one which tends to destroy all confidence in the entire request." [9]

Once this estimate is made, it is added to the known first year expenditure to produce a figure for total estimated expenditure for the biennium for each object category. These amounts are recorded in the seventh vertical column. Amounts shown in column seven which are less than the current appropriation constitute, in effect, a prediction that a "lapse" will occur. When column seven figures exceed the current appropriation, remedial action—sometimes in the form of a request for a deficiency appropriation from the next General Assembly—is called for to prevent expenditures which exceed appropriated amounts. Based on these figures, column eight provides spaces for agency estimates of the money that will be required for the succeeding biennium—which, it ought to be stressed, begins from six to nine months *after* these estimates are prepared and ends somewhere between thirty and thirty-three months later. As the Finance Department points out, column seven (estimated expenditures) assumes great significance in relation to columns two (current appropriation) and eight (estimates for the next biennium): "Significant differences between total estimated expenditures and current appropriations or between these expenditures and the new request should always be explained." [10] As far

---

[9] *Ibid.*, p. 6.
[10] *Ibid.*

as the agencies submitting such forms are concerned, their responsibilities end with completion of column eight. The ninth column is reserved for the amounts recommended for appropriation by the Budgetary Commission and the Governor, while the tenth and last column merely provides some additional space for comment.

In considering the nature of the burden placed upon agencies by the informational requirements of this form, it is apparent that very little calculation is necessary to fill it out. Indeed, only two of the ten columns are at all problematic. Column six requires agencies to predict how much they will spend during the current (i.e., the second) year of the biennium. Except for those agencies which can be affected by a change in economic conditions (e.g., the Public Aid Department) or in commodity price levels (e.g., agencies operating large hospital or prison institutions), this prediction presents few problems. Column eight, which represents agency requests for the new biennium, is the crucial column from the agency point of view and as such requires a great deal of calculation. Considerations of program and political support are important here and are complicated by the need to predict costs for as much as thirty-three months into the future. Apart from this column, however, very little mental effort is required to fill in the remaining information, most of which can be obtained easily from the Department of Finance if it is not already at hand. Even the problem of estimating personnel needs is simplified by the practice of utilizing the agency's latest monthly payroll (in most cases this is the August payroll for each even-numbered year) as the basis for predicting agency employment for the next biennium.[11]

Although this system of accounting and reporting is founded on categories defined by statute, its utilization has been modified somewhat by procedures which partially reflect the outlook of Budget Superintendent Leth. One of his earliest suggestions was the institution of a pre-budget meeting of all agency budget officers. Normally held in July or August, just after the instructions have been distributed, this meeting is used to explain the policy of the Governor and to answer any questions the agencies may

---

[11] *Ibid.*, p. 7.

34

have with regard to the budget instructions.[12] But Mr. Leth takes greater satisfaction in two other devices of considerably more significance, though not of his design. One is the "line-item" appropriation format. Agencies requesting appropriations for new programs that have not been carried on previously are required to make such requests in the form of a separate sum placed on a separate line apart from the other major-object accounts. From an accounting point of view such line appropriations make sense whenever it is impossible to predict the level of expenditure likely to be made from the several object accounting categories. The more important consequence of this device, however, is to enable budgetary decision-makers to isolate such new programs from regular agency operations and to deal with them as items unrelated to other activities. Such easy identification of line items has important consequences for the decision-making process, as will be shown below.

The second device is so important that it must be regarded as a major policy presupposition of the entire budget process. All agencies submitting budget requests are directed by the Finance Department to distinguish between their *basic* and *supplemental* budgets. The most concise definition of these terms was provided in the July, 1960, budget instructions: "The *basic budget request* should not exceed the total appropriated to the agency by the . . . [last] General Assembly. The basic request may be for less than total current appropriations and, the request may propose shifting the amounts between major objects, but all amounts which would increase the grand total requested should be set out separately in *a supplemental budget request*." [13] By July, 1962, when the state was limping along in what appeared to be a serious fiscal crisis, the budget instructions had become much more explicit:

Each agency request will be measured against current appropriations made to that agency and any alternative levels of expenditure will be requested separately. Translated into budgetary terms, this simply means that *current appropriation levels will be the maximum*

[12] For various reasons this meeting was not held prior to initiating preparations for the 73rd biennial budget. The reasons were set forth in a letter addressed to all state agencies dated July 5, 1962, and signed by Mr. T. R. Leth.
[13] "Instructions 1962," p. 2.

limits of the basic request. Any requested amounts, in excess of current
appropriations will be supplemental budgets and the supplemental
requests may be presented in several separate units, or levels, if desired.

The basic budget in the same number, or fewer, dollars presents the
agency's outline of the level of operations which can be maintained
when the dollar cost remains constant. Changes in proposed expenditure of the several major objects are permissible but should be fully explained.

Increased requests which might ordinarily be considered additions
to the agency's basic budget should be presented as the supplemental
request with the highest priority. Examples of this type of increase
would be the staffing and maintaining of new capital facilities, maintenance of added mileage of roads . . . etc.

After presentation of the basic request and a possible supplemental
for increases of a basic budget nature, any other increases should be
requested in separate supplementals. . . .[14]

Both the line-item request and the basic-supplemental distinction are designed to focus attention on increases, conceived in
monetary terms, for either new programs or for expansion of activities that are already carried on. The success of these tools
is frequently emphasized by the Superintendent of Budgets.
"Why, do you know how much money we save every biennium
by getting rid of these supplementals?" he once asked an interviewer. "Every budget period," he continued immediately, "we
cut out some four to five hundred million dollars of supplemental requests from the budget!" Mr. Leth then went on to suggest
that if such reductions were not made, the natural tendency of
administrators to seek expansion of their programs would very
quickly bankrupt the state. From this point of view, techniques
which simplify the job of budget reduction are greatly to be desired.

It is important to note the close parallel that exists between
the accounting and budgetary systems of information. The accounting system is designed to keep track of sums of money expended to purchase specified things, ranging from man-hours
(Personal Services) to automobiles (Equipment). Similarly, the
budgetary system emphasizes dollar amounts to buy certain major objects. Indeed, precisely the same information is utilized in
both systems. If one were to enumerate the virtues of these essentially identical informational systems, simplicity would have

---

[14] *Ibid.*, p. 1. All italics in original.

to come first, since operations more difficult than addition and subtraction are seldom, if ever, required for their use. Furthermore, the emphasis on monetary sums provides a handle that is easily understood and easily manipulated—up or down—should the need arise, without becoming enmeshed in details of programmatic or agency operation. Certainly these attributes are congenial to the financial point of view of the Budget Superintendent, who has not only worked well with existing informational categories but has also helped to institute changes which, if anything, have added to the emphasis on monetary sums. The Budget Superintendent, it must be recalled, views his role as that of watchdog rather than as an advocate of agency or administration programs.

SOME RULES OF THE GAME

But the informational system described here sets out much more than general policies and definitions of categories; it also transmits certain clues regarding the nature of the budgetary game which the wary agency official will be sure to notice. In a sense, the heart of the budget process is the interaction between question and justification. At stated periods of time agencies interrupt their operations in order to present their future operating plans to other officials outside of the agency environment. The interruption itself implies a questioning of the legitimacy of agency activities and calls for a response from the agency in the form of a justification. By reading the budgetary instructions carefully—sometimes between the lines—the agency official can become aware of both the kinds of questions that are likely to be raised and the kinds of justifications that are likely to be accepted.

Over and over again, the budget instructions call for explanations of any proposed changes from the existing level of operations, as measured by the current appropriation. Increases or new programs, of course, are easily identified for questioning purposes through the supplemental and line-item devices, and are dealt with accordingly. But decreases that show up, particularly in the form of expected "lapses" (i.e., expenditures that are less than current appropriations), also require explanation. The penalty for an unsatisfactory explanation is quite clear: "If lapses are shown and the new request is not reduced, an explanation is in order as to why the new request should not be reduced." [15] The obvious implication is that requests similar to the current level of appropriations will require little or no explanation or justification—unless the current appropriation is not being spent. To avoid questioning and its attendant challenge to agency legitimacy, the agency official need only see to it that his request for new money closely approximates his present level of spending authority.

Readers of the budget instructions, furthermore, are left with little doubt concerning which officials will be raising questions. Thus the 1962 instructions begin with a covering note signed by both the Director of Finance and the Superintendent of Budgets, while the textual material makes it clear that the Budgetary Commission and the Governor will be involved in making decisions on agency budget requests.[16] Repeated written warnings against agency attempts to conceal lapses by high estimates of second year expenditures or last minute spending increases underline the competence of these reviewing officials to understand—and be prepared for—some of the more common strategies likely to be followed by agency officials. Throughout, the instructions implicitly assume that, in this questioning situation, questions must be avoided if at all possible. By following the implicit and explicit instructions carefully, agencies gain a reasonable degree of assurance that their current operations will be continued and, by the same token, reviewing officials gain the ability to simplify what could be a complex decision-making problem. Questions of a serious nature serve only to upset this balance. The budget instructions, therefore, make it clear that requests which cause questions are both undesirable and potentially dangerous for the agency involved.[17]

Experienced agency budget officials understand these arrangements, of course, and act accordingly, but even a new budget

---

[15] *Ibid.*, p. 17.

[16] *Ibid.*, p. 2.

[17] Note the implicit bias which appears in the following statement on page 6 of the "Instructions 1962": "Concealment of estimated lapses by 'plugging' second year estimates will probably make for such disparity between the two years as to raise more questions than would be raised by showing an estimated lapse."

officer would have little difficulty in devising a strategy for budgetary success based upon a careful reading of the budget instructions. Such a strategy might include the following rules: 1. Use up
all of your appropriation (to avoid lapses). 2. Avoid requests for
less money than is authorized by your current appropriation. 3.
Avoid requests for large increases. Quite obviously, these are rules
which tend to do little more than preserve the organizational
status quo. Indeed, in a period of inflation and rising costs, the
effect of their application would be to reduce the level of activities
that could be purchased with a constant amount of dollars. More
significantly, they offer little aid to the agency that is anxious to
expand its operations. As a practical matter a variety of other pre-
cepts, derived from experience, are utilized by agencies seeking
appropriations. What these additional rules are, and how they relate to the rules noted above, will be explored in the following
chapter.

ORGANIZATION AND PROCESS

The essential justice of the Superintendent of Budgets' repeated
assertion that budgeting is mostly a matter of common sense
should be apparent by now. Given the watchdog orientation and
a system of information that is easy to use and to understand
(provided one takes the time to do so), there is nothing very
complicated about the budgetary responsibilities carried out by
the Department of Finance. Accordingly, only four men are employed as budget examiners by the Division of Budgets to supervise agency budget preparation.[18] Each of these men is assigned
as examiner to a number of state departments and agencies, with
responsibility for seeing to it that budget estimates are prepared
punctually and accurately. Although the statute envisions a broad
function for the Budget Division, exigencies of departmental operations serve to confine its role within rather narrow boundaries.
As one of the examiners puts it, "We're clerks; that's all we can
be. All we do is take the estimates we get from the departments,
look them over to see that the figures are all right, and send them
on to the Budgetary Commission." In point of fact, the examiners

---

[18] During the 1963 budget period these examiners were responsible for
twenty-one, sixteen, fifteen, and thirteen agencies, respectively.

also put together a written summary for each agency request which indicates the changes, if any, that have been made as compared to the last appropriation. But this does little or nothing to change the nature of the examiner's role which, as suggested above, is described accurately by the term "clerk."

Several factors account for this rather narrow conception of purpose. The most important, of course, is the orientation of the Budget Superintendent, who does not define his—or the Budget Division's—responsibilities to include activities such as management analyses or program advocacy. The job of the Budget Division is to summarize and transmit information which, thanks to ingeniously designed informational categories, is not a task that requires large numbers of professional employees. In part, too, the clerk orientation is a necessary result of the manner in which examiner responsibilities are distributed. Although four examiners are employed, agencies which spend more than half of all funds appropriated by the state are assigned to just one man. Thus the man who is supposed to "review" the billion dollar highway budget, also reviews the budgets submitted by the three state-supported university systems ($500 million), the budget for state aid to local school districts, and the budget for his own department, Finance. When it is recalled that this review must be accomplished quickly in order to enable both the Budgetary Commission and the Governor to examine these proposals prior to the submission of the budget document, it becomes evident that the review process can encompass little more than a check to see that totals are accurate and recorded against the proper fund. Even this is no simple task, however. The highways budget, for example, requires several days' work, according to Budget Division officials.

There is, of course, no reason why the work of the Budget Division should encompass a more comprehensive range of responsibilities. It must be remembered that what is normally thought of as budget review does not take place within the confines of the Finance Department, which holds no hearings, seeks no justification for budget requests from agency officials, and sets no policies. Because Finance confines itself to summarizing and transmitting information, there is little need either for larger staff or for complex procedural guides. Instead, budgetary responsibilities are carried out through a highly informal, but effective, process based upon many years of experience shared by essentially the same group of men. Mr. Leth explained the process as follows: "We don't care how these [budget] requests come in; we take them as they come, and as soon as we get enough of them together then we go ahead and begin holding hearings."

The hearings are held before the Budgetary Commission, but the determination of which agencies will be heard on what dates is normally made by Mr. Leth. His decisions, in turn, depend upon the speed with which the budget estimates come in from the agencies and are summarized by the budget examiners. When enough of these summaries are ready (i.e., enough to hold a good meeting of the commission), the Budget Superintendent simply telephones the Chairman of the Budgetary Commission who then proceeds to complete arrangements for the hearings. Though hearing dates will differ from biennium to biennium, they are generally under way by late November of each even-numbered year. Thus, budget hearings for the 1963-65 budget officially began on November 27, 1962.[19] Mr. Leth, normally accompanied by one of the budget examiners, attends all of these hearings and records the decisions made by the commission on the budget forms. After each hearing is concluded Mr. Leth brings the decisions of the commission before the Governor and, if he approves, preparations are begun immediately to set up the printed forms for insertion into the budget document.

A more detailed discussion of the roles played by the Budgetary Commission and the Governor will be provided below. Here, it is sufficient to emphasize the meaning of this process from the point of view of the Department of Finance. If, for example, Mr. Leth must wait for budget requests to come in before he can begin to arrange hearings, it follows that the agencies themselves have a good deal to say about when hearings shall begin and, accordingly, about the timing of the whole budget process. What this can mean in practice was illustrated in 1962, when many code departments simply ignored a gubernatorial directive to submit all budget requests to Finance by Septem-

---

[19] An earlier meeting was held on October 23, 1962, but was devoted entirely to reports from the Governor, the Public Aid Commission, and the Subcommittee on Economy Measures of the Revenue Study Commission.

ber 10.[20] Indeed, one of the largest departments waited until
January 10, 1963, before submitting its request.[21] Without support from the Governor, of course, there is little that Finance
can do about such tardiness. More significantly, there is little
that Finance would want to do, given its present outlook. As a
result a pattern of many years' standing has developed, in which
the smaller state agencies submit their requests relatively early,
while the largest state agencies tend to wait until the last minute
before giving Finance an indication of what they will request for
the next biennium. Both the Budgetary Commission and the Governor are therefore required to make a great many budgetary
decisions before they have any good idea of what the largest state
agencies will need for the succeeding two years.

This in itself causes no problem for Finance. But the tardiness
of the largest agencies does put a great deal of pressure on the
Budget Division, first, to review and summarize a large number
of documents for each agency and, second, to provide accurate
copy for the budget document once commission and gubernatorial decisions have been made. The fact that many of these decisions are made at the last minute intensifies the pressure during
March and early April, and forces Finance personnel to concentrate all of their attention on "getting the book out." To produce
the budget document in time for the Governor's budget message
becomes the single goal of Finance in this hectic period.

One of the less fortunate consequences of this last minute emphasis on "putting out the book" is the inability of the document
so produced to accommodate the major decisions that are typically made just prior to the presentation of the budget message.
In preparing the 73rd biennial budget, for example, one of the
last decisions made involved a proposed salary increase for state
employees that totaled some $15.8 million. By the time this deci-
sion was made, however, most of the pages in the budget book
had already been set up for printing. Distribution of the $15.8
million figure among the departments according to the number

---

[20] The directive was contained in Budget Superintendent Leth's letter to
all state agencies dated July 5, 1962, and repeated in the "Instructions
1962," p. 15.
[21] The Department of Mental Health. See Chapter 3 for a detailed examination of the budgetary procedures in this agency.

of employees affected would, at that late date, have required the reworking of a great many pages and the recalculation of a great many totals, all of which would have seriously delayed publication of the budget. In order to get the book out on time, therefore, it was decided to insert the entire $15.8 million in the general summary table at the beginning of the budget book as a single lump sum.[22] Budget totals were thereby preserved in the budget book, but the utility of budget recommendations for individual departments was seriously undermined, since appropriation bills drawn later for each department reflected the salary increases that had not been included in departmental budget recommendations. As some legislators noted, the budget book became obsolete the day it was printed.

This resolution of the salary increase problem helps to clarify a conceptual problem of first importance in understanding the role of the Department of Finance. The term "budget," from this department's point of view, means nothing more than a statement of items (classified by object) to be purchased during a given period of time as measured by the dollar amounts devoted to each object, and the funds from which such amounts are to be drawn. Other kinds of meanings, involving consideration of planning or program or fiscal control are obviously not relevant. As the Budget Superintendent has made clear, what the various agencies do and how they do it are matters for others to decide; Finance is concerned primarily with amounts of money that are requested and that are available. What the Department of Finance develops, then, is a money budget or, to put it differently, a biennial statement of the things that state money can buy.

Perhaps the outstanding conclusion to be drawn from this analysis of the Finance Department is that, in practice, there is little distinction between departmental activities as bookkeeper or as budgeter. Identical categories of information are utilized for both purposes under the direction of a single official whose long experience with, and contributions to, their use gives him an unparalleled technical competence. Because of this competence, the added status of an appointive position, long maintained, and

---

[22] The figure appears on page 20-A of *The Illinois State Budget for the Biennium July 1, 1963 to June 30, 1965* (Springfield, 1963).

centralized control over both important channels of financial information, this official has exerted considerable influence over the operations of the department. During his tenure the state organization has developed an almost frictionless system for putting together a "budget" which requires little specialized training and which possesses the further virtue of simplifying potentially complex decisions. Policies and programs are frequently difficult to comprehend; dollars and cents can be understood by all.

Yet despite his protestations of professional neutrality, the Budget Superintendent is far from neutral in the conduct of his responsibilities. His bias lies less in the direction of any particular program, however, than toward hostility for any program which is new or likely to cost the state additional money. As "watchdog" over state funds the Budget Superintendent tends to be suspicious of any new request submitted by an agency and cynical with regard to any change proposed by a political leader —the latter type of proposal is normally dismissed as "just politics." Thus his orientation, like the informational system over which he presides, is toward the status quo and away from anything that might change it. At worst, such an orientation is ultimately incompatible with that of his official superior, the Governor. At best, tension between "neutrality" and the "watchdog" conception is never far from the surface of his relationships with bureaucratic and political colleagues.

CHAPTER THREE

AGENCY
BUDGET ROLES

Strictly speaking, no two agencies are or can be exactly alike. Differences in personnel, program, and purpose—no matter how slight—must exist between each of the separate agencies which make up the state organization. Does it therefore follow that each separate agency must pursue a different course in determining its finances? Not at all, for regardless of differences, every agency must prepare a "budget" every two years, and must do so within a framework established by the central fiscal agency, the Department of Finance. While the operations required by this framework do not produce the same consequences in each agency, they do encourage the development of decision-making rules which appear to differ very little from one agency to the next. These rules, in turn, are based upon certain assumptions made by budget officials concerning the nature of their political-administrative environment. The striking similarity of these assumptions and rules, as revealed in discussions with budget officers from a variety of departments, suggests the existence of what might be called an organizational subculture. We begin here, accordingly, by sketching out the assumptions and rules which constitute this subculture. In order to show the impact of the subculture on budget practices, a rather detailed examination of budget preparation in one agency is then offered.

THE SUBCULTURE OF BUDGETING

Doubtless one of the chief contributing factors to the uniformity of outlook among agency budget officials is the amount of schooling they have had in the operations of the state organization. Interviews in eleven major state agencies revealed that the average length of state service for the budget officers of these agencies was twenty-two years, with individual periods of service ranging up to thirty-four years (Table 2). Not all of these offi-

Table 2. LENGTH OF STATE EMPLOYMENT, BUDGET OFFICERS IN SELECTED STATE AGENCIES (AS OF JANUARY, 1963)[a]

Agency	Budget Officer's Title	Years of State Employment
Agriculture	General Auditor	22
Aeronautics	Controller	16
Conservation	Accounting Supervisor	9
Financial Institutions	Executive Assistant	17
Highways (Div. of)	Chief, Bureau of Administrative Service	34
Insurance	Clerk	28
Mental Health	Deputy Director, Administrative Service	29
Mines and Minerals	Secretary	20
Public Aid	Chief, Division of Research and Statistics	20
Public Health	Assistant to Director	20
Public Safety	Chief Clerk	27
	Average:	22

[a] Agencies in this table include all code departments (except Finance) in which I was able to interview the budget officer.

cials, of course, have spent all their years in the state service as budget officers, but each of them has prepared at least two budgets, and most have been involved specifically in budget preparation for a decade or more. Given this level of experience, and considering the stability of format and control exercised by the Department of Finance, similarity of views among this cadre of officials is to be expected.

Four assumptions are particularly important in shaping the point of view of state budgeters:

1. *The term "budget" refers to the forms distributed by the Finance Department which, when filled out, will appear in the budget document submitted to the legislature by the Governor.* By and large, budget-makers do not see themselves as makers of policy. When asked to describe his approach to the job of budgeting, the typical agency official will simply recite the procedures

he follows in filling out the budget forms and submitting them to Finance. These procedures and forms need not have any necessary relationship to the agency appropriations finally approved by the legislature or, indeed, to any changes in agency policy which may develop after the "budget" has been submitted. As a result there is no need to develop any rationalization of budget development from either a philosophic or strategic point of view. "Budgeting" means nothing more than filling out budget forms and, as seen in Table 2, the skills necessary to accomplish this task are frequently available in the form of a secretary or clerk who can add and subtract and copy figures from Finance Department reports with resonable accuracy. Budget officials who think of budgeting in terms any larger or different from these are exceedingly rare.[1]

2. *The budget is prepared for someone external to the agency itself.* The very fact that the budget is seen as a financial statement that is not necessarily related to agency policies encourages agency officials to view the budget as something essentially artificial, designed for external consumption only. Few of the smaller agencies make any attempt to utilize budget categories to control expenditures, while attempts to fit the budget into some overall management plan are unheard of at this level. Indeed, many smaller agencies rely more heavily on the reports issued by Finance than on their own accounts. Moreover, even those officials who do emphasize their own accounts for use in budget preparation tend to treat budgetary accounts as obstacles to be overcome rather than as constraints to be obeyed. As one such official put it, "Any budget officer with half a brain knows perfectly well that he can cover up any expense he wants to cover up simply by juggling his accounts; I've done it many times myself." Though perhaps exaggerated, this statement does illustrate the widespread disregard for budget categories as mechanisms relevant to internal agency operations.

A similar lack of relevance is characteristic of many of the large agencies, such as Highways, which control their internal operations through highly sophisticated accounting systems. The difficulty at this level is that the relatively simple budget forms

---

[1] One such rare official is employed by the Department of Mental Health. Both the official and the department are discussed below.

cannot easily accommodate more sophisticated systems of information, with the result that budgets prepared by these agencies become little more than watered-down translations of the accounts used to record agency activities. Conscious preparation of such "translations" not only emphasizes the artificial nature of the budget but also underlines its external, rather than internal, relevance. At least one of the largest agencies, for example, prepares two "budgets," one for itself (which is not available for inspection) and one for submission to the external reviewing authorities.

3. *The budget is not taken seriously.* This is a somewhat loose way of stating the twin expectation of budget officials (a) that little time will be devoted to their budgets once they leave the agency itself and (b) that decisions on their budgets will *not* be made according to criteria which are either consistent or relevant to agency operations. Obviously such expectations must be oriented toward a "who" as well as a "how," and as far as agency officials are concerned the "who" is quite clear. All such officials who were interviewed agreed that the Finance Department seldom, if ever, made any changes in the forms submitted, though the examiners were reported to be occasionally helpful in solving technical problems or revealing errors in calculation. Similarly, and perhaps surprisingly, many agency officials did not view the Governor as an especially important decision-maker on budgetary matters. Some, in fact, appeared to have no very clear-cut notion of just what the Governor was supposed to do with regard to the budget. The important reviewing body, from the agency point of view, is the legislature, particularly its surrogate on budgetary affairs, the Budgetary Commission.

According to agency budget officers this commission seldom tampers with requests that do not exceed current appropriation levels. Instead, the commission tends to concentrate on supplemental proposals, almost all of which—again according to agency budgeters—are eliminated. Agency personnel are particularly anxious to point out that the elimination process is normally a quick one (the most common agency estimate of time spent before the commission was five minutes) which appears to have no obvious rationale. Thus one administrator reported that he had experienced hearings at which the only question asked by the commission membership was "Is this budget okay?" Another, from an agency with a long history of reductions imposed by the commission, argued that commission members appear to know very little about the operations of his agency and to have very little desire to learn. As far as he was concerned, hearings before this body are "mostly a joke." Still a third allowed that lengthy consideration and detailed questioning are not altogether unusual in commission proceedings, but when such events take place, policy differences are not the cause. Instead, "Some senator may not like the way a guy combs his hair, or maybe he just wants to get his name in the papers."

The inability of agency officials to see any obvious rationale for commission decisions leads to frequent criticism of the commission as "disinterested," "irrational," or even "ignorant." Inevitably, too, it creates a cynical reaction among agency people, who conclude that "something else" (i.e., politics) motivates commission decisions that they are unable to understand. However critical of the commission agency officials may be, they also assume that the commission is the principal—indeed the only—body likely to pay much attention to their budget requests and this is the principal hazard to the achievement of agency budgetary objectives. The difficulty of this hazard is enormously magnified, of course, by the lack of any publicly recognized rationale for its actions. Lacking such a rationale, decisions made by the commission appear to be completely arbitrary—an appearance which frequently generates considerable apprehension among agency personnel as they look forward to their biennial confrontation with the commission.

4. *The budget will be cut.* To say that agency officials are unable to see any rationale behind Budgetary Commission decisions is not to say that they are unable to predict the actions likely to be taken by the commission. On the contrary, their predictions are freely made, uniform, and, as will be seen below (Chapter 4), generally accurate. Both the uniformity and the accuracy of these predictions stem from their familiarity with the informational categories developed by Finance and their expectation that the decisional rules implicit in those categories will be followed by the commission. With considerable confidence, the typical agency official predicts that his budget will encounter little or no questioning if the new request does not exceed the current appropriation, that any "lapse" that shows up will be closely scrutinized,

and that any request for a supplemental increase will be cut, regardless of the adequacy (from the agency's point of view) of the justification provided.

Underlying such assumptions is a sense of the peculiar significance of the budget in Illinois finance. For any given agency the budget is seen as primarily a financial summary of current operations, designed to provide a financial cover for those operations and, when the occasion presents itself, to make room for some slight expansion. This view does not reduce the importance of the budget, but it does remove budget officers from any necessary connection to major policy decisions and it does permit them to act within the framework of a well-defined subculture of their own. To the extent that maintenance of the organizational status quo is problematic, as is sometimes the case, the rules of this subculture assume an importance that can hardly be exaggerated. For the most part, however, budgeting presupposes that the future is, and of right ought to be, a simple extension of the present and is therefore characterized by rules designed to ensure that result. Fashioned in anticipation of the "review" expected at the hands of the Budgetary Commission, these rules may be thought of as falling into two classes: rules for spending money and rules for preparing budgets.

Rules for Spending Money

Wise budget officers very quickly learn two things. First, they learn that questions concerning their budget requests almost always arise from the record of expenditures made by the agency. Second, they learn that the accounting system is sufficiently ambiguous to offer them considerable leeway in determining charges to be made against particular accounts. Certain rules governing expenditures follow as a matter of course:

1. *Spend all of your appropriation and, if possible, a little bit more.* This rule which has been commented on above, flows directly out of the instructions distributed by Finance. Those who have appeared before the Budgetary Commission and who expect to do so again, however, are in a position to understand its deeper significance. Failure to use up an appropriation indicates that the full amount was unnecessary in the first place, which in turn implies that the Budgetary Commission did not do its job. Such an implicit slap in the commission's face is extremely dangerous and

can lead to a reduction in the next appropriation. Spending slightly more than was appropriated to selected accounts (by a judicious use of accounts in which a surplus is expected), on the other hand, can lay the groundwork for an appropriation increase. At the very least, it can provide justification for maintaining the total over-all appropriation.

2. *Avoid any sudden increase or decrease in expenditures.* Changes in expenditure levels are recorded by the Department of Finance. If brought to the attention of reviewing officials, such records tend to raise questions and create situations in which cuts are likely to be made. To avoid such questioning it is best to maintain a constant expenditure level, even if this requires a certain amount of juggling between accounts. It is particularly important to keep expenditures up during the first year of the biennium, because those figures tend to be given greatest weight by the Budgetary Commission.

3. *In case of conflict between these two rules, the former is to be preferred.* Not infrequently, maintenance of a constant level of expenditure turns out to be impossible with the result that some agencies approach the end of a biennium with large sums of money remaining unspent. Where this situation occurs it is normally better to spend as much of these remaining sums as possible, for several reasons. Chances are that the agency's budget request has already been reviewed, since meetings of the Budgetary Commission usually conclude by February of the legislative year. Thus expenditures which pick up during the final months of the biennium are likely to go unnoticed until sometime after the legislature adjourns. Review of such expenditures will come, if at all, some fifteen to twenty months later, when the commission will be far more interested in new projections than in past excesses, especially if the excesses help to prevent lapses.

Officials who follow these simple rules for spending their money will seldom do worse than to maintain what funds they have, for their careful husbandry of sums available will have created financial records which raise few questions and offer fewer opportunities for criticism. In the event that these rules are not, or cannot, be followed, it is still possible to achieve a similar result through application of an alternative set of rules governing budget preparation.

Rules for Preparing and Submitting Budgets

1. *Avoid requests for sums smaller than the current appropriation.* This rule has been mentioned above and follows from the expected tendency of the Budgetary Commission to give little or no attention to requests that do not exceed the present level of support. In the context of the discussion provided in this chapter, however, it is possible to amplify this basic rule by adding others, as follows:

2. *Put as much as possible of the new request (particularly items with top priority) into the basic budget.* For a variety of reasons it is frequently impossible to avoid "lapses." The imposition of a "freeze" on new employees during the 72nd biennium, for example, made it impossible for many agencies to avoid lapsing considerable sums, since they were unable to replace employees who retired or otherwise left state service. In such circumstances, the new basic budget should include the sums lapsed, even though this is a formal violation of Finance Department regulations for preparing "basic" and "supplemental" budgets. The Budgetary Commission can be expected to be sympathetic to agency desires to maintain what is considered to be "their" money. Or, if a "lapse" in one account provides the basis for a reduced basic request for that account, it is desirable to make up that reduction by asking for an increase in some other account, again on grounds that the increase really does not increase the current level of financial support. The basic principle here is that the current appropriation must be preserved.

3. *Increases that are desired should be made to appear small and should appear to grow out of existing operations (the appearance of fundamental change should be avoided).* If a new program or change in program is desired, a large portion of its cost should be included in the basic budget. The remaining supplemental portion will then appear to be nothing more than a part of ongoing operations and will have an accordingly greater chance of approval.

4. *Give the Budgetary Commission something to cut.* Normally it is desirable to submit requests for substantial supplemental increases. This helps to divert attention away from the basic budget and, more significantly, provides the Budgetary Commission with an opportunity to justify (by eliminating such requests) its con-

tinued existence. The commission and other knowledgeable officials will understand perfectly if you do not press your demand
for supplemental amounts with an extraordinary degree of enthusiasm.

The assumptions and rules delineated here represent a synthe-
sis of ideas and attitudes toward budgeting expressed by numerous agency budget officers. If there is one theme which stands
out, it is that agency budgeting cannot transcend the limits imposed by the conceptual categories used to shape the budgetary
informational system. In addition to defining the kinds of statements that will be treated as "information," those categories
shape the purposes that can be achieved through budgeting, the
strategies likely to be effective in achieving them, and the rules
for selecting strategies. The informational categories, in short,
determine the way officials *think* about finances, and thus structure agency budget roles.

Like all syntheses, however, this one suffers from overgenerali-
zation. To understand its operative meaning requires more detailed information concerning the activities of some agency (or
agencies) which is actually engaged in the job of preparing its
budget request. Accordingly, we turn now to a detailed analysis
of the budget process in one agency, the Department of Mental
Health. In many respects this is an atypical agency: it is large,
highly professionalized, expansive, and unusually self-conscious
regarding the nature and purposes of its budgetary activities. It
is precisely because of these organizationally unusual characteristics that this department has been chosen for intensive analysis,
for Mental Health represents not the typical case, but the hard
case.[2] If the rules of the budgetary subculture break down any-

---

[2] In point of fact, Mental Health represents not only the "hard" case, but
almost the only case. Of the eleven code departments cited in Table 2
above, for example, only Mental Health prepared its budget request according to procedures which were "observable." In the remaining agencies budget
preparation involved nothing more than a clerk or secretary sitting down to
fill in the appropriate figures on the forms, which were then taken in to the
agency head for his review, approval, and signature, though Public Health
indicated that it "sometimes" held formal hearings to complement this procedure. Thus there was nothing that could be observed in these agencies
apart from the activity of a clerk filling in blank spaces on forms. Interviews
with representatives of two of the elected state officers revealed that one of
these—the office of the Secretary of State—followed the practice of holding
formal budget hearings. Through the kindness of officials in both Mental

where, they should break down here. If, on the other hand, the subculture is shown to be an important determinant of Mental Health decisions, its independent significance will have been conclusively demonstrated.

MENTAL HEALTH BUDGETING

The Department of Mental Health is, by a large margin, the largest of the fifteen code departments, with a total payroll in excess of 15,000 persons and a biennial appropriation of nearly $419 million (Table 3).[3] Some twenty-eight separate institutions are operated by the department to provide care for the mentally ill, treatment for the mentally retarded, and a variety of custodial and therapeutic services to disabled and aged veterans and their families, dependent or handicapped children, and physically handicapped adults. In addition, the department provides financial assistance to mental health and child guidance clinics in a number of communities throughout the state. Sheer size, together with the variety of institutions and programs operated, is enough to suggest the complexity of departmental operations.

As shown in Table 3, Mental Health appropriations have increased in each biennium since 1945, with the exception of the period beginning July 1, 1953, when the department suffered a cut of better than $11 million below its previous appropriation. Interestingly enough, that reduction was imposed during the first term of Governor Stratton's Republican administration and became the forerunner of an eight-year period in which total appropriations increased ($149.6 to $214.6 million) by 43.5 per cent. Democratic administrations, on the other hand, appear to have

---

Health and the Secretary of State's office, I was granted access to the hearings conducted in each agency. Since the Secretary of State is a patronage agency performing nonprofessionalized services, there was no reason to expect its budgeting activities to follow rules different from those stated above. The professionalization of the Department of Mental Health did lead me to expect different rules and was chosen for inclusion in the above text on that basis.

[3] The reader should understand that the text treats the Department of Mental Health *as it existed* in the period October, 1962, through June, 1963. A number of organizational changes have been made since that time. These changes are not reflected in the text for the reason that my purpose is to present an account of actors and action *as it occurred* in 1963, rather than to present an up-to-date organizational analysis.

Table 3. DEPARTMENT OF MENTAL HEALTH:
APPROPRIATIONS HISTORY

Biennium	Year	Appropriation	Per Cent Change
73	1963	$418,971,013	+ 8.9
72	1961	384,741,220	+79.2
71	1959	214,665,873	+21.6
70	1957	176,500,621	+18.0
69	1955	149,604,168	+ 8.0
68	1953	138,466,386	− 7.5
67	1951	149,637,598	+10.0
66	1949	135,995,529	+51.0
65	1947	89,854,074	+30.0
64	1945	62,788,165	

been far more generous. Governor Stevenson's first (1949) budget increased the previous departmental appropriation by 51 per cent, and an increase of 66.5 per cent ($89.8 to $149.6 million) was recorded during Stevenson's full four-year term. Percentage increases under Governor Kerner have been even more spectacular, jumping by almost 80 per cent with his first (1961) budget and by more than 95 per cent ($214.6 to $418.9 million) in his four-year term, 1961-65. The bulk of the increase under Governor Kerner, of course, was a direct result of the $150 million Public Welfare Building Bond Issue approved by the people of the state in November, 1960. The resources so provided enabled the newly inaugurated Governor to begin immediate implementation of what a departmental spokesman has called "the largest building program in the department's history." [4] Legislation authorizing much new construction and repair of existing facilities was approved by the 72nd General Assembly, along with the sharp increase in appropriated funds to support this work.

It is against this background of sudden affluence following an eight-year period of relative neglect that departmental preparation of the 73rd biennial budget request must be understood. By mid-July, 1962, when budget preparations began, public assent to the bond issue was not yet two years old, but construction plans embodying a radically new approach to mental health—

---

[4] State of Illinois, Department of Mental Health, *Annual Report 1960-61*, p. 106.

emphasizing smaller "community clinics" rather than the traditional large and isolated "hospital"—were already well advanced, under the leadership of a new and highly respected director.[5] Moreover, the new Governor had indicated from the beginning of his administration that improvement of the state's mental health program would be given top priority. Unfortunately, from the departmental point of view, the poor financial condition of the state had led the Governor to impose a so-called "freeze" on new employment and to withhold his approval of expenditures for capital improvements for which appropriations had been made (see Chapter 5). Thus, despite the availability of resources and strong gubernatorial support, departmental progress on new programs had in fact been retarded to some extent.

The Role of the Deputy Director

Organizationally, the director and his executive and administrative assistants are responsible for the work of the five "services" which operate the various departmental programs. Thus, the Mental Health and Children's and Specialized "Services" operate the numerous institutions and their related services; the Physical Plant Service provides upkeep for the buildings under departmental control; and the Reimbursement Service concerns itself with establishing and collecting charges for the care and maintenance of patients. The fifth service—Administrative Service— is the general staff arm of the department and as such is responsible for a variety of fiscal accounting and personnel functions. Like the other "services" this one is headed by a deputy director who includes among his duties the job of supervising departmental budget preparation.[6]

The present Deputy Director for Administrative Services, Mr. Edward F. Merten, is a long-time employee of the department. Beginning in 1933 at the Anna State Hospital, Mr. Merten moved through a succession of clerical and administrative positions in various institutions until 1943, when he assumed an administra-

---

[5] Dr. Francis J. Gerty, former head of the Department of Psychiatry at the University of Illinois College of Medicine.

[6] Again, the reader is cautioned that this organizational structure existed in 1963. The Mental Health and Children's and Specialized Services no longer exist, with many of their functions now performed by the Department of Children and Family Services, which was created by the 73rd General Assembly.

tive position in the central office. There, in 1955, he took on his present responsibilities. Merten's definition of his responsibilities begins with a realization that, in supervising budget preparation, he is dealing with highly trained professional physicians and psychiatrists who are themselves responsible for institutional programs of great complexity. Because these men are specialists in their own right, he is careful to avoid imposing his own programmatic judgments on budget requests. Instead, he encourages institutional superintendents to be constantly alert for methods of improving their present program operations. If this involves additional costs, they are encouraged to say so and to defend the need for such proposed increases. "We pay some of these men [hospital superintendents] better than twenty thousand each year and we expect them to be knowledgeable enough to know where and how things could be done better and to come in here with requests for improved and expanded programs. If they didn't, we'd probably think that we needed to get new people."

By encouraging concern for program improvement on the part of operating officials the department's administrative staff generates budget requests that are normally expansive. Merten's job is to respond to such requests in terms of what he calls the "political and financial realities." In practice this involves an effort by Merten to induce institutional personnel to set priorities on their needs, again without attempting to impose his own policy preferences. "I've been around long enough," he told an interviewer, "to know that you can't get everything you want in one biennium. And if you can't get everything you want, then you ought to know which things you want to have first, and which things you want to have second." Inevitably, this conception leads Merten to act as a "dampener on requests," reducing them where possible and sometimes eliminating new requests altogether. Asked by an interviewer to give an example, Merten recalled a supplemental request of some $10 million submitted several years ago by one of the larger hospitals for proposed staff increases. While the proposal appeared to be sound, Merten was forced to point out that it would be next to impossible to hire and put to work the number of new employees called for by the supplemental within the space of a single biennium and that, if the additional personnel were found, existing programs would be completely disrupted. Accordingly, the request was reduced by a substantial amount.

Merten's role as "dampener," together with his unwillingness to consciously assert his own policy preferences, tends to confine most of his attention to sums of money. In this respect his orientation is similar to that of Budget Superintendent Leth. But the similarity cannot be pushed very far since, unlike Mr. Leth, the deputy director is officially committed to a department-wide expansion and improvement of program, even if he is content to leave program definition to others. Indeed, Mr. Merten has expressed considerable dissatisfaction over the constraints imposed on program by the basic-supplemental format required by Finance. Conceding, as he does, the utility of basic-supplemental budgeting for agencies that are relatively small, or stable, Merten nevertheless feels that this format, with its inflexible commitment to the "money available" criterion, prevents the budget forms from expressing the true program needs of the operating agency. For an agency such as Mental Health, which is in a period of expansion, this is a particularly difficult problem. Rapid expansion of some departmental institutions and programs necessarily implies a readjustment of priorities within the department, with some activities becoming relatively less significant as others are created or expanded. Existing budget forms cannot easily accommodate such changes with the result that past priorities tend to become frozen. In this sense, basic-supplemental budgeting is more than an inconvenience for Merten; it represents a positive hindrance to an adequate budgeting system.[7]

The Budget Process

As the discussion above has implied, construction of the Mental Health budget is accomplished through a highly formalized procedure. For the 73rd biennium the process was initiated by a memorandum from Merten dated July 17, 1962, and circulated to

---

[7] In this period the department has pressed for expansion of its staff to provide more intensive treatment for patients in its care. While the concept of "intensive" treatment is central to departmental efforts to break away from its past "custodial" approach, the concept cannot be adequately reflected in basic-supplemental budgeting. New staff, for whatever purpose, are requested on supplemental forms which are extremely vulnerable to cuts.

superintendents of all departmental institutions. This was essentially a preliminary document, whose principal purpose was to outline one method of converting existing expenditure records into the new "activity" categories required by the conversion to "functional" budgeting. One month later another collection of documents was sent out for the particular attention of hospital business administrators or business managers. Included were the budget instructions issued by the Department of Finance, partially filled out budget forms for three major-object categories, and a covering memorandum from Deputy Director Merten containing instructions with regard to institutional budget preparation. Significantly, the first "instruction" admonished institutional personnel to pay careful attention to the Finance Department's statement of policy: "Current appropriation levels will be the maximum limits of the basic request."

Note that budget forms for *all* major-object categories were not included in this distribution. The chief omissions were the forms for Personal Services and proposed capital expenditures. In the former case, an IBM runoff from central office records was promised for later delivery, while capital requests were, according to the memorandum, to be developed in conjunction with the Physical Plant Service. A high degree of central involvement and control in the various institutional budget requests was thus assured by the simple device of controlling the nature of the forms that were distributed. Moreover, the forms delivered to the institutions were already partially filled out from records available in the central office. Institutions were permitted some leeway in adjusting predictions of amounts likely to be expended in the second year of the biennium but for the most part, the only column completely open to institutional decision was that which recorded agency requests for the new biennium. The effect was not only to achieve a high degree of central office control, but, more important, to narrow down the focus of budgetary discussion. Review of the returned budget forms by the central office staff would necessarily be confined primarily to the requests for the new biennium.

In keeping with the formality of process begun with two official interoffice memoranda, a third memo dealing with the Personal Services forms was circulated on October 4, 1962. Along with additional instructions, this memo included a schedule for

the formal budget meetings to be held by the department prior
to submission of its 73rd biennial budget request. According to
this schedule meetings were to begin on Thursday, October 11,
1962, and to continue through the following two weeks, ending
on Friday, October 26, 1962. Within this period hearings were
scheduled for nine separate days, including five days of hearings
in Chicago and four in Springfield. Time allotments for the various institutions and services varied from one and one-quarter to
two and one-half hours, with the larger institutions receiving the
larger allotments. On this basis it was possible to arrange hearings for either three or four separate institutions within a single
day, beginning at 9:00 A.M. and running through until late afternoon. To appreciate the diligence necessary to conduct these
hearings in such a concentrated time period, we turn now to an
analysis of the process by which decisions are reached in such
hearings.

Budget Hearings and Budget Decisions

By the time a hospital medical superintendent and his business
manager appear for a budget meeting, the various directions, instructions, and explanations sent out by the central office have
already made it clear that questioning can be expected from
some knowledgeable people. And if for some reason that impression is not made prior to the budget hearing, the circumstances
of the confrontation between agency and central office personnel
would do so. Walking into the meeting room (in either the Chicago or Springfield office building), hospital personnel encounter
a variety of people who they know to be in a supervisory relationship to themselves. Deputy Director Merten, sitting at one
end of a table, is accompanied by several aides, including his
accounting and personnel supervisors, each of whom sits in front
of a large pile of budget forms. The supervisor of the special
Mental Health Fund is also present and, depending on the area
of the state in which the institution is located and the "service"
(Mental Health or Children's) to which it is attached, two or
three other administrative superiors are present. For institutional
representatives, who know that their requests have been available
to the central office for several days, the presence of so many reviewing officials is a forecast of hard questioning ahead. Efforts
to break the tension created by such expectations are frequently

made in the form of humorous comments by institutional representatives who are leaving the hearing room to those who are about to enter. "Better go home and come back tomorrow, Fred; they won't give you a dime today," or "Boy, we're lucky to get out of there alive" are typical.

Though such comments undoubtedly ease tension somewhat, they also reinforce the expectation that budget reductions are about to be imposed. Faced with such a prospect, some hospital superintendents attempt to "manage" the situation by adopting an aggressive posture as they enter the room, in effect "daring" the reviewing officers to propose reductions. A variety of comments and gestures can be used to achieve this posture, whose basic premise is that the institution is insufficiently supported to accomplish its stated objectives. If such a premise can be established at the outset ("I suppose you people are planning to wreck my program again this year" or "I'd have to be a magician to operate a sound program under this budget"), the way is cleared for later objections to any and every proposed cut. Initial aggressiveness, then, is normally accompanied by what might be called the "tactics of objection." Other hospital administrators, however, make no attempt whatever to control the situation. They appear before the reviewing officials as meek and passive subordinates, who seldom question the decisions imposed by their superiors.

Attempts to establish control of the reviewing situation normally have little practical effect, for the reviewing officials represent the authority of the central office and are thus in a position to completely ignore institutional protestations if they so desire. This is not done, largely because reviewing officials share the program goals of the institutional representatives, but both sides understand that it can be done, and this knowledge enervates any attempt to challenge the situational control of the reviewing officers. Firmly in command, and knowing it, the reviewing officials adopt a relatively uniform response to each institutional representative, emphasizing a quietly competent neutrality and a desire to get the job done according to the rules. Though nowhere written down, these "rules" appear to be well understood by all participants. For each agency budget, forms for each major-object category are taken up one by one, usually beginning with "Contractual Services" and concluding with "Personal Services." Each of these "object" sheets, moreover, is examined line-by-line and, when the occasion demands, item-by-item. The process is always initiated by Deputy Director Merten, who raises most of the questions that are raised and makes most of the decisions that are made, with occasional assistance from his aides. Within the limitations of the informational categories utilized, the process is inherently both comprehensive and exhausting.

The existence of "rules" to determine the kinds of questions that are raised and the manner of raising them is equally apparent. To a considerable extent, these rules are a natural outgrowth of the pre-hearing preparations of the various agencies, following central office instructions. As noted earlier, those instructions provided agencies with little freedom to manipulate figures. Indeed, the only column on the budget forms which was completely open to agency decision was that provided for estimating financial needs for the new biennium. Thus it is less than surprising to discover that questions and discussion focus almost exclusively on institutional requests for the new biennium. But such requests become meaningful—and questionable—only in comparison with some other standard. In the context of the budget review situation, this standard is provided by two other columns on the various budget forms: current appropriation and estimated total expenditures for the current biennium. A quick glance by Deputy Director Merten at these three columns enables him to compare the present appropriation against the sum now being spent and the sum which the agency would like to spend in the next biennium. Where the latter two sums are approximately the same, or where the new request does not exceed the present appropriation, they are passed over quickly—frequently in seconds. Whenever the new request exceeds current expenditure by a considerable amount, however, some explanation is requested by the deputy director. It is precisely this process of raising questions about the increased sums of money requested for the new biennium that constitutes the heart of budget review in Mental Health.

One of the principal consequences flowing from the use of such rules to govern the process of review is the frequent expenditure of quantities of energy which are disproportionate to the sums involved. Again and again, increases measured in hundreds or thousands will be discussed and debated for periods ranging up to thirty minutes or more, while requests measured in millions will be passed over in seconds as long as no increase is involved. Thus in one instance, a "Commodities" request of some $3.4 million was approved in just three words: "Commodities are okay." On another occasion an $8.8 million Personal Services request was approved inside of a minute, with reviewing officers pausing only long enough to cheer the ability of the institution involved to add twenty-nine positions to its budget without increasing its request over the current appropriation. On still another occasion, involving a similarly magical addition of eighty-four positions without exceeding the current appropriation, a $12.7 million Personal Services request was approved by the words "That's remarkable." Yet numerous smaller items, involving perhaps a $3,000 increase in Travel, or a $40,000 change in fuel are haggled over for many minutes, occasionally consuming the better part of an hour.

None of this should be taken to mean that such quickly approved large items are not "reviewed" by central office staff. The fact that little time is devoted to such items *during the hearings* means only that a prior examination by Merten or his staff has failed to reveal anything questionable in such items. If, for example, a prior examination shows a current appropriation of $3.4 million for Commodities which looks as though it will be entirely used up and if the new Commodities request is approximately $3.4 million, give or take a hundred thousand, and if there appear to be no unusual changes in expenditure for the several accounts that comprise the "Commodities" category, then there is simply no reason to waste valuable hearing time on a discussion of this object. The controlling criterion, in other words, is not size of appropriation request, but change of appropriation request. Hearings, in this context, are designed to justify increases, or, if justification is not possible, to eliminate them.

But who decides whether an increase is "justified," and according to what criteria? Normally it is Deputy Director Merten who determines the acceptability of such requests, with an occasional assist from administrative officials representing the two major "services" (i.e., Mental Health and Children's and Specialized). The effect, of course, is to involve the central office even more deeply in the affairs of each operating agency. Questions involv-

ing relatively small sums of money in specific categories—a
$2,000 increase in Equipment, or a $30,000 addition to Commodities, or a $7,000 increase in Printing—are frequently determined
by the deputy director or even his accounting supervisor. In
this sense, no account, large or small, is immune to central office
scrutiny. The result is that many decisions are imposed on the
operating agencies by their administrative superiors.

It follows from what has been said above that the criteria for
making these decisions must be related to the need to "justify"
budget requests, particularly when they involve increases. Observing the activities which produce these decisions suggests that
justifications based upon the merit of the proposed increases,
though always offered by institutional representatives, are not
always controlling. Instead, the deputy director and his aides
tend to be acutely conscious of the extradepartmental agencies
—particularly the legislature—which will scrutinize the departmental budget and tend to base their decisions regarding what
is or is not "justified" on their own estimates of what will be acceptable to these external agencies. Thus the final request reflects
not so much "what the department needs" as "what the department can defend." Since questions are directed primarily to proposed increases, final figures ultimately boil down to "the increases
that can be defended by the department."

Quite obviously, decisions that are, in effect, predictions of
what will or will not be supported by the legislature can only
be based upon judgment—a quality or ability that is inherently
imprecise and perhaps nondefinable. This is not to say that there
are no rules to guide the exercise of judgment. On the contrary,
the entire review process, focusing on the search for justification
of increases, may be thought of as a product of rules which indicate to departmental officials that they are safe if they confine
most of their attention to increases. And, as we shall see below,
there are a number of rules which help to make decisions in
specific kinds of problem situations. Ultimately, however, the
question of "what to question" can be answered only through
the exercise of judgment. Only this "sense" or "feel" can determine whether to pass over a $3,000 increase or cut it back, or
whether to ask for higher salaries or more people at the same
salaries. Viewing the process for the first time, the outside observer is likely to be struck most of all by the extent to which dis-

cussions appear to be initiated by statements reflecting this vague "sense" or judgment. Thus the deputy director, glancing across a budget form, will suggest that "Travel looks a little high," or "There's an awful lot of money in postage," or "Maybe we'd better cut down on some of that commodities money."

Though vague, such statements are far from capricious, for they rest on the comparison between appropriation, expenditure, and new request that has been noted above. Far and away the most damaging comparison, from an agency point of view, is one that reveals a projected surplus in appropriated funds at the end of the current biennium. Where such a surplus—or lapse— is shown, it is extremely difficult for the "lapsing" agency to secure an increase in its new request. Indeed, the agency in such circumstances is more than fully occupied in preventing a reduction in the new request. Failure to reduce the request could easily produce embarrassing consequences if discovered later on in the budget process for such a discovery would tend to raise doubts about the honesty of the departmental budget. To avoid such a loss of confidence, Merten and his aides are particularly careful to make the necessary adjustments. As one of these aides put it, in reducing an institutional request, "You'd better cut it because you can be sure that if you don't somebody else will."

That the confidence game is an internal, as well as external, matter is illustrated by the differential treatment accorded to the several institutions whose projections revealed "lapses" of considerable sums. Cuts of varying amounts were freely dictated by Merten and his accounting supervisor in the budget of one institution, whose representatives admitted what was obvious: that they were "playing it safe" in submitting a "padded" budget. The budget of another institution, whose projected biennial expenditures for Contractual Services totaled some $34,000 less than its appropriation, was reduced by some $22,000 after it was discovered that the institution had budgeted the same item under two object categories. A different course was followed, however, for a third institution, whose budget appeared to be frugal and whose representatives pointed out that much of the expenditure they had planned was halted by the Governor's order to cut back on spending. In this case the institution was advised to submit some purchase requisitions quickly in order to use up more of the current appropriation before the first of the year (when the budget would be submitted). In this fashion the lapse, the questioning that might have resulted from the lapse, and the new request were all reduced in a single stroke.

The desire to preserve a high level of confidence is also evident in other kinds of "judgmental" decisions made by central office personnel, particularly decisions relating to increases. Several institutions, for example, submitted supplemental requests in anticipation of new buildings or new programs or both. To a considerable extent, accurate prediction of expenditures likely to be made are simply impossible in such cases, depending, as they do, on imponderables such as date of opening (for buildings), ability to recruit and hire staff, etc. In the face of these imponderables institutions tend to base requests on what they feel to be "safe" estimates—by which they mean estimates that assume full staff operation of the new facilities beginning on the day of predicted openings. Such predictions are not "dishonest" but they do frequently overlook unexpected delays in construction, or difficulties in staff procurement. To permit such requests to go through would not be "dishonest" either, but it would be unwise, for if expenditures failed to keep up with appropriations made on the basis of such estimates, large lapses would show up during the following budget period, with potentially harmful consequences. Merten's efforts to avoid such consequences produced instructions to one institution to base its estimate of Personal Services requirements for an almost completed facility on the assumption of a full staff complement, but to assume employment for only eighteen months. Another institution's request for 814 new positions was challenged on the ground that so many new positions simply could not be filled within a single biennium. In such instances, where the presence of imponderables destroys all possibility of developing the "right" answer, decisions must be based on inexact judgment. This, in turn, is weighted heavily in favor of what might be called the "rule of avoidance": avoid embarrassment by avoiding the things that cause it, such as large and hard-to-explain lapses.

Anxious as the deputy director may be to avoid embarrassment, he is at least as anxious to promote request for increases that he considers to be justified. Consideration of the kinds of increases which are accepted is sometimes revealing. Thus several agencies, in explaining new requests that were substantially in excess of projected current expenditures, reported that existing appropriations from state funds had turned out to be inadequate and that federal funds available to the agencies were being used to carry on programs so affected. One agency pointed out that resort to federal funds was a bookkeeping problem, in part, because of the state requirement that limited expenditures to 75 per cent of appropriated sums during the first eighteen months of the biennium. In short, he had state money available but was unable to use it until the first of the year.

Requested increases of this kind, which are easily defended in terms of past appropriation inadequacies, are normally granted with little trouble, though the exact amount of each increase is hardly a matter of precision. After listening to an explanation of federal-state fund juggling by one institution in connection with its $360,000 requested increase in Travel, Merten agreed that the increase was justified, but wondered "whether to ask for all of it now or to ask for half now and half next biennium." Following his superior's thoughts exactly, an aide suggested "Well, why don't we say $180,000? That's halfway—a compromise." After a slight hesitation, Merten decided, "I guess that's all right."

These kinds of increases, flowing more or less naturally out of inadequacies in existing programs, suggest that the lack of sufficient funds to carry out present responsibilities provides a "defendable" basis for requesting more money. It also suggests that program adequacy is of considerable concern to central office personnel. Not infrequently, the deputy director will provide a measure of this concern by suggesting that institutional requests are not high enough. Responding to one institution's claim that it would be able to "manage" with the amounts requested, for example, Merten was stern. "If your goal is to operate a therapeutic program," he asked, "will it be all right to 'manage'?" His own reluctance to accept such a limited conception was revealed in the several increases he dictated later in various categories on the budget forms. Even more striking was the following exchange, which took place in the course of a discussion which emphasized the difficulty faced by another institution in recruiting adequate numbers of nursing personnel.

Medical Superintendent: [to Merten] Are you suggesting that we should have asked for more help?

Deputy Director Merten: I guess what I'm saying is that you people ought to give some consideration to the question of whether your present staffing is sufficient to carry on an adequate medical care program. If you don't think it is, and if you think you could do a more adequate job with more people, you ought to ask for them.

Further discussion produced agreement that this institution would submit a supplemental request for enough new people to bring their staff up to a reasonable level. Once again Merten's skilled judgments concerning what would or would not be acceptable were decisive, as he advised institutional personnel to ask for a large number of new employees at the same—or only slightly higher—rates of pay rather than much higher pay rates for roughly the same number of employees. "This might be finagling a little bit," he admitted, "but it would stand a better chance of approval." [8]

"Is there much chance of getting the supplemental approved?" asked the superintendent. Merten's reply was interesting:

I don't know, but I do know this: you won't get it if you don't ask for it. Most of the financial experts say that the state will have to raise an extra two hundred fifty to three hundred million dollars for the new biennium even if no increases are made in the distribution of state school aid or in the level of support for public aid or the universities. Now you can be sure that most of these agencies will be asking for increases—the teachers colleges and the University of Illinois have already announced that they will ask for more money. Unless we are willing to ask for what we need to run an adequate program, we will not be able to get our fair share. [9]

---

[8] In a later letter to the author, Deputy Director Merten explained the thinking behind the recommendation as follows: "Budget instructions provide that funds for new employees requested in the budget are to be computed at Step I of the salary range. In 1963 many of the salary levels for professional and technical personnel were entirely inadequate (many have since been revised upward). As a practical matter we knew that we would have to start physicians, psychologists, social workers, nurses, etc., well above the minimum salary range; therefore the decision to request a slightly higher number of employees rather than listing high starting salaries."

[9] Use of the term "fair share" does not imply a well-developed idea of what Mental Health should get in comparison to all other agencies. This was the first and last time that I heard the term mentioned by anyone. On the other hand, the concept does reflect the attitude that this department deserves some adequate (or fair) portion of the increases likely to be appropriated by the legislature to the largest agencies. Mental Health keeps abreast of what these increases are likely to be (an announcement of the increase to be requested by the state universities appeared in the press on the day before this meeting) and uses that information to develop its judg-

This entire exchange makes it clear that the department is willing to give strong support to increases that can be defended in terms of program adequacy and improvement. More significantly, it also suggests that considerations of program improvement are likely to carry more weight when other large state agencies are known to be pressing for increases themselves. The Mental Health Department, in short, does not and cannot make its decisions in a political-administrative vacuum; it is alert to what other state agencies are doing and tailors its actions accordingly. The strategic value of late budget submission—and remember that these decisions were being made some five to six weeks *after* the Governor's September 10 deadline—now becomes apparent, for the later the date of submission, the greater the ability of department officials to gauge the temper of the budgetary situation with accuracy.[10] And the more accurate this estimate is, the greater are the department's chances for formulating an effective budgetary strategy. In this instance, faced with the certainty of requested budget increases from other agencies, and anxious to spur its own plans for expansion, the department encouraged increased requests whenever it felt confident of its ability to defend them.

All this, perhaps, may suggest that decisions regarding what to ask for are made less according to the "merits" of particular requests than according to considerations of "what the department can get." To a considerable extent this is true, though it would be quite unfair to suggest that departmental representatives are interested in more money simply for the sake of more money. It is essential to bear in mind that, short of providing a doctor and equipment for each patient under departmental care, standards of patient care are limited only by availability of funds. Professionals in this highly professional department are fully aware of proper standards of care for the patients they treat. Their "budget" problem does not revolve around the need

ment about how much it should request. Compare Aaron Wildavsky, *The Politics of the Budgetary Process* (Boston: Little, Brown and Co., 1964), pp. 16-17.

[10] I do not mean to suggest that Mental Health consciously plans to submit its budget request as late as it can. I merely wish to note that one consequence of taking so much time to prepare its budget is to vastly improve the quality of departmental judgment on the vital question: "How much can we get?"

to gain legislative approval for better standards—indeed they would just as soon keep the legislature away from that problem for fear of what these "laymen" might do to carefully devised "professional" programs. Their real problem is to get the money to be able to do what they know they would like to do. In this sense, the "merits" of particular requests are not so much unimportant as assumed, and assuming that "merit" is established, the central question becomes "How much can we get, and how can we guarantee that we get it?"

From this point of view, of course, a budgeting system that tends to assume the legitimacy of existing appropriation levels is very useful to the department, for it both focuses strategic planning on increases and offers some obvious rules for making strategic decisions. Some of the rules, such as avoiding lapses or large increases except where they are easily defended, are fairly obvious. Others are less easy to detect, partly because they represent more conscious efforts at manipulation. Though some of these strategies have already been hinted at in the above discussion, it will be useful to provide a more systematic, if brief, review of them here.

Strategies, of course, cannot transcend existing budget categories and procedures, but they can be built upon the opportunities provided by the existing forms and processes. More precisely, it is possible to control the kind of information submitted to external reviewing authorities by (a) Manipulating payments from the "accounts" set up by appropriations; (b) Manipulating the items included in the "basic" and "supplemental" budgets; and (c) Manipulating the use of various funds to support expenditures.

Should an ophthalmologist brought into a state hospital to examine patients' eyes be paid from the "Personal Services" or "Contractual Services" appropriation? Or perhaps the "Travel" appropriation should be used, particularly if the specialist is located some distance away from the hospital and if both the Personal Services and Contractual Services accounts are running short of funds. Certain employees of this same hospital, who live in buildings that are part of the institutional complex, are granted a reduction in rent as compensation for overtime work. Should this be recorded as an increase in "Personal Services" or as a decrease in "Maintenance" allowance? Depending on how such transactions are recorded, the figures contained on the budget forms submitted by the various institutions can vary a great deal. Since statutory definitions of the kinds of expenditures properly supported by each of the "object" appropriations cannot hope to cover the variety of ambiguous expenditure situations which arise, institutional officials necessarily have considerable leeway in determining which accounts to use for which payments. Though this freedom need not be used for strategic purposes, such uses are not at all uncommon, particularly in that hazy region between "Personal Services" and "Contractual Services." A careful use of one account to support activities normally paid from another account can accomplish a number of strategic purposes, ranging from avoidance of suspicious questioning to creation of the *raison d'être* of a proposed increase.

Even more important, from a strategic point of view, is the existence of what amounts to two budgets: the basic budget and the supplemental budget. Because the basic budget is defined solely in terms of money, it is frequently possible to reduce, expand, or otherwise modify programs or purchases without exceeding the limits imposed by the basic budget. And because it is assumed that the basic budget will be given little scrutiny as long as money limits are not exceeded, most institutional officials are anxious to put as many of their requests into the basic budget as they can. Central office personnel, following the same assumptions, are normally happy to cooperate, and issue frequent instructions to move requests for equipment or new personnel from proposed supplementals back to the basic budgets "because you're not spending up to your appropriation." Sometimes, particularly with regard to the "Personal Services" category, these shifts have the effect of actually increasing the dollars to be included in the basic request over the current appropriation level. In one such case, the deputy director and his aides expended a great deal of effort in moving items from a proposed Personal Services supplemental request into the basic request. The supplemental was materially reduced, but the basic increased from a $10.1 million current appropriation to a $10.5 million new request.

If basic-supplemental budgeting does not always follow the pattern dictated by the Finance Department (i.e., no increases in the basic budget), it is nevertheless instrumental in creating the feeling, among departmental officials, that the basic budget figure represents the amount to which the department or one of its sub-units is "entitled." In a very literal sense, the phrase "your appropriation," when applied to an agency's basic figure, means just that; it connotes a sum of money which "belongs" to the agency as a matter of right and is therefore not to be tampered with. Thus if central office personnel reduce one account in a basic request, they will frequently increase another, in order to maintain the level of financial support to be requested in the basic. Institutional spokesmen for their part assume a proprietary interest in sums allocated to their various accounts, and are quick to protest past or present reductions. "Our Travel," said one hospital superintendent, "was cut in 1960 and we have never gotten it back up."

The drive to "put it in the basic," coupled with the notion that agencies are "entitled" to the appropriated sum currently authorized helps to explain the pattern of continued appropriation increases exhibited by the department. If an expanded program can be placed under the covering umbrella of a basic budget calculated in dollar amounts, it will become part of the "property" to which the agency is "entitled." And if this can be achieved, the chances are good that few, or no, questions will be raised about it in the next budget period, when attention will focus once again on the proposed increases. Knowing this, central office personnel are led to soften their skepticism over requests for large increases by adopting the attitude that "if you don't use all of it [the increase] for this, you can use it for other work." Even here, however, the all important desire to preserve confidence is operative, for while the central office will frequently approve large shifts (and even increases) in the basic requests, they will do so only when persuaded that such shifts can be defended if necessary. Blatant attempts to begin completely new programs by hiding new personnel in a basic, for example, are patiently weeded out by the deputy director, who normally advises submission of a supplemental request in such cases.

Changes within the basic request or shifts between the basic and supplemental requests are difficult to detect, and sometimes cause confusion even for so experienced a hand as the deputy director. Further complications arise from the use of several different funds to support departmental activities. While the bulk of the department's operating expenditures are paid out of the General Revenue Fund, and the bulk of its capital expenditures out of the Public Welfare Building Fund (Bond Issue), appropriations are also made from the *state* Mental Health Fund and from *three federal* funds (Child Welfare, Mental Health, and Veterans Bureau). Though use of these additional funds is partially restricted to certain purposes only, in practice their use is subject to a variety of more or less strategic designs. Thus federal funds used to support the salaries—but not operating expenses—of persons operating certain programs can create the impression of low-cost service. With such service firmly implanted as part of the ongoing departmental program, it is then possible to switch the salary expense over to state funds in the next budget. Instead of a suspiciously large one-shot change, a less noticeable shift in smaller increments can be made. Or, programs or agencies for which no specific appropriation has been made can be operated entirely on federal funds. Similarly the availability of a substantial special state fund (the Mental Health Fund) can permit program expansion or new construction even when general funds are not available.

Most important of all, the availability of alternative sources of support provides a constant opportunity to control the flow of financial information available to external sources. A judicious shifting of purchases or salary payments from a state to a federal fund, or from one state fund to another, can produce expenditure records that suggest the inadequacy of state appropriations, or the consistency of state spending (despite periodic fluctuations), or even the frugality of agency officials (e.g., "lapsing" amounts from minor accounts such as Travel). Few institutional officials attempt to exploit such strategic opportunities, but those who do are in a position to create a desired financial "image" through day-to-day decisions to charge expenditures to one fund or another. Together with the control that can be exercised over expenditures from the various object accounts, and used in conjunction with basic-supplemental budgeting, this strategic tool places great informational power into the hands of institutional and departmental spokesmen.

Most of the decisions made during the course of these formal hearings are final—in the sense that they ultimately appear in the request submitted to the Finance Department. Roughly another month is required, however, to clear up the few items which, because of poor agency preparation or inadequate information, are found to be unsatisfactory to the deputy director. Consultations between the various institutional representatives and central office personnel are common during this "clean-up" period, at the conclusion of which the completed forms for each agency are presented to the Director of Mental Health for his approval. Though largely a formality in terms of specific amounts, the director's participation can be and is influential in determining the degree of expansiveness that will be reflected in institutional requests. During the course of budget preparation for the 73rd biennium the director had made it clear that he would give strong support to plans for improving existing institutional programs. As a result, the operating budget submitted to the Department of Finance on January 10, 1963, included an increase of $17.2 million in the basic budget request (from a current appropriation of $196.5 to a request of $213.7 million). Supplemental requests of some $36.9 million brought the total of increases requested from the General Revenue Fund up to $54.1 million. Slight decreases in reappropriations and expected contributions from the U.S. Veterans Bureau fund diminished the over-all increase requested, but the jump from an appropriation of $206.2 million to a request of $259.7 million indicated that the department was taking its program responsibilities very seriously indeed.

SUMMARY: AGENCY BUDGETS AND AGENCY STATUS

To look closely at the way decisions are made in the preparation of a Mental Health "budget" is to recognize, once again, the extent to which the budgetary discourse is shaped by the informational categories controlled by the Department of Finance. Because these categories reflect a desire to know *how much* money was or will be spent for *which* things, budget presentation and review is rarely accomplished in any terms but these. And because these categories place such heavy emphasis on the distinction between money that *is* and money that *will be* available, all other bases for comparison are effectively squeezed out of consideration. What remains, from the observer's point of view, is little more than a series of financial "before and after" snapshots from a camera that appears to be aimed rather indiscriminately at everything—from the largest to the smallest sums. Lacking discrimination, the camera of departmental review gives precisely the same attention to every appropriation item, which is to say that each item is treated as an entity completely within itself, related to nothing except its own past record of sums appropriated and spent. Necessarily, the resulting "budget" is little more than a series of sums, whose chief relationship is their appearance on the same printed page.

Equally apparent is the extraordinary degree to which the central office staff imposes its financial and strategic judgments upon requests made by the operating agencies. This is an important point to consider, for the imposition of central office judgments concerning finances and strategies contrasts sharply against the general unwillingness of the central office to offer judgments concerning the substance of institutional programs. Departmental and institutional *policies*, in other words, are determined elsewhere, through procedures distinct from the process of budget preparation. Given the nonprogrammatic orientation of Deputy Director Merten and the inability of the existing budget categories to accommodate programmatic conceptions, this conclusion is hardly surprising. Nevertheless it must be emphasized, in order to make clear that program and policy innovation normally do *not* originate in the process of budget preparation. Budgeting in Mental Health is essentially negative and defensive, designed to protect departmental assets and, if possible, expand them slightly, but not to break new paths or propose radical increases in expenditure. Specialized skills are necessary to perform these budgetary tasks well, but precisely because these skills are related more to a particular situation than to an organized body of knowledge, it is both feasible and strategically desirable to gather them together in the central office. Budgetary specialization thus becomes an adjunct to organizational power, concerned with maintaining a given status, rather than a rationalized technique for planning future policies and expenditures.

The conclusion that budgetary activities in the Department of Mental Health are primarily directed toward the maintenance of organizational status seems applicable to other agencies as well, for despite unusual organizational attributes such as large size and professionalization, budget roles in Mental Health clearly reflect the very same presuppositions and rules which organize budget roles in other agencies. Mental Health officials are more conscious of what they do, and thus more careful in doing it than are the secretaries and clerks in many of the smaller agencies. But regardless of the manner in which the activity is carried out, the nature of the activity in all agencies is determined by existing informational categories and the subculture that has developed around those categories.

By suggesting that the activities of this subculture are not particularly relevant to organizational expansion, the experience of the Mental Health Department raises this further question: "Through what role or roles does this form of organizational change take place?" Some possible answers to this question already have been suggested in the above discussion and will be dealt with at some length in a later chapter. It will be useful to keep the question in mind, meanwhile, as we move on to consider other budgetary roles.

CHAPTER FOUR

THE ILLINOIS BUDGETARY COMMISSION: STATUS IN SEARCH OF A ROLE

The Illinois Budgetary Commission is perhaps the best known, and least understood, of all the agencies officially involved in budgeting for the state organization. Its notoriety rests primarily upon its historic practice of recommending reductions on the appropriation requests submitted by the various state agencies. This practice, carefully publicized in biennial announcements of the millions of dollars "cut" from budget requests by the commission, has established the commission's reputation as *the* source of budgetary strength in Illinois. As one knowledgeable official put it, "We may not do much budgeting around here, but what we do is done by the Budgetary Commission." And yet next to nothing is known about the manner in which the commission conducts its work, or the reasons for its actions, or the relationship between what it does and the activities of other budgetary actors. In part this is a result of the commission's own failure to maintain records of its deliberations. To an even greater extent, however, confusion about the role of the Budgetary Commission has arisen out of unresolved ambiguities written into statutory provisions which define the nature and purpose of the commission itself.

ORIGINS

Open conflict between the Governor and the legislature provided the impetus for the development of the Budgetary Commission as another fiscal agency.[1] In 1937 Democratic Governor Henry Horner, searching for a way to cope with pressures for increased state expenditures, submitted to the legislature a proposal for a 3 per cent tax on the sales of utility companies. The proposal passed the Senate easily enough, but in the House the Republican minority was able to stall the bill long enough to force the Governor to submit his budget before he was ready to do so. Although Horner indicated that the early budget could not be construed as a set of "recommendations" in view of his own lack of sufficient preparation, House Republicans used these preliminary figures as the basis for prolonged attacks on both the budget totals and the form in which they were presented. House Democrats from Cook County, meanwhile, were preparing their own rebellion against Horner's plan to prevent assignment of responsibility for the collection of driver's license fees to the Secretary of State, an office then held by a Cook County Democrat. This dispute, too, affected the state budget situation, for the House Majority Leader announced, on May 20, that "the Governor won't be able to move a single appropriation bill until the driver's license bill is advanced."

Given the continuing pressure for increased state spending and the similarly intractable hostility between Horner and his Cook County Democratic colleagues, it appeared that neither of these problems would be solved in a single legislative session. But they could be temporized. And one way to temporize was to create a commission to look further into the matters. Accordingly, on July 9, 1937, the Governor signed a bill to create the Illinois Budgetary Commission. The provisions of the new law clearly reflected the breakdown in executive-legislative relations which had taken place during the 1937 legislative session. Of the new commission's seven members, one was to be the Governor, serving in an ex officio capacity, two were to be the respective chairmen of the House and Senate Appropriations committees, and the remaining four were to be chosen by the House Speaker

[1] The following brief summary of the origins of the Budgetary Commission is drawn primarily from the *Chicago Tribune* of January to June, 1937.

(two) and the Senate President (two). The commission was authorized, first, to "make a thorough study and investigation of all State expenditures and income from any source" and, second, to "make a study of all license tax fees, and where such fees are for services rendered by the State, shall determine if said fees are inadequate for the services so rendered." Recommendations flowing from such studies were to be submitted to the Governor "not later than the first day of September prior to the convening of the next regular session of the General Assembly," while a duplicate of this report was to be submitted later to the legislature itself. No further specification of duties and no further provisions for staffing the commission were made.[2]

In light of this statement of the responsibilities of the new commission, use of the term "budgetary" in its title presented something of an anomaly. Nothing in the statute took away any of the Governor's clear-cut authority to determine the content of the budget document. Nor did the statute assign the commission any authority to determine appropriations. Indeed it could not do so without a change in the Illinois Constitution, which assigns exclusive authority to determine appropriations to the legislature. At best the "recommendations" required from the commission could have advisory status only, with implementation left entirely in the hands of either the Governor or the legislature, or both. Moreover, since the procedures to be followed by the commission in preparing its "studies" were not spelled out, and since no provision for staff services was made, the statute left considerable doubt with regard to the meaning to be attached to the "budgetary" work it authorized.

The statute clearly was not a product of a legislative consensus to improve the quality of legislative participation in budgeting. Instead, the commission appears to have been designed to provide a vehicle capable of dealing with the two very specific problems that had arisen in the 1937 session. From a political point of view the new agency could keep channels of communication open between the Governor and the legislature—or at least the legislative leadership. And from a fiscal point of view, the commission was specifically empowered to concern itself with the license fee dispute that had created such a heated intra-

---

[2] *Illinois Revised Statutes 1949*, Ch. 127, Secs. 193-199.

party controversy. Application of the term "Budgetary Commission" to this vehicle did little more than foster expectations that do not appear to have coincided with the expectations implicit in the body of the statute itself.

In determining the uses to which this new statute would be put, the commission chose a course of action which emphasized its limited interest in an expansion of the legislative budget role. Constitutional and statutory limitations, to be sure, prevented the commission from exercising direct authority over either the Governor's budget or legislative appropriations. But the commission could easily and legitimately have established formalized procedures for fiscal investigations, or developed and publicized various kinds of financial data, or chosen to put together its own comprehensive budget recommendations for public consideration. Yet the commission did none of these things. Instead, it chose to act as little more than a medium of consultation between the Governor and the legislative leadership. The commission obtained no staff of its own, its deliberations were arranged informally and conducted largely in secret, no records were maintained, and such recommendations as were made were normally made privately to the Governor, but not to the legislature, on the basis of information provided by one of the Governor's own executive departments (Finance). Thus by 1952 the role of the commission could be summarized in the following succinct terms: "(1) it provides a means for general executive-legislative liaison in budget preparation, (2) it conducts budget hearings with the aid of the Department of Finance and makes recommendations regarding appropriations on the basis thereof, (3) it supplies, through regular staff studies, comparative data on biennial expenditures and a listing of state taxes and license fees, and (4) it maintains a file of audit reports." [3]

To a large extent, of course, the stance adopted by the commission was a direct consequence of the Governor's involvement in its work. An enlarged conception of commission responsibili-

[3] Illinois Legislative Council, *Legislative Budget Staffing* (Legislative Council Publication 111, October, 1952), p. 5. This report points out that the commission, until the mid-1940's, had occasionally issued biennial reports of some consequence. A report issued on September 1, 1944, for example, dealt with a variety of topics such as office space rentals, relief, inheritance taxes, and others.

ties necessarily would have created another center of budgetary influence capable of challenging the Governor. As long as the Governor remained a member of the commission, the development of such a conception was bound to be inhibited, perhaps not so much by direct political pressure as by the erosion of motivation for an alternative arrangement. By confining itself to a liaison role that offered no public challenge to the Governor, the commission could fairly claim participation in the budget process and could, depending on the cooperation of the Governor, claim to have had an impact as well. For his part, the Governor could ensure the cooperation of legislative leaders simply by accepting—or appearing to accept—the recommendations made to him by the commission. Thus, the commission, with status conferred by the Governor, could gain considerable prestige as a powerful budget agency while the Governor, in return, could encourage legislative acquiescence to his financial proposals.

Something like this system of mutual reinforcement seems to have marked the first decade or so of the commission's existence. Though it is difficult to document, scattered newspaper accounts suggest a close relationship between the Governor and the commission throughout this period, with the commission playing an especially significant part in the postwar expenditure of an accumulated wartime revenue surplus. As long as a close relationship was maintained between the commission and the Governor, there was no particular need to develop a more rationalized or systematic definition of the commission's purposes and procedures. The commission cooperated with the Governor in preparing the budget and did so with relative informality—and that seems to be as much as anyone knew, or cared to know.

But the presumed strength conferred upon the commission by its close relationship to the Governor was also its greatest weakness. Failure to develop an independent point of view meant that the commission would be forced to drift aimlessly whenever it failed to reach some form of accommodation with the Governor. No governor, of course, could be forced to pay any attention to commission recommendations if he did not choose to do so, and if he did not, the principal foundation for the belief in the "power" of the commission disappeared. During the decade beginning in 1950, this foundation was progressively weakened as the relationship between the commission and the Governor became increasingly distant. As far as Republican Governor Stratton was concerned, budgeting was his responsibility, and his alone. The hearings conducted by the commission were occasionally useful as forums for the expression of different points of view, he thought, but were largely "window dressing" in terms of their impact on specific budgetary decisions. Stratton himself made those decisions and normally incorporated them into budget messages which he wrote with his own hand.[4]

By ignoring the commission, except for a polite biennial expression of appreciation for its good work on the budget, Stratton eliminated the principal justification for the role it had chosen to play. Curiously, the commission refused to attempt a new formulation of its role, preferring instead to continue old procedures that had been based upon its self-image as a consultative body. Meetings continued to be arranged informally and conducted privately, recommendations continued to be made to the Governor—who ignored them or not as he saw fit—and record-keeping of any sort continued to be overlooked, except for the periodic biennial announcements of the amounts cut from budget requests by the commission. If the commission members were reluctant to examine their activities, however, others were not, perhaps because of a general recognition that the earlier justification for the commission's behavior no longer existed. Citizens' organizations joined legislative agencies in expressing dissatisfaction with the commission and in proposing alternative conceptions of its proper role.[5] As in 1937, when an unusual combination of events provided a catalyst for the creation of the Budgetary Commission, another catalyst was required in the mid-1950's before any attempt was made to formulate a new definition of the obligations of the commission.

This time the catalytic agent was the discovery, in 1956, that well over a million dollars in state funds had been embezzled by an elected state officer, Auditor of Public Accounts Orville

---

[4] Interview with former Governor William G. Stratton, May 10, 1962.

[5] In addition to the above (note 3) report of the Legislative Council, see Roger Henn, *Control of the Purse Strings—Part I* (Springfield: Taxpayers' Federation of Illinois, September, 1952), for an excellent critique of Illinois financial procedures in general and the Budgetary Commission in particular.

Hodge. The investigation that followed this discovery proved to be a severe embarrassment for the Budgetary Commission, which not only had approved the regular appropriation requests submitted by the Auditor, but also had permitted a $500,000 supplemental request to slip by virtually unnoticed, thus adding to the funds available for the Auditor's illicit purposes. Commenting harshly on the commission's failure to review the Auditor's requests for money, an investigating committee led by a former president of the University of Illinois suggested that the commission "is wholly without the staff necessary to perform thoroughly critical budget request studies" and that both "the Commission and the legislature were without staff, funds, facilities and means to make the needed investigation and analysis of the Auditor's requests." [6]

To remedy these deficiencies the investigators proposed "a legislative redefinition of the duties of the Budgetary Commission." Noting perceptively that "except for use of the word as part of the name of the Commission, there is not a single reference in the Act to budgets or budgeting," the report submitted by the investigating team went on to list a series of recommendations which provided a basis for amendments to the commission statute which were adopted by the 1957 legislature. The 1957 amendments enlarged legislative membership on the commission from six to fourteen (including the two Appropriations committees chairmen), provided specifically for a professional staff in the form of an executive director "experienced in government and in management and fiscal analysis," and attempted to define the budgetary duties of the commission with greater precision. On the one hand, the commission itself was authorized to investigate both budget procedures and budget requests and to report its conclusions in the form of a published report to the Governor and legislature no later than the first of March in each legislative year. And, on the other hand, the duties assigned to the executive director included items such as "cost studies and management analyses," as well as any other studies the commission might desire. During legislative sessions, moreover, the

---

[6] Lloyd Morey, Albert E. Jenner, Jr., and John S. Rendleman, *Report and Recommendations to Illinois Budgetary Commission*, December 4, 1956, pp. 44, 45.

executive director was assigned the duty of analyzing all appropriations measures introduced and submitting his analyses to members of the House and Senate Appropriations committees.[7]

Here, then, was a considerable expansion of the original statutory conception of Budgetary Commission responsibilities, directly related to the budget, and conceived within the framework of what obviously was a professional approach to governmental "management." The new conception, however, represented something imposed upon the commission from the outside. In 1957, as in 1937, there simply was no ground swell of legislative opinion in favor of a more active—or more professional—budgetary role for a predominantly legislative agency. On both occasions the desire to "do something" about a very specific problem took precedence over whatever desire there may have been to construct a theoretically sound system of budgetary responsibilities. Indeed, it was only because these reforms offered an acceptable way out of a very difficult problem situation that they were considered at all by the legislative leaders. But while such reforms were being considered on paper, the fundamental structure of the commission remained very much the same: the Governor retained his membership, and control over the remaining participants remained in the hands of the legislative leadership. And the Governor, at least, was clear about his own view of the commission's role, as his later veto of an expanded commission appropriation revealed. Hodge scandal or not, the position of the commission after the 1957 session remained essentially what it had been during its previous twenty years.

Not until 1959 were funds appropriated to the commission for the purpose of obtaining a full-time director to carry out its expanded statutory responsibilities. And since the enlarged appropriation did not become available until July, 1959, when work on the 1959 biennial budget already had been completed, whatever impact the new arrangements were to have could not begin to be felt before late 1960, when work on the 1961 (72nd) biennial budget was scheduled to begin. But 1960 was also an elec-

---

[7] For a detailed account of other changes proposed at this time and their subsequent disposition see Steiner and Gove, *op. cit.*, pp. 134-163.

tion year—a fact which added a further dimension to the uncertainty surrounding the future activities of the commission. When Democrat Otto Kerner was elected to replace Republican Governor Stratton in November, 1960, the commission was faced with a situation calling for a twofold accommodation. It had not yet attempted to exercise its expanded responsibilities, although it now had sufficient resources to at least begin to do so. Whether and how such an exercise would take place would depend, in turn, on the commission's relationship with the new Governor. Kerner, who was both new and inexperienced, and who had given no indication of his own expectations with regard to the commission's activities, was the unknown quantity.

In the face of these uncertainties the commission avoided the requirements imposed upon it by the recent statutory amendments. Although it now had an executive director, he was used as little more than a clerk. The commission once again conducted itself as a consultative body, holding its hearings and transmitting its recommendations for cuts to the Governor without the benefit of any formal report. This approach had been workable in previous years when governors actually consulted with the commission, or when, by ignoring the commission, governors themselves assumed full responsibility for the budget document. On this occasion, however, the new Governor neither consulted with the commission nor assumed personal responsibility. Enmeshed in his own difficulties, Governor Kerner followed a course which ultimately produced a last minute conflict between his budget recommendations and the legislature's willingness to finance them. (See Chapter 5.)

A special legislative economy committee was hurriedly created during the last week of the 1961 session in order to bring about a reconciliation between anticipated expenditures and revenues. Though the committee failed to achieve its objectives, it had a dual significance for the position of the Budgetary Commission. First, the failure to include the leadership of the commission as members of the special economy committee represented a serious, if implicit, criticism of the structure and functions of the commission itself. Such criticism became much more open and frequent during the next (73rd) legislative session, stimulated largely by members of the so-called "Economy Bloc." Second, the failure of the special committee to bring expenditures and revenues into line created what appeared to be a serious fiscal crisis throughout the latter part of 1961 and early 1962. This crisis eventually strained relationships between the Governor and the Budgetary Commission to the point of open hostility. Once again, the very foundation and justification for the commission's consultative or liason role had broken down.

As the 1963 (73rd) budget period approached, then, a basic ambiguity concerning the proper role of the Budgetary Commission persisted. The commission did not possess, and (short of Constitutional or statutory changes) could not be given *authority* to determine budget or appropriation figures. But it did have broad investigatory powers and was authorized to make *recommendations* to both the Governor and the legislature. Traditionally such recommendations had been made informally to the Governor in a nonpublic fashion which suggested that the commission saw itself as a liaison agency only. Although the desire for such a liaison agency appears to have been the principal motivation for the original creation of a body composed of both the Governor and legislative leaders, gubernatorial participation in the commission's deliberations had ceased to exist by the early 1950's, thus destroying the basis for the commission's early orientation. Despite this, and despite repeated efforts to impose an alternative orientation on the commission, the original choice of a liaison role was maintained and promised to continue throughout the 1963 budget period. To understand this reluctance to change it is necessary to know more about commission personnel and to develop a deeper understanding of the mechanics of commission behavior.

THE PERMANENT ELITE

From the beginning the Budgetary Commission was structured to draw its legislative membership from the Senate and House leadership groups. Chairmen of the two Appropriations committees automatically qualified for membership, while the remaining places were at the disposal of the Speaker, elected by the majority party in the House, and the Executive Committee, controlled by the majority party in the Senate. During the first twenty years of its existence, when commission membership was confined to only three legislators from each house, selection of commissioners necessarily was restricted to the small group of men who were themselves the leaders of the two houses. The commission thus assumed the quality of a legislative power elite. As the commission and the Governor drifted further apart, this quality reinforced the increasingly popular notion that the commission was primarily—if not exclusively—a legislative agency. Curiously, acceptance of this view by the commission itself led to no change in the actions of the commission. There was not a little irony in this, for now the commission, as well as the Governor, had repudiated the consultative orientation—without any apparent impact on commission behavior.

By 1957, when the commission statute was amended, this joint repudiation of the consultative idea had become firmly established. In attempting to modify the ideas which might determine future commission behavior, however, the 1957 amendments neglected to deal with the bases of commission practice, which remained firmly rooted in the control over commission personnel available to the legislative leadership. Though legislative membership on the commission was more than doubled, the method of selecting that membership was unchanged. Given this fact, and in view of the extraordinary stability of legislative membership in general, it is less than surprising to learn that control over the commission remained in precisely the same hands after 1957 as before that date. Nor is it any more surprising to learn that the members added to the commission as a result of the 1957 amendments were all carefully screened to ensure commission harmony.

A closer look at the membership of the commission during the preparation of the 73rd biennial budget presents a revealing insight into its character. Perhaps its best-known member was Representative Paul Powell, an almost legendary southern Illinois politician then serving in his thirtieth consecutive year in the lower house. A colorful politician, who had been downstate Illinois campaign manager during the Truman campaign of 1948, Powell had distinguished himself in the House as a hard-working and extremely knowledgeable legislator whose chief concern was to increase the share of tangible state benefits available to his southern Illinois constituency. Powell had been more than usually successful at this pursuit, using the experience and power built up during his three terms as Speaker (1949, 1959, 1961), long-time service on important legislative committees, and a position of some importance in the state Democratic organization. Powell always had paid particular attention to state jobs and state money, and chose his committee assignments accordingly. Obtaining a seat on the Budgetary Commission in 1945, Powell had maintained his membership continuously since that time and had served several terms as vice-chairman. Although Republican control of the lower house in the 1963 session cost him the speakership for that session, Powell assumed the job of House Minority Leader and remained one of the two or three most influential members of the General Assembly. Powell's experience, reputation, and power added considerably to the political weight of the Budgetary Commission, which Powell was once again serving as vice-chairman.

Though less flamboyant as a politician, and therefore less well known to the public, Senator Everett R. Peters was the most important member of the 1963 commission. Like Powell, who was his close political ally, Peters was a veteran of thirty years in the legislature who had moved to the Senate in 1940 after three terms in the House. In the Senate Peters quickly became a spokesman for the University of Illinois, which is in his district, and gradually assumed a position of prominence within the small circle of Republicans who led the Senate Republican Caucus and thus controlled Senate affairs. Peters, too, was concerned about increasing the share of tangible state benefits —jobs, buildings, highways—flowing to his district and busied himself with the details of state finance. By the middle of his second Senate term Peters had become Chairman of the Budgetary Commission at a time when the commission appears to have worked closely with Republican Governor Green in determining the budgetary implications of the shift from a wartime to a peacetime state government. Though Peters lost the chairmanship in 1947, he regained it in 1949 and, in 1963, was serving his eighth consecutive term as chairman.[8] Throughout

---

[8] After the close of the 1963 legislative session, Peters lost the chairmanship to Representative William J. Murphy. Murphy was subsequently dropped from the Republican slate of candidates for the 1964 at-large election and thus lost his position both in the legislature and on the commission. Murphy was replaced at the beginning of the 1965 session by Senator A. L. Cronin. Peters, meanwhile, continued to serve on the commission.

this period Peters maintained a strong leadership position in the Senate as sometime chairman of the influential Committee on Committees, member of the Executive Committee, and member-chairman of the Appropriations Committee. Informally, Senator Peters acted as the chief expert and spokesman on state finance for the Republican Senate majority.

The presence of these two members of the legislative elite on the Budgetary Commission roster for such an extended period of time reflected the intimacy of the relationship between the commission and the leaders of the House and Senate. Powell and Peters, of course, were themselves leaders and therefore in a position to maintain their membership. Beyond that, they had been in a position to exert considerable influence over the kinds of persons selected for the additional places on the commission. Thus, the 1963 commission membership from the House included Appropriations Committee Chairman Lloyd (Curly) Harris, a veteran of twenty-six years in the legislature and long-time southern Illinois ally of Powell. Democratic Representative Clyde Choate, a sixteen-year veteran from southern Illinois, was a well-known Powell protégé, while Democratic Representative Joseph DeLaCour was an agreeable sixteen-year veteran representing the Cook County organization. When the Republican majority organized the House in January, 1963, Harris was replaced as Appropriations Chairman by Peter C. Granata, another thirty-year veteran friendly to Powell. And when DeLaCour moved to his newly won Senate seat at the same time, his Republican replacement was George S. Brydia, a twenty-five year veteran who, despite his nominal Republicanism, had helped engineer the election of Democrat Powell as Speaker in 1959. Brydia's Republican House colleagues on the commission were Representatives William E. Pollack, who was a close personal associate of Senator Peters, and Charles K. Willett, who was the only member other than Powell to have served a term on the commission prior to its enlargement in the 1957 session. Like Willett, who joined in 1955, Pollack and Choate, who joined in 1957, were reappointed to the commission for each session which followed.

On the Senate side, Republican commissioners in addition to Peters included Arthur Bidwill, T. Mac Downing, and Fred Hart. Of these, Downing was a twenty-five year Senate veteran in his retirement year who had served four terms as commissioner in the period 1945-53. Hart was a near seatmate and close associate of Senator Peters, and Bidwill was the Senate Majority Leader and President Pro Tem serving his twenty-eighth year as a state senator. Bidwill's confidence in the leadership given the commission by Senator Peters, incidentally, was so great that he rarely attended meetings. An unfilled vacancy left only two Democratic senators on the commission, A. L. Cronin and Edmund Sweeney, both of whom represented the Cook County organization. Except for Senator Downing none of these men had served on the commission prior to 1957. Bidwill joined in that year and remained, Cronin and Hart joined in 1959, and Sweeney served for the first time in 1961.

If we put these several observations on commission personnel together, we can begin to appreciate some of the behavioral characteristics noted earlier. Peters and Powell, alone among the 1963 commissioners, had served for a significant length of time prior to the 1957 rearrangement. The experience gained in these years of service coupled with the powerful position each man continued to hold in his respective legislative chamber made it exceedingly unlikely that other commissioners would have either the ability or the desire to challenge the high status enjoyed by these two men, formalized in their official positions as chairman and vice-chairman. What the other members lacked in commission experience, however, was made up for by the long experience most of them had had as legislators. As men who had come to the legislature twenty to thirty years ago, who were members of the same legislative generation as Peters and Powell and who in most cases had either demonstrated their loyalty to or acquiescence in the leadership given by these two veteran legislators, the other commissioners could be expected to share the outlook of the commission leaders.

If, then, the activities of the commission do not appear to have changed very greatly in the past twenty years, one reasonable explanation for this stability surely lies in the fact that during this same period commission leadership has not changed at all. More significantly, perhaps, commission "followership" clearly had been carefully screened, as of 1963, to maximize internal harmony and minimize internal pressures for an alternative conception of purpose. Though such an alternative conception now existed as a result of the 1957 statutory amendments, the failure of those amendments to alter the method of selecting commission personnel had enabled the existing legislative leaders to confine commission membership to those who were likely to be in agreement with them. Legislators who were not likely to be agreeable were simply ignored. One representative who had been active in the so-called "Economy Bloc" of the 72nd General Assembly responded vigorously when asked if he had ever taken any part in Budgetary Commission activity. "Hell no!" he said. "You don't go there unless you're asked. That's the inner sanctum." Thus, despite the virtually complete breakdown in the conditions necessary for successful pursuit of the liaison role, and in the face of considerable external pressure for change, the Budgetary Commission had succeeded in protecting itself against change. As the 1963 budgeting period approached, the commission's leaders were the same as they had been for two decades, its ostensible purposes were the same, and its actions promised to be the same.

COMMISSION ROLE ORIENTATION

Observations made in 1963 suggest that the commission does not organize its activities according to any clearly defined rationalization of purpose. To begin with, the commission itself does not schedule the hearings in which it determines its recommendations. Instead, it relies on Budget Superintendent T. R. Leth, from the Department of Finance, to indicate that he has accumulated a sufficient number of budget comparisons to warrant a full meeting of the commission. The availability of the comparisons thus determines both the timing and the substance of the hearings, during which the commission reviews the requests for appropriations prepared by the various state agencies. Beginning on November 27, 1962, and concluding on March 4, 1963, eleven such hearings were held to consider requests for the 73rd biennium. Decisions reached at each hearing were, with only a few exceptions, recorded and transmitted immediately to the Governor by Budget Superintendent Leth.

Use of these procedures limits the commission to a *seriatim* review of separate agency requests, which treats each request as an item separate from all other such items. By "taking them as they come," the commission frequently deals on the same day with requests ranging from the largest to the smallest state agencies and programs. Moreover, since decisions on each agency request are normally made on the day of the hearing itself, the commission's final recommendations for a variety of agencies are made as early as November or December, before it has any precise idea of the total amount to be requested or the amount of revenue likely to be available. Only once during the eight hearings attended by the author was the question of total state revenue even raised, and then only as part of a general discussion. Thus the commission does not deal with a "budget" but with requests for appropriations submitted by specific agencies; it takes such requests one-by-one and it disposes of them on their own terms, without recourse to total sums or to abstractions such as "the budget" or "fiscal policy."

The absence of a more abstract definition of commission responsibilities is reflected in other characteristic actions. No systematic attempt is made, for example, to review requests for capital expenditures. Close to $22 million in requests for new capital expenditures for the 73rd biennium was never considered by the commission. There is some evidence that Chairman Peters is conscious of this lack of official interest in capital spending: on one occasion he remarked that "We [the commission] only deal with recurring items here." On the other hand, the commission is inconsistent in applying this rule. Requests for funds totaling some $38.6 million for such items as dam construction were, in fact, considered and disposed of during the 1963 hearings.

Perhaps the key to this apparent inconsistency lies in another more uniformly followed precept which limits the commission's attention to current programs and proposed extensions of current programs. Among the significant innovations which the 73rd General Assembly was called upon to consider were the following: the creation of a new Department of Children and Family Services with an initial appropriation of $4.5 million; a new method of financing capital construction projects valued at some $70 million, and a new appropriation in excess of $12.5 million for judicial salaries following public approval of an amendment to the judicial article of the state constitution. None of these innovations was considered by the Budgetary Commission.[9] This marked reluctance to deal with items which represent a departure from existing routine is reflected in the hearings as well. Agency proposals for completely new programs are normally eliminated, but such action is frequently accompanied by the suggestion that if the new program is really desired it can be introduced in a separate bill. The commission, in short, is not interested in accepting responsibility for any proposal that represents a change in policy or an increase in cost.

Yet even this conclusion must be qualified in the face of commission willingness to approve increases for certain agencies —most notably those supported by special funds. The obvious case in point here is the Division of Highways, whose billion dollar budget request for the 73rd biennium was based upon funds from the federal government and from the state's Road Fund. Following the normal inclination of most state officials to allow programs supported by special funds to spend as much as they expect to receive in income from the special fund, the Budgetary Commission approved the highway budget in minutes, and thus gave its blessing to an increased sum amounting to one-quarter of the total state budget.

The phrase "gave its blessing to" may seriously misrepresent the facts, however, since it implies a positive approval of some known set of circumstances with which the commission agreed. In one sense this is precisely true. Revenues from state motor fuel taxes and automobile license and registration fees are automatically deposited in the Road Fund and automatically allocated to the state and to localities according to a statutory formula. Commission approval of the highway budget can thus be thought of as a simple reaffirmation of a policy established long ago by the legislature. But this line of reasoning focuses on the statutory formula for apportioning funds rather than on the policy content (i.e., where, when, and how to build highways) of the budget. Careful review of Highway Division policies and expenditures is simply beyond the competence of the commission —expenditures are too large and policies too complex for detailed review by the commission's limited staff.

---

[9] No one, in fact, ever "reviewed" the judicial salaries item. It appeared in the budget simply because one of the budget examiners decided to put it there after realizing that the item had been ignored.

In this sense it is probably more accurate to view the commission's quick approval of the highway request as nothing more than a sign of its unwillingness to accept the responsibility of attempting to control an agency whose size and complexity is quite overpowering. This too, is characteristic, for the degree of financial control attempted by the commission over various agencies appears to vary inversely with the size of the agency. Consider the treatment accorded the request of the Department of Mental Health, which was discussed earlier in some detail. After a hearing of some fifteen to twenty minutes, during which a series of questions failed to dent Director Francis J. Gerty's spirited defense of his full budget request, the commission decided to take no action on the request at all. Or again, although the commission dutifully scheduled a whole afternoon for consideration of the requests of the various universities, it concluded by accepting all of the recommendations proposed by the newly created Board of Higher Education, which had reviewed the requests prior to their submission to the commission. An independently derived commission viewpoint simply did not exist.

As far as the commission is concerned, then, there is no such thing as a "total budget" or an over-all "financial program." The commission deals with specific amounts requested by individual agencies on a piecemeal basis, it fails to give systematic attention to capital requests, it avoids requests for new programs, and it gives only the barest kind of formal review to programs supported by special funds and the largest state agencies. Despite these characteristics of commission activity, the record made by the commission in 1963 appears impressive: requested increases totaling $631 million were presented to the Budgetary Commission, but only $358 million in increases were presented later to the Governor. Thus, the commission can be credited with eliminating some $273 million from original budget requests for the 73rd biennium. Or can it?

Table 4 provides a list of the principal reductions recommended by the commission, in descending order of magnitude. Note, incidentally, that the table is confined to requests supported by the state's General Revenue and Common School funds, thus avoiding special funds altogether. Note, also, that very close to 90 per cent of all the reductions credited to the commission are accounted for by the four largest items alone.

Table 4. BUDGETARY COMMISSION REDUCTIONS: 73RD BIENNIUM (GENERAL REVENUE AND COMMON SCHOOL FUNDS)

Agency or Program		Amount of Reduction
School Aid to Local Districts		$106,148,110
Public Aid		63,433,337
State Universities		51,034,550
State Employees' Retirement System		23,577,081
Subtotal, these four items:	$244,193,078	
Public Health		5,318,695
Labor		4,915,120
Universities Retirement System		4,912,600
Vocational Education		2,785,081
Youth Commission		1,940,769
Registration and Education		1,633,972
School Buildings Commission		1,515,079
Vocational Rehabilitation		640,814
Financial Institutions		504,536
All Other		4,640,441
Subtotal, these items:	$ 28,807,107	
Total Reductions		$273,000,185

But the $51 million reduction in the universities' requests was not "made" by the commission; as has just been pointed out, the commission merely acquiesced in reductions that had previously been determined by the Board of Higher Education. Nor did the commission "make" the decision to remove $63 million from the request of the Illinois Public Aid Commission (now the Department of Public Aid). The initiative for that reduction came from the Senate, which had been engaged in a running battle with the administrators of the public aid program. Indeed, the Budgetary Commission's Executive Director, Francis Whitney, knew nothing of the cuts until they were announced by Senator Peters.[10] It is worth noting here, too, that the $23.5

---

[10] Whitney earlier had been directed to prepare recommendations for reducing the public aid budget. He did so, but the final figures used were not his; they were figures developed in secret sessions of the Senate. The public aid fight was one of the most controversial political issues of the session. While a detailed account is beyond the scope of this report, some of its budgetary implications will be discussed below. A running account of the battle can be obtained in the Chicago daily newspapers from Janu-

million cut from the request of the State Employees' Retirement System—like the $4.9 million reduction imposed on the University Retirement System budget—was more shadow than substance. In both cases the funds eliminated represented the amounts necessary to give actuarial soundness to the retirement systems. Though such funds must be requested, the legislature has not approved their appropriations for years. The large ($106 million) reduction in aid to local school districts was initiated by the commission,[11] but the significance of this action is open to some question in view of the subsequent legislative decision to restore these funds—a decision which no commission member opposed (see below). Thus 90 per cent of the reductions for which the commission can take "credit" turn out to have been initiated elsewhere or without substantive effect.

This analysis provides little occasion for surprise, for it has been pointed out already that the commission normally pays only scant attention to the largest programs and agencies, from which the great bulk of the above reductions were taken. Thus, if we list the largest requests made in the budget book and then inquire into the amount of attention given them by the Budgetary Commission (as is done in Table 5), we learn that well over half of the total budget presented to the legislature was considered by the commission in just two hearings, and that only four hearings (of eleven held) were required to dispose of almost 80 per cent of the total budget. When it is recalled that these hearings seldom exceeded two and one-half hours in length, and when it is further recalled that numerous other requests in addition to those listed above were considered during the February 4 and 12 hearings, it becomes apparent that commission review of the largest budget requests was "review" in name only.

The conclusion is thus inescapable: the Budgetary Commission devotes the bulk of its attention to a relatively minor portion of the total spending program of the state. Seven of its eleven hearings were devoted to just 20 per cent of the total budget, and

---

ary through May, 1963. The problem has an interesting budgetary history, part of which is recorded in my earlier article, "Some Budgetary Aspects of the Illinois Fiscal Crisis," *Illinois Government* (Urbana: Institute of Government and Public Affairs), No. 14 (August, 1962).

[11] The best account of this action appears in the *Chicago Sun-Times* of March 5, 1963.

Table 5. BUDGETRAY COMMISSION HEARINGS
FOR LARGEST BUDGET ITEMS

Agency	Date of Hearing	Budget Request
Highways (Div. of)	Feb. 4, 1963	$ 986,392,750
Mental Health	Feb. 4, 1963	273,591,556
Subtotal, these 2 requests:	$1,259,984,306	
Public Aid	Feb. 12, 1963	638,123,146
Finance	Feb. 12, 1963	308,124,754
Subtotal, these 2 requests:	$ 946,247,900	
Universities	Feb. 27, 1963	440,181,068
Common Schools	Mar. 4, 1963	433,090,000
Subtotal, these 2 requests:	$ 873,271,068	
Total		$3,079,503,274[a]
Total, entire budget:		$3,890,164,676

[a] 79.16 per cent of total budget.

produced only 10 per cent of all the reductions recommended
by the commission. These facts must be kept in mind as we look
more closely at the manner in which it accomplishes the bulk
of its work.

THE PROCESS OF DECISION

It is clear from the preceding analysis that, whatever the
nature of the commission's recommendations, the process by
which such recommendations are determined does not require
a great deal of time. A total of eleven two-to-three–hour hearings, after all, was sufficient to accommodate commission action
on a spending program that embraced sixty-five separate agencies
and ultimately stood at just under $4 billion. Such rapid-fire
decision-making is made possible, in part, by commission disinterest in the substantive aspects of agency programs. To some
extent this disinterest is balanced by the knowledge already
available to the experienced members of the commission, particularly Chairman Peters. Most commissioners are neither as experienced nor as knowledgeable as the chairman, however, and
the result is a frequently surprising absence of the most elemen-
tary forms of information about the agencies whose budget

requests are being reviewed. Thus numerous commissioners, at various times, were unaware of items such as the status (permanent or temporary) of a major state commission, the source of funds for another such commission, or even the identity of the director of one of the major code departments.

Statements revealing the absence of information of this order are commonly expressed during commission hearings, but they seldom lead to extended probing of agency operations. Such probing is discouraged by the chief unwritten rule by which the commission operates: "Don't ask too many questions." Although there is no fixed definition of what constitutes "too many" questions, members who exceed the limits of what their colleagues are prepared to tolerate very quickly notice the pointed stares aimed at them, or the buzzing which indicates that other commissioners are no longer paying any attention, or even the gruff intervention of the chairman. One new member, who had the effrontery to ask questions during his first meeting as a commissioner, was given a mild rebuke in the form of a comparison linking him to another member who owned a reputation for "asking too many questions."

The commission is at least equally hostile to information that is volunteered by agency officials in excess of what it is prepared to accept. Here the guideline is more clear, based as it is on the distinction between oral and written information. A brief oral presentation by a representative of the agency being heard is expected and normally requested by Senator Peters. Except in rare instances, however, a written document acts as a red flag of warning to commissioners, who typically begin talking between themselves or leave the room while the written statement is being read or summarized. Sometimes such written statements are not tolerated at all. On one occasion, for example, an agency appeared before the commission with several witnesses who had been brought along to add their support to the agency's request. After listening to the agency director and then to roughly half of a statement that had been prepared by one of the witnesses, Senator Peters interrupted. "Excuse me," he said, "we're running behind. Could you just state—one, two, three—why you think they ought to get what you want them to get? We're all in favor of this here. We know they do wonderful work and all that, but we've got a hundred more people outside waiting to get in." The witness finished quickly and, nothing daunted, another rose immediately from his chair to approach the table, simultaneously unfolding his own prepared statement. "Do you have to read that?" asked Senator Peters. The statement was not read.

Such apparent disinterest in extended presentations of the details of agency operations strongly suggests that commissioners do not look upon hearings as a vehicle for the development of knowledge or the exercise of legislative oversight. Instead, hearings are treated primarily as occasions for making decisions as quickly as possible. Detailed knowledge of agency programs is not required for the bulk of these decisions, which are made according to a formula that provides a small number of very simple rules to follow in determining commission recommendations. These rules, in turn, are based upon the categories of information utilized by the Department of Finance and made available to the commission.

It will be recalled that commission hearings do not begin until a sufficient number of agency requests have been summarized by Finance and made available to the commission. These "budget comparisons," as they are called, summarize the relationship between appropriation, expenditure, and new request—including supplemental requests—for each agency, and present this information as briefly as possible. Though obviously designed for easy use by members of the commission, commissioners themselves almost never see the comparisons. What they see are brief summaries, prepared and distributed by the commission's executive director, Francis Whitney. These summaries, rather than the more detailed comparisons, are the principal informational resource used by commissioners and the principal stimulus to interrogation during the hearings. The brevity of his summaries is suggested by Executive Director Whitney himself, who says, "I try not to write more than one page. Anything more than that just will not be read."

As long as the commission relies on comparisons provided by Finance, of course, it is necessarily bound to the intellectual framework on which such comparisons are built. That framework, as pointed out in an earlier chapter, is the essence of simplicity: sums of money provided the informational common denominator for discussion; sums devoted to existing operations are assumed to be legitimate; deviation from legitimacy is measured in terms of unexpended sums or requests for additional sums. Within such a framework, there is no occasion to raise questions unless there are deviations—i.e., lapses or new requests. Where these kinds of deviations do not show up in the budget forms, there is very little that Director Whitney can, or does, write about. Where they do show up, the director's memoranda consistently follow this standard pattern: probable lapses in relation to the requested sum are noted first; requests for supplemental appropriations, if any, are noted second; other unusual features, such as accounting or organizational changes, are noted as necessary, along with suggestions for possible questions. The simplicity of this framework permits Whitney to dispose of a $4 million request in ten lines, or a $270 million request in one page.

As a practical matter, however, even these modestly sized reports are ignored much of the time. Although Whitney prepares his reports well in advance of the hearings, commissioners normally do not see them until the day of the hearing itself. Indeed, except for Senator Peters, commissioners do not see the report for any given agency until just before representatives of that agency are summoned into the room, when they are distributed by Director Whitney. If they are to be read at all, therefore, the commission reports must be read at the very moment when their subject is being openly discussed. In this contest between the written and the spoken word, the latter usually wins. For most of the time, most commissioners are unprepared for anything but the exchange of pleasantries.

Given these two conditions—the lack of advance preparation by commissioners and the reliance on brief, one-page reports emphasizing lapses and supplemental requests—it is to be expected that interrogation focuses almost entirely on lapses and supplementals. There are exceptions, of course, particularly when a commissioner is at odds personally with an administrator or when a commissioner wishes to explore some administrative detail which has become known to him through sources other than commission memoranda. But these personal antagonisms and occasional explorations into administrative detail seldom affect decisions, for the information that structures commission interrogation also structures the rules followed by the commission in determining its recommendations. These rules, which operate quite independently of any additional information generated in the hearings process, may be expressed as follows:

1. *Approve the new basic budget request.* Unless the new basic budget exceeds the current appropriation figure by a substantial amount, it is normally approved with little or no questioning. Somewhat more scrutiny is given to basic budget requests which represent large increases over the current appropriation, but even these are normally approved. Where the new basic is the same or less than the current appropriation, of course, it is approved without question.

2. *Cut the supplementals.* The tendency of the commission is to look with disfavor upon any supplemental request. This is particularly the case when an agency expects to lapse a large portion of its present appropriation. An agency which requests a supplemental appropriation while showing a large anticipated lapse has a negligible chance of obtaining commission approval for the supplemental request.

3. *Approve slight increases.* This rule, which can be viewed alternatively as a subcategory under either of the two preceding rules, results in frequent commission approval of requests which exceed the current appropriation—but not by much. Sometimes these slight increases appear in the basic budget. More typically they are presented in the form of supplemental requests. Although the commission rarely approves an entire supplemental, it is not unusual for the commission to approve a portion of a supplemental, especially when the agency requesting the supplemental appears to be spending all, or nearly all, of its appropriation. An agency anticipating a reasonably small lapse can expect to receive approval for at least some of the supplemental requests that it submits.

Commission application of these decisional rules does not require knowledge of agency operations. Regardless of the statements presented to the commission in its hearings, the most predictable decision-making response—usually verbalized by Senator Peters—is "Let's give them the basic and cut that supplemental." Normally such a statement needs no further amplification, but when additional comments are volunteered, they typically refer to other financial facts: "they're not spending what they have now" (i.e., a lapse) or "they already increased their basic." The fact that such statements can be made without any knowledge of agency programs is one reason why commissioners seldom exhibit great interest in the testimony offered at hearings —the financial data available in commission memoranda provide everything necessary to the decisions that will be made. Indeed, commissioners sometimes appear to have made up their minds before any testimony is offered. One agency head, whose five-minute explanation of his budget had been given at a time when Senator Peters was out of the room, attempted to recapitulate his statement for the chairman when he returned. Peters, however, was not interested. "That's all right, Director," he said. "I've already made up my mind."

Though perhaps an extreme case, the above is not at all unlike more typical exchanges, which reveal a similar gap between the monetary formulae which structure decisions and knowledge of agency operations. Consider the following exchange, which occurred at the conclusion of another five-to-ten-minute presentation by a welfare agency, and after the agency representative had been dismissed:

Chairman: What do you wish to do, gentlemen, cut that supplemental?
Commission Member: Yeah, cut the supplemental.
Chairman: That all right?
Other Commissioners: (Express general agreement.)
Commission Member: What do they do, anyway?
Chairman: Nothing. (Others laugh.)
Commission Member: Well, these guys even increased their basic. As long as they're sitting around with nothing to do, why don't we trim some more off their basic?
Chairman: No, it's all right. We have to go along with a little reform once in a while.

Whatever else may be said of this exchange, it is clear that none of the commissioners was strongly moved to appeal to the programs conducted by the agency. The agency head had, in fact, attempted to sketch out his program in his brief presentation, but the commissioners were not then very attentive, just as their later "decision" treated the programmatic question with the half-humorous spirit in which it was offered. Some commissioners, of course, may have known a good deal about agency programs, but such knowledge, if it existed, was not expressed, and in any event was unnecessary for the decision that was made. That decision was interpreted within the framework of dollars for basic and supplemental requests, and made by applying a predetermined formula to which all commissioners agreed.

The typical commission decision is thus made by applying a formula to a given agency request. Such a procedure is easy, since it avoids potentially complicated questions of substance, and quick, since the formulae can be applied without listening to lengthy testimony or reading lengthy budget request justifications. Indeed, it seems apparent that commission hearings themselves could easily be eliminated without seriously affecting the substance of commission recommendations. The commission, it will be recalled, makes no decisions at all with regard to expenditures supported by special funds, nor does it attempt to impose its own views on the largest state agencies. Why, then, are hearings held at all?

One possible answer, implicit in the preceding argument, is that hearings are considered to be necessary, not so much to "make" decisions, but to determine whether or not decisions that are already made should be altered. Since decisions are made by formula and since the formula is built into the information used by the commission, it can be argued that all of the commission's determinations are made automatically and in advance of the hearings. The purpose of hearings, from this point of view, is to ratify these prior decisions or, if witnesses are sufficiently persuasive, to modify them in some way. Thus, it is fairly safe to assume—as most agency officials do—that the commission will be inclined to cut any supplemental unless persuaded otherwise. Hearings offer opportunities to persuade and to be persuaded.

The difficulty with this explanation is that it does not explain enough. Though it offers a plausible explanation of commission behavior with regard to the marginal increases approved by the commission, it does not indicate what utility hearings may be thought to have for the major decisions of the commission— which appear to be made according to predetermined formulae. Indeed, if these predetermined formulae are as important as I have suggested, it would seem necessary to question the accuracy of referring to the actions of the commission as "decisions." An action can be called a decision when it controls the future actions of some persons with regard to some objects. But what persons and what objects are controlled by the activities referred to above as "commission decisions"? And in what sense can the actions described here be attributed to the commission, as opposed, say, to the Department of Finance, or to pure chance? In order to answer such questions we need a deeper, and more precise, specification of the commission's perceived role.

A RATIONALE FOR RITUAL

Although commission procedures frequently appear to be haphazard at best, there is nevertheless a deeply ingrained rationale implicit—and sometimes explicit—in what the commission does. It is a rationale of power, representing a sort of intellectual hangover from earlier days, which makes good use of the informational categories available to the commission. To appreciate this rationale it is useful to recall briefly the nature of the commission's work. The commission sits as a self-defined legislative agency to pass judgment on requests for appropriations submitted by the various agencies which comprise the state organization. These requests normally total several hundred million dollars more than current appropriation levels. After listening to the various agency spokesmen, the commission deliberates in the fashion described above and then makes its decisions. The effects of these decisions for any given biennium can then be summarized in terms of the amounts cut from agency requests and the increases over current appropriation levels approved by the commission.

But the commission does not summarize its work in this way. Instead it places virtually all of its emphasis on the reductions it recommends, ignoring the increases approved. Thus, while the commission approved requests for the 73rd biennium which exceeded current appropriations by some $358 million, its public statements made little or no mention of these approvals. As far as the commission was concerned, its work was best summarized in statements reporting the $273 million that had been cut from agency requests. Strategically, of course, this emphasis is perhaps to be expected, since the commission would be hard put to justify increases on the basis of its severely limited information. Reductions, on the other hand, serve to justify themselves, particularly within an intellectual framework that equates appropriation with dollar sums.

More significantly, however, commissioners define their work solely in terms of cutting requests. Large increases, which involve the largest agencies and programs, are not so much approved as accepted, for they are viewed as beyond the ability of the commission to control—witness the typical lack of action with regard to the largest agencies or the *pro forma* consideration they are given. Commissioners do attempt to deal with the smaller agencies by searching for cuts that can be made. Increases are frequently approved for these agencies, to be sure, but that is not of great moment to the commission. What matters most is that some reduction be imposed on each total request. As Senator Peters frequently remarks, "We like to cut something out of every request we get." From the point of view of commissioners, the commission is a cutting agency.

It is this purpose—conceived, it must be emphasized, as the job of changing dollar amounts on the budget forms for the specific agencies which come before the commission—which gives unity, consistency, and predictability to commission behavior. For such a purpose the financial categories provided by Finance are extremely useful, in that they provide both the motivation for reductions and the specification of where reductions can be made. By revealing lapses, these categories suggest that a current appropriation is excessive, which in turn provides a satisfactory motivation for a reduction. And by separating supplemental requests from current appropriations, this information indicates precisely where cuts can be made. Such information does not indicate how much to cut, of course, but neither does it avoid this problem altogether, for it does provide the basis for a useful rule of thumb which may be expressed as follows: the larger the lapse, the less likely it is that the commission will approve a supplemental.

Despite its single-minded emphasis on cuts, however, the commission does not appear to take its recommendations for reductions very seriously. Indeed, commission reluctance to make any recommendations at all with regard to the larger agencies suggests very clearly that, as far as such agencies are concerned, the commission expects someone else (i.e., the Governor) to make appropriation decisions. Such an attitude is understandable enough in light of commission realization that its decisions can be no more than recommendations and that the limited information it has would probably be of little use to the Governor. What is more curious is the commission's refusal to take seriously the recommendations it does make. Thus commissioners as legislators freely vote in favor of appropriation bills containing the very items which, as commissioners, they had agreed to cut. Perhaps the most glaring case in point which occurred in 1963 concerned the controversial proposal to increase the level of state aid to local school districts. When such a proposal was made to the Budgetary Commission, it was promptly rejected. Yet no member of the commission later voted against the same proposal when it passed the Senate and the House. Far from controlling the future actions of others, then, the "decisions" of the commission do not even control the future actions of the commissioners themselves.

This analysis indicates that the importance of commission activities is not to be understood in terms of anything that happens after commission hearings are concluded. Nor are commission "decisions," which appear to have little binding effect on commissioners, to be understood in terms of their contributions to state financial policies. What is important to commissioners is not so much the cuts, as the act of cutting. The commission, it must be recalled, represents the principal leaders of the legislature, several of whom are viewed by other members of the state organization as powerful men and all of whom desire to be so viewed. In order to promote and maintain the image of power, some visible evidence of that power must be available. One technique of providing such evidence, of course, would be to engage in lengthy investigations and to publish numerous reports of the results obtained, perhaps including within them a variety of recommendations for budgetary action. The commission does none of these things, relying instead on its traditional technique of holding hearings and making its private recommendations for reductions to the Governor. As long as its hearings are held and agency representatives compelled to attend, the commission offers visible evidence of its power. And as long as its recommendations remain essentially private, except for public statements summarizing total amounts cut, there is no way for potential challengers of commission power to find grounds for questioning decisions that are presumably made on the basis of expert knowledge, particularly since the "experts" are the leaders of both legislative houses. What happens to these decisions in later stages of the budget process is unimportant, for almost no one other than commissioners and commission staff (including Budget Superintendent Leth) knows what they were to begin with. All of the relevant budgetary actors, however, know that the hearings have been held and that so many dollars have been cut by the powerful commission.

Hearings are thus important in and of themselves as occasions when the commission cuts and, by cutting, demonstrates that it is exercising the power it is reputed to have. On the one hand, the interaction between witnesses who are commanded to appear and a group of men who can issue such commands takes the form of interrogation which emphasizes the superordinate position of the commission. Sometimes the commission chooses to explicitly underline the differentiation it makes between itself and other, less powerful, groups. One commissioner, after listening to the introduction of four relatively young and inexperienced legislators who had come to request funds for a construction project in their districts,[12] clearly was unimpressed. "Ha!" he snapped. "What a powerful group!" On the other hand the cuts which result from this interaction create a record that can later be used as evidence of work accomplished. The existence of such a record has been considered especially important since the 1956 Hodge scandal, which so bluntly and so publicly challenged the value of the activities carried on by the commission. In the period since, the commission has been particularly sensitive to the charge that it fails to perform adequately. During the 1963 hearings, for example, commissioners frequently asked questions which began with the following kind of prefix: "Now we're always being criticized for not doing our job, and yet you come in here expecting us to . . . [approve a supplemental or say nothing about a large lapse, etc.]."

It is this sensitivity which explains much of the commission's

---

[12] The appearance before the commission of several legislator groups of this kind during the 1963 hearings indicates the extent to which other legislators view the commission as a powerful influence over budget decisions. Commission reaction in such situations was to instruct such legislators to bring their projects to the proper administrative agency for insertion into their budget if possible. Inexperienced and uninformed legislators were thus "taught" by a group of experienced and presumably knowledgeable old-timers.

concentration on lapses, which imply commission failure to give adequate review to a previous request, and on cuts, which seek to eliminate the bases of such a failure with regard to the next budget. The political embarrassment caused the commission by a large lapse was made especially clear by Auditor of Public Accounts Michael J. Howlett who, shortly after he assumed office in 1961, announced publicly that he would not use all of the money appropriated to his office for his Republican predecessor. He would, he then averred, lapse several hundred thousand dollars. When his subsequent appearance before the commission substantiated his earlier claims, the loudest, angriest shouting match of the year ensued, and produced a substantial cut,[13] despite the Auditor's status as an elected state officer.

Only rarely does the commission fail to achieve unanimity on the need to impose a cut. Indeed, disagreement among commissioners was observed just once during the eight hearings attended by the author. The agency involved was the Department of Mines and Minerals, whose expenditure of less than $700,000 per year indicated that it was among the smallest of the code departments. Moreover, the departmental budget request for the 73rd biennium revealed that there was no disposition on the part of the department to attempt a major change in this status. Prodded by Senator Peters, Director W. J. Orlandi explained that the $32,000 increase in the new basic budget was caused by his decision to hire an additional mine inspector for work he considered to be "absolutely necessary." The $76,000 supplemental request was predicated on his desire to add three mine inspectors plus a research chemist for the department's coal-sampling program. After several more minutes of testimony, occupied primarily by Orlandi's explanation of the mine inspection and coal-sampling programs, the director was dismissed by Senator Peters.

After Director Orlandi had left the room, Senator Peters suggested that the increase in the basic budget be approved but that the supplemental should be eliminated to conserve the state's fis-

---

[13] The term "substantial" here must be understood in relative terms, for the commission's "cut" was only $100,000 from a total request of $8.9 million. No cuts, however, were imposed on the budgets submitted by the Lieutenant Governor, Attorney General, Treasurer, and Superintendent of Public Instruction, while only a token reduction of $50,000 was recommended for the Secretary of State's $12.5 million request.

cal resources. Several commissioners objected, beginning with two from the southern (coal-mining) part of the state, who made clear their unwillingness to have any future mine disasters traced back to the state's refusal to give sufficient support to a mine safety program. When Commissioner Harris noted his deep concern for mine safety and suggested further that "Powell would feel the same way if he were here," [14] the case was clinched, or nearly so. Retreating, Senator Peters agreed that mine safety was important, but remained opposed to giving the department everything it had requested. "Goddamit," he insisted, "we've got to cut something out of this budget—how about that chemist?" With the way thus cleared for compromise, the appropriate suggestion was made and the commission approved funds sufficient to pay the cost of the additional mine inspectors—but not the chemist.

This incident offers a striking insight into the motivation of Senator Peters and, through him, the entire commission. Here was a case in which the amounts involved were trivial and in which, given the reaction of other commissioners, approval of the entire request would have been both easy and financially harmless. Yet Senator Peters insisted on imposing a reduction. Moreover, the nature of the reduction—what was to be cut—was clearly of far less interest to him than the fact of the reduction itself. Nor should it be assumed that the commission's decision was based on programmatic criteria. Many of the commissioners were seeing the new director for the first time, and, judging from the questioning, few had any detailed knowledge of the programs for which the director sought more money. Furthermore, it is essential to bear in mind that the recommended reduction, though ostensibly aimed at "that chemist," was recorded as a sum of money smaller than the amount requested. Whether or not that sum would be used for chemists, inspectors, or other personnel was left to the discretion of the department. The commission did not seek to do more than reduce a total sum of money and would not be in a position, during the next budget period, to inquire into the nature of departmental discretion. By that time, these discretionary decisions would be safely recorded in

---

[14] At the time of this hearing, Powell was hospitalized following a heart attack.

another basic budget request which would be given little or no attention. This cut, like other commission cuts, was important chiefly for what it was, rather than what it did. It was a cut, after all, and as such provided both an expression of power and a justification for the commission's existence.

SUMMARY: THE FRAGILITY OF POWER

The Budgetary Commission can fairly be said to represent the legislative establishment in Springfield. Members of this elite group share many common experiences: they come from "safe" districts, they measure their legislative service in decades rather than years, and they cherish the power to gain their ends through legislative activity which they have built up during their years of service. In firm control of the Budgetary Commission since the close of World War II, they have maintained control through a careful selection of members to screen out the expression of points of view and purposes different from their own. For almost all of this period their spokesman has been Senator Peters, their purpose has been to maintain their access to great legislative power, and one of their principal tools has been budget cuts. Utilizing an informational system which offers both incentive for and identification of reductions (lapses and supplementals) plus the staff services of the Budget Superintendent and, recently, the commission's own executive director, the commission has continued to impose substantial cuts on budget requests. These cuts, in turn, have maintained the belief—widespread among legislators and administrative officials alike—that the commission is a center of great budgetary power.

And, ironically enough, the commission *is* a center of considerable budgetary power, at least as measured by the number of agencies whose budget figures appear to be determined by commission recommendations. Thus, the original requests of forty-one administrative agencies were reduced in some way before they appeared in the budget book. Of these reductions, twenty-one were made initially by the commission and later accepted by the Governor. In the remaining twenty cases the Governor reduced agency requests beyond the levels recommended by the commission. The Governor's cuts, however, focused primarily on capital requests, many of which were not heard by the commission and which, in any event, had little impact on current administrative operations. If the commission is viewed as a powerful agency, then, it is largely because its recommendations do in fact determine the figures which appear in the budget book for a large number of administrative agencies.

Yet this power must be properly understood, for the commission's traditional and habitual insistence on cuts is doubly defective. It provides neither an accurate statement of what the commission does (recall the $358 million in increases approved) nor a statement of the grounds by which such actions can be defended. In 1963 as in previous years, the high status enjoyed by commissioners, together with the absence of information concerning what they did, was sufficient to stifle an effective legislative demand for a defense of commission recommendations. In the absence of such a demand the commission continued to impose piecemeal reductions by formula, before it had any specific notion of total requests or total revenues, and without regard for such abstractions as the "state budget" or "state financial policy." Without a conscous concern for such abstractions, the commission could not insist on dealing with *all* items of expenditure; it was satisfied to deal with only those requests which it received through the Department of Finance. Even here, however, the commission was reluctant to determine recommendations for the largest programs and agencies, preferring to allow others the burden of such choices. To speak of the commission's power, therefore, is not to speak of its ability to determine over-all budgetary policies or the amounts to be allocated to the most costly state activities. Power, as far as the commission is concerned, is measured primarily in terms of impact on the small-to-medium state agencies. In short, the commission's financial power is small, though its power to affect a variety of administrative agencies is —or was, in 1963—considerable.

But this conclusion may itself be misleading, for the role the commission has chosen to play cannot resolve the ambiguity inherent in its organizational position and thus cannot establish a power base that is independent of other budgetary actors. By acting as nothing more than an agency which reduces some requests for appropriations, the commission implicitly defines its focus in narrow terms while at the same time it assumes a broad budgetary authority which it does not have and cannot get. And by continuing to maintain the official fiction that it works in co-operation with the Governor, the commission enables the Governor to exercise full control over the budgetary power that the commission can claim. Thus, if the Governor wished to change every recommendation made by the commission, he could do so and thereby eliminate even the crude measure of commission power utilized above. Indeed, the commission depends upon the Governor not only for such measures of power, but also for the techniques by which they are achieved: the information utilized by the commission is supplied by an executive agency (Finance) and the same agency is largely responsible for the timetable followed in commission hearings.

In a profound sense, then, the Governor and his agencies are able to structure the alternatives open to the commission and to control the criteria available for choice. Possessing no authority to determine budgeted amounts and lacking the expertise which would be necessary to develop and apply decisional criteria other than the criteria implicit in the executive's system of information, the commission is unable to formulate an independent judgment of its own. Such power as it does have with regard to budget book decisions is a function of gubernatorial charity. Such power as it has with regard to later appropriation decisions is due almost entirely to its status in the legislative system.

CHAPTER FIVE

THE GOVERNOR: OUTSIDER ON THE INSIDE

The state organization, like most large organizations, is perfectly capable of running itself. Offices and responsibilities are delineated by statute, while day-to-day operations are activated by a programmed flow of work which rarely requires intervention by executive action. This situation presents a serious problem to a governor, for it forces him to seek changes in the organization as a means of becoming relevant to it. Unless he does change the organization in some way, there will be nothing for which the Governor can "take credit" and nothing to show that his tenure in office had any impact on the organization. The Governor is thus a focal point for change, not so much because he is personally interested in reform (though he may be), but because implementation of some change is the only way that he can demonstrate his presence as Governor.

But there are no rules which tell the Governor what to do to promote change, nor are there, in the Illinois context, any bureaucratic units established to search out potential areas of change. If change is to come, therefore, it must come as a product of the Governor's own resources. The office of Governor is thus cast in an intensely personal light, in which gubernatorial role performance seems to be relatively more dependent upon the personality traits of incumbents than upon situational or organizational characteristics. Reviewing gubernatorial "styles" in Illinois since 1933, Steiner and Gove conclude that "There is no 'model' or accepted way of being governor in Illinois. . . . Governors are individuals, they have each achieved an important degree of political success, and they play their roles according to their individual perceptions of what constitutes success." [1]

LIMITS OF GUBERNATORIAL POWER

From a financial point of view the Governor is provided a number of tools by which he can transform his perceptions of success into achievements. Through the Department of Finance, which is responsible to him, he is in complete control over the preparation of the biennial budget and can, moreover, command the preparation of whatever supplemental information, in whatever form, he desires. Through his budget he can determine the content of all major appropriation bills introduced into the legislature. Since practically all moneys received by the state can be expended only by appropriation, the Governor is in a position to exercise great control over all proposals to spend such funds. The Governor's power to veto legislation in whole or in part, furthermore, gives him the last word on legislative decisions to authorize expenditures.[2] Finally, the appropriation bills themselves contain several provisions which enable the Governor to oversee the spending process itself: neither capital expenditures, nor expenditures from contingency appropriations, nor transfers of funds between departmental subunits can be made without the Governor's written consent. These controls over both financial planning and execution, coupled with the Governor's right to issue executive orders that have financial implications (e.g., to curtail the replacement of departed employees) appear to give the Governor the status of a virtual financial czar.

But here again, appearances can be deceiving. To begin with, there are a number of agencies that are not, in practice, affected by these controls. The political independence of the six other Constitutional officers, who, like the Governor, are elected by the people of the entire state, is reflected in their freedom from gubernatorial interference. Although their budget requests must be

---

[1] "Governors, Issues, and Styles: 1933-1960," *The Office of Governor* (Urbana: Institute of Government and Public Affairs, 1963), p. 47.

[2] The veto power is virtually absolute since the legislature normally has adjourned by the time the Governor receives the numerous bills passed during the closing days of the legislative session. Legislative reconsideration of a veto, therefore, is impossible.

channeled through the Governor, little attempt is made to tamper with them. Thus their inclusion in the Governor's budget is primarily a matter of bookkeeping convenience. As a matter of record-keeping convenience state officers make expenditure information available to the Department of Finance, but, beyond that, they budget and spend as they, and they alone, wish. By the same token, the General Assembly and its various commissions, together with judicial agencies, are equally unaffected by these gubernatorial controls. Some idea of what this means in terms of the Governor's financial power may be gleaned from the fact that appropriations for these agencies totaled $257.2 million for the 73rd biennium.

A second group of agencies is only partially subject to control by the Governor. In this group are a number of minor boards plus the various state universities which are governed by their own boards of trustees. The University of Illinois, for example, is governed by a board whose members are elected, on a staggered basis, at each general election. Members of the Teachers College and Southern Illinois University boards are appointed by the Governor, but in all three cases it is the boards, not the Governor, which determine both the long- and short-run financial operations of their respective institutions. What control the Governor can exercise is a product of his budget, through which he can grant or deny requests for increases in state appropriations. Once appropriations have been made, however, the Governor can influence expenditures primarily through persuasion; he cannot control expenditures because authority for such control is vested in the various boards.[3] Appropriations for the 73rd biennium for this group of agencies totaled some $453.9 million.

The full range of gubernatorial controls theoretically can be exerted only over the code departments and the various boards and commissions which report directly to him, but even here, the Governor faces serious practical limitations. These limitations basically are of two sorts. On the one hand, a great many state activities are financed by special funds which can be used for no other purpose. Many of these are created by state law; others

---

[3] Capital expenditures by the universities are subject to the Governor's written release of appropriated funds. This does give the Governor the ability to determine *when* such expenditures will be incurred. *What* the expenditures will purchase, however, is determined by the boards.

come in the form of grants-in-aid from the federal government.[4] These funds and activities are not completely outside the scope of gubernatorial influence, but in order for such influence to be exercised, the Governor must move beyond simple administrative action, either to press for changes in statutes, or to revise existing fiscal relationships between the state and the federal government. Since money from both sources is frequently intermingled—as it is in the gigantic Road Fund—even a minor alteration in statute or in an existing federal aid relationship can have major consequences. The pressure against such tampering is thus understandably great and effective in reducing the Governor's freedom of action. Since roughly half of all state expenditures are supported by these special funds this limitation must be regarded as very severe indeed.

Second, additional limitations are imposed through statutory provisions which provide for automatic expenditures from the General Revenue Fund. State aid to local school districts, for example, is governed by a statute which guarantees minimum per-pupil statewide spending and which requires state contributions to local districts to maintain that minimum standard. This statute not only causes a heavy drain on the general purpose revenue of the state but, so long as the number of school children continues to increase, the financial requirements imposed upon the state will continue to increase. Thus, while there was no change in the statute's distribution formula made by the 73rd General Assembly, the appropriation nevertheless jumped $40 million, to the sum of $433 million. A similar situation exists with regard to expenditures for the various federally assisted public aid programs. Here again, statutes require maintenance of minimum levels of health and decency. So long as the state accepts the responsibility for maintaining these levels, and so long as it participates in the various categorical assistance programs supported by the federal government, expenditures for these purposes will be controlled more by the numbers of persons who become dependent than by any actions available to the Governor.

It is possible, then, to argue that the Governor's great financial

---

[4] Federal grants are appropriated, but appropriation bills typically permit expenditure of federal money even if federal contributions exceed the amounts appropriated. Federal funds thus lessen gubernatorial control while simultaneously increasing the pressure to spend money.

powers are more apparent than real. If we add 73rd biennial appropriations made to agencies independent of the Governor or only partially subject to his controls to appropriations made from special funds or according to automatic statutory formulae, we learn that these appropriations total $3.1 billion, or 80 per cent (79.81 per cent) of all appropriations made for the 73rd biennium. The remaining 20 per cent—or $791.3 million—represents the portion of state spending which is subject to full gubernatorial control.[5] On this basis one could easily argue that the Governor, far from being the master of his own financial house, is a virtual prisoner within its walls.

But let us be clear about the nature of his imprisonment. No legal or Constitutional provision prevents the Governor from attempting to overcome any of the financial limitations noted above. Nothing prevents him from proposing changes in the statutes which create special funds or which specify formulae for school aid and public aid. Nor does it seem likely that a determined Governor could be denied a greater degree of control over the expenditures of agencies, such as the universities, whose finances are governed by their own boards, particularly since the Governor is already in a position to have a substantial impact upon the budgets of such agencies. Similarly, the obligation of the so-called "independent" state officers to submit their budget requests to the Governor suggests that it is within the Governor's power to do more to those requests than simply to reproduce them. If such attempts to exert his influence are not made by the Governor it is not because he *cannot;* it is because he *will not.* We are back, in short, to the Governor's own perceptions and motivations, particularly with regard to his vision of political customs, traditions, and opportunities.

It is precisely for this reason that the office of Governor appears to be so thoroughly colored by the personal politics of the incumbent. The limits on gubernatorial action are essentially political, rather than legal or administrative. Whether those limits

---

[5] These figures, like the figures cited in previous paragraphs, are taken from the very useful booklet published by the Department of Finance and titled *Financial Program for Illinois for 73rd Biennium* (Springfield, 1963). Table V, pages 35 to 42, lists 72nd and 73rd appropriations according to agencies which are independent or under the control of the Governor.

are accepted or challenged, and how a challenge is made, if it is, are questions whose answers ultimately depend on what the Governor wants and what he does to get it. If the Governor chooses not to challenge those limits, he can lead a serene life at the head of an organization that really does not need his presence in order to function. If, on the other hand, he decides to press for change, he will encounter a political obstacle of the first importance: the reluctance of other members of the state organization to provide the information he needs to determine the best method for achieving his goals.

The Governor, after all, is likely to appear somewhat wet behind the ears to bureaucrats and legislators who have spent decades in the state organization. Indeed, since most recent Governors have been recruited from outside the state organization itself, this appearance will probably be fully realized in practice. Though the Governor can surround himself with aides to develop information and advice, it will be some time before they, and he, are sufficiently aware of the "rules of the game" which guide complex state activities to assume control over those activities. In the meantime, numerous veteran employees will be in the somewhat ambiguous position of "teaching" their official superiors how to do their jobs. Unless the Governor knows what these jobs and rules are, he will be unable to formulate plans for change and unable to recognize it if and when it comes. But if the Governor's intentions to challenge the existing order are widely known (or even suspected) he will face deeply ingrained obstruction, for he and his aides will be "learning" their jobs from persons whose jobs are threatened by any plan for change. The Governor, in short, is normally an outsider coming into an established system. If he also chooses to be a reformer of that system, he will require great skill to overcome the superior knowledge and hostility to change characteristic of those who control the existing order.

Seen in this light, the Governor's formally complete power to determine the content of the budget assumes enormous political importance, not so much because it enables him to control state expenditures (which it does not) but more simply because it enables him *to know* what is going on in the state organization. Since every agency, from the smallest to the largest, must submit its request to him, the Governor has it within his power to demand an explanation of every line of every request, if he so desires. And since preparation of his budget is among the first major responsibilities to face the newly elected Governor, an inexperienced outsider can use the process of budget preparation to quickly develop what he needs most: comprehensive information about state operations. Mere possession of such information will not solve all—or even most—of his financial problems, but unless he has it, his chances of implementing meaningful change will be minimized.

The above discussion has suggested that the basic alternatives which confront the Governor are two: to accept the existing organizational order or to seek changes within it. Postwar developments within Illinois, however, have made it apparent that these alternatives may no longer exist. Whether or not the Governor acts as a proponent of change, it is increasingly unlikely that he can avoid the consequences of population increases, accelerating technological advances, and newly developing standards of governmental service. Each of these has spawned its own peculiar financial pressure: for more state aid to education; for more state aid to the dependent; for more and different state attention to the mentally ill, to the control of highway traffic, or to the stimulation of economic growth. In some cases these pressures find a voice within the state bureaucracy. In others their voice is provided by private and public agencies external to the state organization. But whatever their source and whatever their voice, these pressures are demanding more and more satisfaction from the state organization. If the Governor does not provide it, perhaps the bureaucracy or the federal government will, carrying the Governor along as need be. Astride this tiger, the Governor's alternatives are no longer to act or not act for change. His real alternatives are to lead or be led. And in order to lead he must know where he is and where he can go.

GOVERNOR KERNER AND THE
73rd BIENNIAL BUDGET

During the period under study the Governor of Illinois was Otto Kerner. Son of a former Attorney General of Illinois and married to a daughter of a former mayor of Chicago, Kerner had deep historical and personal roots in Illinois politics, particularly the "machine" politics of Cook County. At the same time, Kerner's education at Brown, Cambridge (England), and the North-western University law school had helped to develop commitments to the professional and business world of Chicago. Prior to his wartime service as an artillery officer the latter commitments were the more prominent as Kerner worked to establish his corporate law practice. After his release from active duty in 1946 the former ties came to the surface, first as he was appointed U.S. attorney for the Northern District of Illinois, and later as a county judge of Cook County, a position to which he was elected in 1954 and again in 1958. These factors in Kerner's background, coupled with his proven ability to attract votes, helped to secure his nomination to oppose Republican incumbent Stratton's attempt to win an unprecedented third term as governor. On November 8, 1960, the precedent was again upheld as Kerner overwhelmed Stratton by a margin of better than a half-million votes.

While on the county bench, Kerner had given some indication that he would adopt a "good government" stance. He had improved the operation of his court, spoken freely about the need to keep the election machinery free from political interference, and taken an active interest in improving court treatment of juvenile offenders. Campaigning for Governor in the fall of 1960, Kerner enhanced his liberal, good-government image. He castigated the Republican administration for its wasteful use of large numbers of unnecessary political employees, thereby implying not only needless state expenditures, but worse, corruption. He emphasized the need for greater economic development within the state and for additional state aid to local schools. Perhaps most significant of all, he threw his support behind the pending bond issue proposals for construction of additional mental health and university facilities and promised to give top priority to mental health should the people approve his candidacy. Though it would be stretching a point to assert that Kerner campaigned as a "reformer," it was clear that he viewed political activity as instrumental to the achievement of good works for the public interest, and that without these larger purposes, political office was barren of meaning.

This stance obviously was an effective campaign device, but it did little to prepare the Governor-elect for the specific problems he would face upon assuming his responsibilities. Indeed, it very probably hindered Kerner's ability to deal with those problems, for he was sufficiently unaware of the rules of the game to assume that others shared his beliefs and would cooperate with him in every way to ensure their realization. This assumption was quickly shattered when, on entering the Governor's office for the first time, he discovered that his departed predecessor had removed all of his files and papers, leaving the Governor-elect with absolutely nothing to suggest what to do or how to do it.[6] Given the fact that Kerner was also bequeathed a projected deficit of some $12 million in the General Revenue Fund by the end of June, the new Governor's predicament was considerably less than comfortable.

Lacking any experience which might have provided guidelines for coping with this situation, Kerner could not avoid floundering. His first problem was to develop a staff. On the assumption that the transition period would be a period of orderly and cooperative introduction to his new duties, Kerner had not planned for or recruited a large staff. His campaign manager and most trusted lieutenant, Theodore J. Isaacs, had been given the job of Director of Revenue—a position that forced Isaacs to spend most of his time in Chicago, thus reducing his ability to handle the vast organizational problem confronting the Governor. Kerner's press secretary was available and former Governor Stratton's office manager was retained to handle the routine office chores, but apart from these two men, there was no one available as yet to advise the Governor on either day-to-day problems or the more difficult problem of translating some of his campaign ideas into a program for legislative action. After some consultation, two university professors were pressed into service on a part-time basis and by mid-March of 1961 a legal assistant was hired. But it was not until the end of March—when almost half the legislative session had been completed—that the Governor was able to

---

[6] Sometime later, former Governor Stratton justified his behavior in an interview: "When I came in I didn't ask Stevenson for anything but the key to the mansion and the key to the office. I wouldn't expect to do any more than that for any other Governor." Interview, May 10, 1962.

present a detailed statement of his program.[7] In the meantime, the process of budget preparation was being completed with little possibility for any detailed gubernatorial attention.

That the budget was completed at all was largely due to the efforts of just two men. Within the circle of his own aides, Kerner assigned chief financial responsibility to Revenue Director Isaacs and made it clear that others on his staff need not become concerned with the matter. But Isaacs was located in Chicago, which insulated him from the daily decisions on the budget. Furthermore, the principal concern of both Isaacs and the Governor was not so much the content of the budget as it was the problem of finding additional sources of revenue. For the first time in the state's history, money would have to be borrowed in order to pay the bills for the 71st biennium, while estimates of the additional revenue needed to balance the new 72nd budget ranged upward from $265 million. Finding solutions to problems of this magnitude was enough to fully occupy both Isaacs and his financial "task force" of professors and lawyers, a group that had been established in order to find revenue-producing changes in existing statutes. While this activity was taking place, the pages of the budget book were being filled up by the same persons who had always handled that job, guided by the sure hand of Budget Superintendent Ted Leth, on whom the novice Governor leaned heavily for advice.

Separated by this informal division of labor, the revenue and expenditure portions of the budget came together for the first time on March 31, when agency requests were shown to Isaacs. Though the Budgetary Commission had cut some $291 million from original requests, Isaacs was not satisfied. "I looked at them," he said later, "and told the Governor they were too high —that we couldn't raise that much money. So we began to cut things down." A week later, the "cutting" had progressed to a point at which the remaining requests were within $20 million of the additional revenue anticipated from Isaacs' proposed modifications of the tax system. Cheered by this progress, Governor

---

[7] Kerner's inaugural address, delivered on January 9, 1961, was a brief, vague, and frequently trite statement of general purpose which lacked specific recommendations. His so-called "second inaugural," delivered on March 28, 1961, was designed by his staff to remedy these defects.

Kerner determined to ease the fears of some of his more liberal supporters and told an April 6 press conference that a much opposed increase in the sales tax would not be necessary. But the Governor had spoken too soon. When the final requests for capital improvements were received, Isaacs realized that their total of $101 million was far in excess of what he had expected. And even as he began the process of reducing these capital items, Isaacs realized further that his plan for increasing corporate taxes would, if enacted, produce only half the amount he originally predicted because of the lag between assessment and collection. This oversight, together with the capital budget surprise, made it very clear that anticipated expenditures would exceed anticipated revenues by a considerable margin. Additional revenue, in substantial amounts, would have to be found.[8]

Isaacs broke this news to the Governor on April 12, and Kerner was forced to choose: either impose large additional reductions on budget requests or recommend a new source of revenue. Seven days later, Kerner revealed his choice in his first budget message to a joint session of the Illinois House and Senate. Flatly contradicting his thirteen-day-old press conference statement, the Governor proposed a half-cent increase in the sales tax. Together with statutory changes to broaden the base of the sales tax and new or increased levies on corporations, cigars and cigarettes, and hotels, this increase brought the Governor's recommendations for new taxes up to $378 million to finance proposed expenditures of just under $3.5 billion. The Governor took issue with editorial writers and politicians who had urged reduction of state spending to meet the fiscal crisis by arguing that the problem was not that simple. He pointed out that the major state programs—education, welfare, and highways—consumed 73.7 per cent of the total budget and implied that these activities could not be reduced. "Let us not deceive ourselves," he pleaded. "We can economize in areas of state government; we can become more efficient, but we cannot turn back the clock to a society of fewer people and less expensive programs." What was needed was a thorough overhaul of the state's financial system to provide a more adequate revenue structure in a more intelligi-

---

[8] An excellent summary of this activity, including the quotations referred to above, can be found in the *Chicago Daily News* of April 21, 1961.

ble setting. To these ends, Kerner announced his creation of a revenue study commission and proposed adoption of a performance budget for the next biennium.[9]

In many respects the budget message was curious. Though the Governor clearly seemed to be interested in promoting some rather fundamental changes in state finance, he seemed also to be strongly impressed by the near impossibility of effecting major changes. Moreover, his obviously inadequate preparation and resulting budgetary vacillation left the impression that he really knew very little about was going on within his administration— an impression which could only compromise the strength of his recommendations for reform. In the weeks that followed the absence of firm gubernatorial control became the dominant image of the new administration, fed by almost daily occurrences: the Governor repeatedly changed positions on matters ranging from very little to very great importance, his chief legislative representatives frequently opposed him and got away with it, he seemed unable to develop legislative support for his chief revenue proposals and, finally, newspaper reporters dwelled at length on the manipulation of "padded" budget requests and extravagant expenditures of various agencies which they were able to report but about which the Governor apparently knew nothing.[10] Through it all the Governor remained serene, insisting that he and his financial program were above politics. His interest was to secure what was right for all of the people and he would not resort to ward heeling for partisan gain.

Unfortunately, perhaps, the image of gubernatorial impotence had real consequences, for there was no one in the legislature equipped to provide the leadership that the Governor was unwilling or unable to give. The result was almost complete stalemate on Kerner's financial program marked by unusual, and occasionally chaotic, demonstrations on the part of the legislature.

---

[9] The Governor's budget message of April 19, 1961, can be found at the beginning of the 72nd budget document.

[10] Ever alert to potential public scandal, the *Chicago Daily News* ran a series of stories "exposing" the content of selected budget requests. The lead story, printed on June 19, 1961, was given the large headline "How Kerner's Budget Got Loaded with Fat." Earlier another Chicago newsman, impressed by Kerner's vacillation and self-contradictions, wrote a feature story which publicly wondered, "Are Kerner's Aides Failing Him?" See the *Chicago Sun-Times,* June 11, 1961.

For the first time in history, the Republican-controlled Senate defeated an appropriation bill for one of the code departments, causing the Democrat-controlled lower house to "sit on" the appropriation bill for the Republican Secretary of State.[11] Speaker Paul Powell was forced to call in the state police to control an outbreak of physical violence in the House during a Republican filibuster against the sales tax increase. At the last minute a special House-Senate economy committee was created in an attempt to bring requests for appropriations into line with anticipated revenues.[12] In a feverish four days of almost around-the-clock meetings with agency heads just before the General Assembly was due to adjourn, the committee managed to trim an additional $14 million from appropriation requests, but this sum was far too small to have much of an impact. When it was all over, the legislature had passed appropriations which exceeded the Governor's budget by some $54 million, while simultaneously failing by 38.5 million to enact all portions of the Governor's revenue program.[13] Though the Governor's budget for the 72nd biennium was thus out of balance by more than $90 million, this result was probably better than anyone had a right to expect. The sales tax *was* both broadened and increased, the cigarette tax increase *was* approved, and higher corporate taxes *were* approved. Given the political situation in May and June, the outcome could have been far worse.

The budget, however, remained seriously out of balance. Governor Kerner immediately announced that he would veto as many appropriations as he could and halt expenditures from other appropriations wherever possible. By mid-December, 1961, predictions of an impending crisis had become commonplace. Budget Superintendent Leth told a December 19 meeting of the Budgetary Commission that the General Revenue Fund balance had fallen to $178,000—a tiny fraction of the $5 million that was considered to be a "safe" balance to meet daily state obligations. Both Budgetary Commission Chairman Peters and the Governor predicted that new taxes would have to be voted by the middle of the next year (implying the need for a special session of the

---

[11] *Chicago Sun-Times,* June 21, 1961.
[12] *Chicago Daily News,* June 22, 1961.
[13] *Chicago Daily Tribune,* July 7, 1961.

legislature) to meet mounting expenditures for public aid. That afternoon Kerner told a meeting of his cabinet that construction expenditures from general revenue would be halted, except for emergencies, and that jobs becoming vacant in their departments were not to be refilled: the "freeze" was on. Eight days later, Kerner announced his appointment of a special economy committee to police these restrictions.

The failure of the Governor's "freeze" order to reduce state employment through the early months of 1962 produced caustic newspaper comment but little surprise for observers who, by this time, had become accustomed to the Governor's style. Meanwhile Revenue Director Isaacs announced a series of steps designed to provide the greatest possible returns from the new tax laws. As public and legislative demands for a special session increased in intensity, the Governor planted himself firmly on both sides of the question. During a press conference held in the last week in March Kerner said that the state would be able to get by on its current resources until January, 1963, thus avoiding the need for a special session. Seven weeks later he challenged himself in a commencement address at Quincy College. The cash, he said, had run out. "The account is not only empty, it is in the red and it is going further into the red." The problem could be solved, he urged, only if politics were buried "for the common good." But instead of arranging for the burial, the Governor repeatedly criticized legislative leaders, particularly the Budgetary Commission, for failing to offer solutions, while simultaneously refusing to initiate either a conference with the commission or a call for a special session. The question of where the Governor stood and why became even more mystifying as he publicly disavowed not only proposals put forward by Budget Superintendent Leth but also proposals put forth by his personal assistant, Dr. Norton E. Long.[14] Observers began moving beyond the

---

[14] In a speech before the Government Affairs Council of the Chicago Association of Commerce and Industry on May 16, 1962, Professor Long urged that a special session be called in June. On the following day, Governor Kerner refused to comment on Long's proposal. On May 22, 1962, Budget Superintendent Leth proposed a plan for meeting the crisis. Significantly enough, Leth's plan was offered to the Budgetary Commission. Two days later the Governor dismissed his Budget Superintendent's plan as nothing more than "his own opinion."

question of who was minding the store to the equally confusing question of who, if anyone, was in the back room checking the stock.

Ultimately the Governor did call a special session, carefully timed to begin on November 12, six days after the general election. By this time, however, the worst appeared to be over. Spurred by a favorable court decision on the tax broadening bills and aided by some juggling of funds and accounts,[15] the financial condition of the General Revenue Fund was sufficiently recovered to meet state financial requirements until well beyond the beginning of the new legislative session, less than two months later, at which time additional deficiency appropriations could be voted as necessary. These considerations were not lost upon the Republican Senate, which paid little heed to the Governor's urgent plea for additional appropriations to care for the human needs of persons on the public assistance rolls. Amid muttered complaints that "nobody seems to know" exactly how much money was available or necessary, the Senate approved only $28 million of the Governor's $131 million recommendation and forced the Democratic House to go along with the lower figure. More than a little frustrated by it all, the Governor reacted by characterizing Republican legislators as "do-nothings." "If I submitted a bill that was against sin," he said, "they would vote it down."

The somewhat checkered history of Governor Kerner's first budget demonstrated quite clearly that the Governor, though universally respected as an honest and upright man, was beyond his depth in a political system dominated by veterans whose rules of behavior were unfamiliar to him. Since his closest advisors were also outsiders who shared the Governor's own point of view, there was no alternative but a long and sometimes painful period of on-the-job training, marked by hesitation, vacillation, and inconsistency. The experience also made it clear that Revenue Director Isaacs was the man to see as far as the Governor's financial actions were concerned. Indeed, much of the Governor's vacillation was traceable to the conflicting viewpoints expressed by Isaacs on the one hand, and members of the Gov-

---

[15] For example, recipients of relief payments, supported by state funds were switched over to the federally supported ADC-U program wherever possible to diminish the drain on the General Revenue Fund.

ernor's personal or official staff (Long and Leth in particular) on the other. As it gradually became clear that these staff assistants disagreed among themselves, Isaacs assumed the commanding financial position in Kerner's administration.

Strangely enough, the results of this first Kerner-Isaacs financial effort were increasingly promising, in spite of the many false starts and self-contradictions. As the new legislative session approached, it began to appear as though the new revenue measures could live up to, and possibly exceed, all original expectations. If this were in fact the case, the next step was clear, for both Kerner and Isaacs had learned a valuable lesson the hard way: they simply were not in a position to know, and therefore control, the bases of agency expenditures. "At present," Kerner had written some months earlier, "we are largely at the mercy of the agencies for their discretion and restraint in asking for jobs and money."

THE 73rd BUDGET

To some extent the Governor's information gap was a mechanical problem arising, in the first months of his administration at least, partly from the separation of revenue estimation from expenditure estimation and partly from the customary procedures followed by Budget Superintendent Leth. Pressed by the need to complete the budget book, Leth normally seeks to achieve gubernatorial approval of requests as soon after Budgetary Commission action as he can. Shortly after each meeting of the commission, therefore, Leth brings the recommendations made at that meeting before the Governor for his signature after which the decisions are set up on forms ready for printing. Following this procedure for the new Governor, Leth was able to offer valuable advice on the actions open to the Governor. But the procedure itself forced the Governor to make many decisions before he had any good idea of what total requests might be, and before he could develop a reasonable estimate of total revenue. And since the decisions had to be made immediately (from Leth's point of view) there was little or no opportunity to probe deeply into the contents of the forms presented to him. Indeed, as noted earlier, it was not until the first week in April that either the Governor or Isaacs saw the capital requests. By that time, of course, it was apparent that cuts would have to be made —and made quickly—if the budget was to be presented on schedule. The cuts were made, of course, but again, they were necessarily made in the semidarkness caused by the lack of opportunity to closely examine the budget forms.

Quite apart from the mechanics of gubernatorial decision, however, there was another, and deeper, problem which became apparent to both Kerner and Isaacs. This was the problem of whether the budget forms themselves offered a meaningful basis upon which to determine what should and should not be recommended. Impressed by his recent difficulties, the Governor chose the occasion of his first budget message to describe the budget as "a great mystery to all of those who have been required to read and attempt to understand it," adding perceptively that "There are some who have felt that it was better that way." His recommendation for a performance budget was thus put forward as an "attempt to prepare a more meaningful document." Some months later identical themes were echoed by Revenue Director Isaacs. "The budget document," he told an interviewer, "really cannot be understood by anyone. It reveals very little to a governor and very little to the people of the state."

If this complaint was fully justified by the experience of the 72nd biennium, the Governor's successful effort to secure legislative approval of the performance budget idea was nevertheless destined to have little impact on the 73rd budget. The 73rd would be the first budget to implement the "performance" idea. Since several years would be necessary before the performance categories could accumulate sufficient data to permit decisions based upon those categories, financial choices for the 73rd biennium would unavoidably be based on the same budgetary data as had been used in the past. Agencies would prepare two budgets—performance and major-object—but comparisons could be made only within the older budget framework. As the 73rd budget period approached, therefore, prospects were for "business as usual" and a potential repeat of the Governor's 1961 performance.

In mulling over this dismal prospect with his recently appointed assistant, Harry Hulman, Revenue Director Isaacs conceived what he later described as a stroke of "pure genius." Why not, he thought, organize a "task force" of high-level business accountants to assist the Governor in preparing the 73rd budget? Unless some other source of information could be developed, the Governor was certain to be handicapped again in dealing with budget requests, the more so because relationships between Kerner and Isaacs on the one hand, and Budget Superintendent Leth on the other, had become strained. A more "business-like" system of financial control was the administration's long-run goal anyway, and what better source of advice could there be than a group of experienced businessmen, whose point of view was bound to be congenial to Kerner and Isaacs alike. There was also politics to consider. The Governor would be up for re-election in 1964, and it would be important to persuade the "opinion leaders" of the business community that the Kerner administration was determined to give a dollar's worth of service for every dollar of revenue collected. Again, what better way to do this than to involve a group of highly placed businessmen on the "Kerner Team."

Presented with the idea, the Governor gave his approval and Isaacs set to work. At a fall, 1962, dinner meeting held by the State Chamber of Commerce, Isaacs sounded out a few business leaders as well as Chamber officials. Their reception was enthusiastic enough to warrant the scheduling of another luncheon meeting to which representatives of several large companies, all members of the State Chamber, were invited. Isaacs later recalled that he had "laid it on the line" to his luncheon guests. The state's financial system was in serious need of repair; their help as experienced businessmen would be invaluable if they could give it; if they did help, he would see to it that they had his—and the Governor's—complete cooperation: the administration did not intend to trifle with this matter. Some initial skepticism—normal for a predominantly Republican business group—was cleared away by Isaacs in a question-and-answer period, following which an agreement was reached: the group, coordinated by the State Chamber, would help.

Shortly afterward, officials of the State Chamber contacted fifteen firms requesting the services of one of their top financial executives for the projects. All fifteen agreed to cooperate. In the meantime, Isaacs was arranging to conduct a "school" for the businessmen. By early December, 1962, the "school" had begun operations. At two luncheon meetings held in Chicago, Budget Supintendent Leth and his chief budget examiner, Vernon Shontz, explained the budget forms and process in detail, and outlined the fund structure supporting state appropriations. After each of the meetings the budget group—now officially styled the "Budget Advisory Committee"—broke up into smaller groups to discuss what they had learned and to lay plans for the best use of the time available to them. Isaacs held to his promise of "full cooperation" by giving the businessmen complete access to the budget that had been prepared by his own department and suggesting to the group that a detailed analysis of this one budget could provide a sort of "practice run" over whatever larger target they might select.

By January, 1963, the target had been chosen. Governor Kerner revealed its nature in a talk before a luncheon meeting of the State Chamber of Commerce in Springfield on January 15. The task force, he said, had three objectives:

Its first function is to make the budget format intelligible for the average layman by analyzing the requests for these agencies. They then eliminate thousands of figures and tables and present the agency budget request to the policymakers in a form most readily understood.

Its second function calls for them to go beyond the budgetary process as dictated by statute and make recommendations as to how our performance budget can be improved procedurely.

Its third function is a long range one calling for them to supply the working details—the staffing and functions—of a proposed Budget Department which I discussed in my address to the legislature last week.[16]

Perhaps by inadvertence, the Governor's discussion of a new Budget Department included a public confession of his own relative helplessness to deal with agency demands. Comparing the proposed new department to the federal Bureau of the Budget, Kerner suggested that "It would give us an independent voice in the executive branch and also provide us with the ways and means to impartially check the operations of all our government bodies."

Even as this ambitious program was being announced by the

---

[16] Illinois State Chamber of Commerce, *Current Report,* Vol. 18, No. 4 (January 1963).

Governor, the task force was in the midst of its review of requests from forty-three of the major state agencies. As examiners in the Finance Department completed their summaries of agency requests, copies of the summaries were forwarded to the task force through the Revenue Department. Task Force review of these summaries enabled the businessmen to generate some ideas for a new, presumably improved, format, but the question of whether or not the amounts requested were justified remained beyond their reach. To get at this deeper and more sensitive question required access to at least the detailed budget forms, and probably access to agency officials as well. But access to the detailed forms customarily had been discouraged by Budget Superintendent Leth and the Governor was hesitant to risk a further deterioration of his relations with Leth by ordering him to do what he clearly was reluctant to do. If the task force was to realize its full potential, therefore, some way would have to be found around this formidable barrier.

An opening was provided by the Budgetary Commission itself when, at its February 4 meeting, it decided to take no action on the budget request submitted by the Department of Mental Health. "I told the Governor," Isaacs said later, "that this was a God-send. The thing for us to do was to accept the budget politely, thank the commission for its work, and tell them to send us all the forms for the department—and while they were at it they could send us all the other forms as well." The success of this maneuver was a major breakthrough, for it made documents which had traditionally been kept within the confines of the Department of Finance available to the Governor's staff for the first time.[17] This, in turn, opened a new dimension in the work of the task force. With more detailed information available, the task force could now reasonably hope to go beyond mere matters of form to the question of substance: overbudgeted activities might now be uncovered.

This prospect was sufficiently attractive to the employers of the task force members to persuade them to release their employees for a period of thirty days, during which the business-

---

[17] Actually the documents never left the offices of the Finance Department. Task force members simply were given access to them by the budget examiners.

men-on-loan would be able to devote full-time attention to the job of probing into the requests submitted by the various state agencies. Beginning in mid-February, 1963, and running through mid-March, various members of the task force journeyed to Springfield to spend as long as two weeks reviewing budget forms and discussing them with agency and Finance Department personnel. Following these investigations, memoranda summarizing the results of the investigations were prepared and submitted to the Governor. As one statehouse wag put it, the "thirty-day wonders" were hard at work.

And work hard they did. Indeed, it is probably safe to say that not since the administration of Adlai Stevenson had budget requests been given the intense review undertaken by Governor Kerner's task force. According to the task force member assigned to the Department of Mental Health, some forty man-hours were devoted to that budget alone. Yet the result of all this effort, from a budget point of view, was almost painfully insignificant. A miscalculation in the request for school aid was caught by the task force which enabled the Governor to reduce the request by some $11 million. And, after the businessmen had completed their work, the staff coordinator from the Department of Revenue continued his work on the financing of new capital expenditures. But apart from these, admittedly important, contributions, there is little evidence to suggest that the task force had a significant impact on the budget. In point of fact, the bulk of the budget already had been formulated and made ready for printing by the time the task force began its investigations. To have required major changes in late March would have imposed a nearly impossible burden on the limited staff of the Finance Department, then striving to "get the book out" in time for the Governor's budget message.

From the Governor's point of view, however, whether or not the task force had any significant impact on the substance of the budget may have been relatively less important than its ability to devise a format to improve the information available to the Governor for decision-making purposes. This, after all, was the principal initial motivation behind the task force idea. Here, the task force did suggest one change which apparently had not been thought of previously. Instead of comparing the new request against the current *appropriation,* as is done in the Finance De-

partment's summaries, the task force memoranda for the various
agencies compared the new request against *projected current
expenditures*, and provided, in most cases, comparisons of appropriations and expenditures for the previous two biennia. This
simple device would permit the Governor to take account of
lapsed funds in planning his revenue requirements for the coming
biennium. Its significance as a way of relieving the pressure to
find new revenue sources is suggested by Table 6, which reveals
an average lapse of almost $59 million in the General Revenue
Fund for the 67th through the 72nd biennia.

Table 6. GENERAL REVENUE FUND LAPSES: 67TH TO 72ND BIENNIA

Biennium	Lapse
72	$78,352,722
71	82,843,882
70	42,089,182
69	47,738,513
68	29,389,030
67	73,068,028

Average Lapse: $58.9 million

But note that the attempt to predict a lapse is useful only for
purposes of revenue estimation: it does nothing to cope with
the problem of expenditures and how they are determined. If the
Governor expected his task force to improve his own understanding of the bases for expenditure requests, he expected too much,
for the task force found it impossible to overcome the limitations
imposed by the existing categories of information. Thus the
task force memoranda contained precisely the same kind of
information as is included by the Department of Finance on its
budget comparisons. Basic and supplemental requests were
listed, by fund, and the totals compared to the previous appropriation and expenditure figures. Major increases (or decreases)
were then listed and reasons for supplemental requests were
briefly explained. Finally, comments by the reviewer were included whenever such comments were felt to be necessary. For
the most part, however, task force members did not feel themselves qualified—as indeed they were not—to comment on the

"reasonableness" of the requests and confined whatever comments they made to technical problems. Though this information
was expressed by the task force according to a shorter format
than that used by Finance, it is doubtful, considering the nature
of the Governor's problem, whether brevity was a virtue. For
the 73rd budget, as for the 72nd, the Governor's budget would
necessarily be built upon the uncertain foundations of the old
informational categories.

Between the 72nd and 73rd budget periods, however, there
was this difference: 1964, the second year of the 73rd biennium,
was an election year, and Governor Kerner already had decided
to stand for reelection. And Revenue Director Isaacs, who had
managed Kerner's previous campaigns for elective office, was
already planning the 1964 campaign as well. Recalling the
scandals that had embarrassed the previous Republican administration, Isaacs expressed considerable determination to an interviewer in February, 1963. "Kerner's got to be reelected," he
said crisply. "The state will be in for trouble if he isn't." By this
time, of course, Isaacs had assumed the commanding position
in the Kerner administration on matters affecting state finance.
In this capacity, as well as in his impending activity as campaign
manager, Isaacs saw one clear-cut path to Kerner's reelection.
Above all else, the Kerner budget for 1963-65 would have to
avoid any request for new taxes.

Just how this was to be accomplished was not yet clear in
February.[18] Though the new revenue measures enacted in 1961
were proving to be as productive as Isaacs had said they would
be, it did not seem likely that they would be productive enough
to support the additional demands that would be made on the
General Revenue Fund for the 1963-65 fiscal period. Even at
existing rates the school aid appropriation would have to be increased because of an increase in the school age population.

---

[18] Isaacs resigned as Director of Revenue in September, 1963. However,
he continued to manage Governor Kerner's reelection campaign until the
first week of October, 1964, when it was disclosed that his Chicago law
firm had represented a company doing business with the State of Illinois
during Isaacs' tenure as Revenue Director. This disclosure—made only five
weeks before the November election—prompted Isaacs to resign as campaign manager for Governor Kerner. Kerner was nevertheless reelected by
a substantial majority.

Worse, it was virtually certain that the Governor would come under heavy pressure to increase the state's level of minimum support. Similarly, mounting relief roles, unaffected by a generally healthy economy, would require a substantially higher state contribution. Nor would it be possible to avoid demands for large increases from the state universities or the Department of Mental Health. For these agencies alone, requests totaling upwards of $300 million over the present appropriation levels could be anticipated.

Amid growing public speculation that a one-cent increase in the sales tax would be necessary to support state programs through the new biennium, Isaacs moved to prevent such a result. Early in January several bills designed to close various loopholes in the sales tax were introduced in the Senate, which quickly passed them. By mid-February the bills had passed the House as well. The emergency provisions written into these measures gave them immediate effect and by March 1 they were being enforced by the Department of Revenue, which estimated that an additional $100,000 per day, or $70 million per biennium, would accrue to the state. At the same time efforts were begun to impose additional reductions on the requests available. Taking the opportunity offered by the Budgetary Commission, Governor Kerner instructed Budget Superintendent Leth to investigate the possibility of reducing the Mental Health budget. Leth himself crossed the street to the department's general office and there, meeting with Director Gerty and Deputy Director Merten, an agreement was reached to reduce the request by some $7.6 million.[19] Through March the Governor continued to search for changes, but his principal problems centered on whether or not to accept the large reductions already imposed upon the school aid and public aid requests by the Budgetary Commission. In addition, Isaacs and his aides were giving detailed consideration to the possibility of changing the state's method of financing the bulk of the new requests for capital expenditures. The Illinois Building Authority had been created by statute in 1961 and

---

[19] Interesting enough, this agreement was brought to the attention of the Budgetary Commission by Leth. Newspapers immediately credited the commission with having slashed the Mental Health budget by this amount. See the *Chicago Daily News*, February 28, 1963.

given authority to float bonds to finance capital items. If this device could be made to work, a substantial sum could be eliminated from the budget.[20]

By April 1, these decisions had been made. Speaking before a luncheon meeting of his budget task force, the Governor presented a broad outline of his financial plan for the 73rd biennium. Obviously pleased about what he had to say, the Governor boasted that the state, under his administration, had come out of the "fiscal doldrums." With $65 million in the General Revenue Fund account as of March 31, the Governor expected "to finish this biennium with sufficient funds to repay the money we borrowed and still be able to go into the next biennium doing business on a normal basis." More important, the cuts he had ordered made in budget requests had made it possible "as of the present time, to say that there should be no new taxes for the next biennium." The Governor made it clear, however, that continued increases for education and welfare, which were beyond his control, could not be avoided in the future. Since the "constrictions of the existing Revenue Article of our [state] Constitution" would ultimately make it impossible to continue to meet these growing demands, Kerner urged that the article be amended and promised to "have more to say about this in a presentation to the legislature." In the meantime, the Governor summarized the "different attitude toward budget practices" which his administration, stimulated by the task force, had adopted.

The approach that would be acceptable to a reasonable and prudent businessman is what we are undertaking to adopt throughout my entire administration. For example, we must stop depleting the General Revenue Funds for long-term capital expenditures. New structures that require many months to build and that will be used for 25 to 50 years, or more, must be financed on a long-term basis rather than by undertaking to pay for these projects out of current revenues. In your business, long-term financing is what you would resort to for such projects.

So, in our case, the General Revenue Funds should be used ex-

---

[20] The building authority idea had been discussed for some years and had actually been approved by the legislature, only to be vetoed by Governor Stratton. For an early analysis of the notion in relationship to Illinois finance, see Gilbert Y. Steiner, "A State Building Authority: Solution to Construction Needs?" *Current Economic Comment* (Urbana: Bureau of Economic and Business Research), Vol. 17, No. 1 (February 1955), pp. 22-30.

clusively for current operating costs. By the same token, capital expenditures should be amortized out of income or revenue to be received during those years that the improvements are being used. It is a combination of such recommended financing for capital items and economics over and above the savings already effected . . . that will enable us to continue the business of the state throughout the next biennium in an economical manner.[21]

On the following day a highly placed spokesman for the Kerner administration clarified the implications of the Governor's remarks. In addition to utilizing the Building Authority to support extensive capital construction for the first time, the administration would accept the large school and public aid reductions announced by the Budgetary Commission.

Three weeks later Governor Kerner invited legislative leaders to an evening meeting at the mansion to explain to them the details of his budget, due to be presented on the following day. What he and Revenue Director Isaacs said to the assembled legislators is summarized in Table 7, which reveals the increased demand on the General Revenue Fund for the 73rd biennium and the manner in which that demand was disposed of. Altogether, requests for appropriations from the General Revenue Fund for the 73rd fiscal period exceeded 72nd appropriations by some $685.7 million. A reduction of some $272.5 million (including the public aid and school aid reductions) from this total figure was credited to the Budgetary Commission which, combined with $87.5 million in federal money, left the Governor to face increases of some $325.7 million. Prior to March 26, however, the Governor had restored some $7.7 million of the reductions made by the commission, and had made other adjustments which added another $4.2 million to the requests. The total increase before him at that time, therefore, was $337.6 million.

Even with the additional revenue of $170 million which Isaacs promised would be available to the state in the 73rd biennium, the state would still fall short of the requested increases by some $167.6 million. A further reduction by this amount was thus unavoidable. To accomplish this, $83 million in capital requests—including $15.5 million in requested reappropriations—was cut, largely from the state universities. The items included in these

[21] Text taken from a news release distributed by the official Illinois Information Service dated April 1, 1963.

Table 7. GOVERNOR'S CALCULATIONS FOR A BALANCED BUDGET, 1963-65 (GENERAL REVENUE FUND ONLY) [a]

Total increases to Governor		$685.7	
Less: Anticipated Federal Aid		87.5	
Budgetary Commission Cuts		272.5	
		325.7	
Plus: Governor's Restorations and Adjustments		11.9	
Total Increases at March 26:			$337.6
Less: Estimate of Added 73rd Revenue			170.0
Balance Needed at March 26:			167.6
Less Governor's Reductions:			
Federal Public Aid Adjustment	$ 1.1		
New Capital—Reduced	67.5		
Reappropriations Cut	15.5		
Airport Grants	3.0		
Common School Fund	16.0		
School Building Commission	4.0		
Mental Health	10.0		
Judicial Article	.7		
Insurance	.3		
Revenue	.6		
Public Safety	.6		
Commerce (new)	4.0		
Manpower Training Program (new)	7.1		
Total			130.4
Available from Budgetary Balance June 30, 1963			37.2
RECAPITULATION			
Increases Requested as of March 26, 1963		$337.6	
Less: Governor's Final Reductions		130.4	
			207.2
Plus: Estimated Federal Increase			87.3
Total General Revenue Increase in Budget			$294.5

[a] In millions.

reductions were to be incorporated into a building program which would make use of the Illinois Building Authority. A $16 million reduction in the Common School Fund request, coupled with the $4 million taken out of the School Building Commission proposal reduced state obligations to local schools by another $20 million, while a late decision removed another $10 million from the Mental Health request. Several other minor reductions, together with the Governor's abandonment of plans to recommend a new Commerce Department and to provide high-level state support for a new manpower training program brought these late reductions to a total of $130.4 million. Removing this much from the new requests left increases of $207.2 million, which could be supported by the additional $170 million in expected revenue plus $37.2 million from appropriations that would "lapse" on June 30, 1963. The total general revenue budget, including the $87.3 million in estimated federal moneys, would increase by $294.5 million, but it would also "balance" at that level.

Thus the Governor, largely through the efforts of his Revenue Director—chief political advisor—had accomplished what almost no one believed could be accomplished. On the following day, April 24, 1963, he presented the accomplishment to a joint session of the legislature. "This is the largest budget ever presented for the State," he said. "It totals in excess of $3.8 billion." Despite the Governor's recommended increase in total appropriations of $363.7 million, however, no new or additional taxes were proposed. The substantial increases budgeted for welfare, mental health, education, and highways were to be financed "through diligence in the collection of revenues and an efficient tax administration," together with federal aid amounting to more than $1 billion for the 73rd biennium. If proponents of welfare and education programs were disappointed in the Governor's failure to recommend larger increases for these programs, there were others who could find satisfaction in what the Governor had done for them. Some $34.3 million was proposed for increasing salaries of state employees, including a $15.8 million salary increase for employees of the code departments. An appropriation of $4.5 million was proposed for a new Department of Children and Family Services, while a $6.75 million appropriation for educating gifted children, cut by the Budgetary Commission, was restored in the Governor's budget. Not everyone with a stake in state finance was satisfied, of course, but not everyone could be, particularly when the twin values of "fiscal responsibility" and "reelection" superseded all others.[22]

---

[22] The best brief analysis of the 73rd budget is found in a news release dated April 24, 1963, distributed by the Illinois Information Service. The release was organized to answer specific questions submitted beforehand by newsmen.

Over all, Governor Kerner's second budget performance presented a rather sharp contrast to his first attempt. This was not because he instituted any fundamental changes or developed any new information. Indeed, it is worth emphasizing at this point that the Governor's fundamental budget "problem" centered on the need to reduce *increases*, which is precisely the same problem faced by other participants in the budget process. Nor could the Governor's task force hope to overcome his information gap in the absence of a different set of informational categories. The difference, rather, was that both Kerner and Isaacs had gained two years' experience, in which they had begun to realize that no one but the Governor could do the Governor's job. If a balanced budget with no new taxes was thought to be necessary for reelection, therefore, the Governor himself had to act to ensure this result, for no one else had either the desire or the authority to do so. And if this meant imposing reductions without really knowing why or what the consequences on the program would be, so be it: that was a condition of the existing system that had to be lived with. The Governor, in short, had begun to realize that the budget was basically *his* problem, which required the generous exercise of *his* authority. The changes made in Budgetary Commission recommendations and the cut of an additional $130 million from agency requests were partial measures of this realization.

But in another sense, Kerner's second budget represented a victory for "the system" over one who had originally sought great changes in it. The Governor's first budget message had spoken repeatedly—and rather grandly—of the need for change. "We have tried too long," Kerner said in 1961, "to co-exist with a financial situation brought about by our refusal to accept the necessity for change." Decrying the policies that had produced the status quo, jerry-built budgets of the past, he pleaded for a new revenue article, a performance budget and an end to "outmoded methods" that looked to the past rather than the future. Now, in 1963, the same Governor adopted a decidedly different tone. Instead of the defects of the system, he spoke of the many accomplishments made within it; instead of the need for change, he spoke of the difficulties in the way of its achievement, emphasizing the "factors beyond our control" and his own lack of maneuverability. Perhaps he had come to accept, with most others, the statehouse axiom that "change comes hard in Illinois." Or perhaps he and Isaacs both were coming to the view that mastery of the system itself was a necessary prerequisite for changing it.

AFTERMATH

The euphoria produced by the near-magical submission of a budget that was both balanced and significantly increased could only be short lived, for the "gimmick" that was chiefly responsible for the balance had yet to be implemented. In presenting his budget message Governor Kerner had repeated his earlier declaration that "new structures that require many months to build and will be used for many years will be financed on a long-term basis instead of by undertaking to pay for the construction of these projects out of current revenues." The Governor had also made a promise: "I shall present a program to carry out this provision for capital requirements at a later date." The "later date," however, was not specified. As days, and then weeks, passed without any further word from the Governor, uneasiness grew stronger among the agencies whose requests for new capital items had been eliminated from the budget. Some of the more cynical among the agency officials noted that the Governor could ease his financial problems a great deal by refusing to submit any capital program at all, thus relieving his administration of an $83 million burden. When it became known that the Governor had requested a joint session for May 22, it was quickly assumed that the Governor had finally worked out the details of his capital construction program. But the assumption was wrong. The Governor's address dealt instead with his proposal to amend the revenue article of the state Constitution. There was still no public indication of what the Governor's capital program was to be—if it was to be at all.

In point of fact the capital construction program was in serious trouble, for reasons that were in part technical and in part administrative. Technically, use of the Building Authority device meant that bonds would be issued to raise the funds necessary for capital items declared by the legislature to be in the public interest. Annual rental fees, paid by the users of the capital facilities to the Building Authority, would then be used to amortize the bonds. But in order to ensure the marketability of the bonds in the first place, potential purchasers would have to have some guarantee as to their legality. This guarantee traditionally had been provided for other state bond issues by the firm of Chapman and Cutler, bonding attorneys. When presented with the Governor's plan, however, a number of difficulties were immediately apparent to the attorneys. Capital requests submitted by the state agencies included such items as movable equipment for buildings or planning costs for new projects which appeared to stretch the meaning of "capital" to barely tolerable limits. Other items, such as paint shops or driveway surfaces, were so small as to question the advisability of using ten-to-forty–year maturity bonds to finance them. Chapman and Cutler would have to satisfy itself as to these kinds of expenditures, and satisfaction required a great deal of time. Beyond this there was a further administrative problem. The program was being handled from Chicago by Isaacs and his assistants, none of whom were overly familiar, or friendly, with officials from other state agencies. Not only delay, but a good deal of confusion, was the result.

The delay was resolved on May 29, when Senate Bill 1177, declaring $67 million in capital items to be "in the public interest," was finally introduced—without the benefit, incidentally, of any formal declaration of program by the Governor. Confusion blossomed, however, when the Senate Executive Committee met to consider the bill and its companion, Senate Bill 1161, on June 11. Isaacs and his assistant assigned to the capital items program, Harold Caswell, were present, along with officials from the Building Authority and the Chapman and Cutler firm. Also present were officials from the state agencies whose capital requests had been included in Senate Bill 1177. The administration was prepared, it seemed, to bring up the bill, provide testimony in its favor from several expert sources, and move the bill out of committee for final Senate approval. Further delay could not be tolerated, in fact, since adjournment was only two weeks away and the Senate would very shortly move to table all bills in committee as a means of expediting last minute business.

The appearance of advance preparation was quickly dissipated. Presenting the bill to the committee, Senator Edward C. Eberspacher, its sponsor, mistakenly described it as a plan to finance capital construction projects from funds which had been approved by the people in the referendum of November, 1960. Then, in moving forward to explain the bill, Mr. Caswell presented an amendment which deleted the mention of specific sums of money to be allocated to each project. The amendment was offered, a Chapman and Cutler representative explained, weakly, to provide "greater flexibility." But no one in the administration had taken the trouble to give any advance notification to the committee that this amendment would be offered. Indeed, it later turned out that the agencies themselves were unaware that such an amendment was planned.[23] Isaacs and Caswell, working with the bond attorneys, had simply drafted the amendment in Chicago and then come to Springfield to present it, for the first time, to the committee.

Predictably, the reaction of the Republicans who dominated the committee was heated. Describing the proposal as an "insult to the legislature," Senator Russell Arrington was clearly upset. "I can't understand," he said, "how an administration could submit this kind of a proposal without giving us any advance notice and without giving us any indication as to how much money it wants and what kinds of projects it wants to put up and where it wants to put them." Other Republicans echoed these sentiments in arguing that the amendment—and indeed the Building Authority concept itself—replaced legislative control over appropriations with what amounted to a blank check authorization. "What were these projects, and how or why were they chosen?" were questions repeatedly asked of Caswell, whose best reply was that the projects were all submitted by state agencies as part of the process of budget preparation. Strangely enough, the officials from the agencies who could have provided detailed answers to these questions were never asked to do so.[24] Lacking the details, the "hearing" became a contest between Republican senators to see which of them could most imaginatively abuse the bill and the administration alike. On a

[23] Among those caught unawares were representatives from the University of Illinois, who learned of the amendment as it was being presented, and whose first look at the proposal came after the hearing had concluded, when a copy was hastily made. With $18 million in capital facilities at stake, university officials were more than a little concerned.

[24] Why agency officials were not called upon for testimony is unclear, unless Isaacs and his assistants did not realize they were there.

motion to report out the bill with a favorable recommendation, the vote was 13 to 10, against.

Thus was demonstrated the complete failure of communication between the Isaacs team on the one hand, and both the Republican senators and agency officials on the other; the demonstration needed only to be completed, this time with regard to the Democratic senators (who were sponsors of the legislation). With 1177 defeated, at least temporarily, Senate Minority Leader Donald J. O'Brien suggested that the companion bill, 1161, might as well be considered anyway, since it could be treated as a separate item. Accordingly, Amos Watts of the Chapman and Cutler firm began his explanation of the bill which his firm had drafted to correct some technical problems in the Building Authority statute. Watts had not proceeded very far when Senator John P. Meyer interrupted to request copies of the amendments being explained by him. Apologizing for his oversight, Watts indicated that Mr. Caswell had brought copies of the amendments with him, and turned to ask Caswell for them. But Caswell was no longer in the room! As soon as 1177 had been voted down, Caswell, Isaacs, and Assistant Revenue Director Hulman all had stalked out of the room, leaving Watts without the amendments that were the subject of his testimony, and leaving a severely embarrassed group of Democratic senators who had argued strongly in support of the administration program, only to find the administration itself absent when most needed. Obviously displeased, O'Brien moved to postpone consideration of the bill to a later date.

Two days later both bills were reported out favorably by the committee, after the monetary sums were put back and after detailed letters of explanation were submitted by each of the agencies involved. Almost as an afterthought, Senate Bill 1233, appropriating $7.2 million to various agencies to pay rent on facilities constructed by the Building Authority, was introduced on June 13. With the initial ambiguities cleared away, the three bills were quickly passed by both Senate and House, giving effect to the capital program by which the Governor had balanced his budget.[25]

---

[25] By accident or design, funds for projects begun, but not completed, during the 72nd biennium were not reappropriated, causing numerous construction projects to be halted by the fall of 1963. See the *Chicago Sun-Times* of November 3, 1963, for a report on this matter.

SUMMARY: THE UNCERTAIN STRANGER

The history of Governor Kerner's first two budgets suggests strongly that hard and fast generalizations about the Governor's role in making financial decisions are impossible. A governor's interpretation of his powers and responsibilities will necessarily differ from man to man and may, as in Governor Kerner's case, differ from one period to the next within the same man. Entering the state organization with no knowledge of the rules by which legislators and bureaucrats reached their budgetary decisions, Kerner simply assumed that other participants in the budget process shared his own "public interest" orientation. He had only to state a problem—be it a new revenue article, a budget department, or a performance budget—to his newly acquired colleagues and they, sharing his interest in the public good, would work toward its solution. But other definitions of the public interest were as real as his own, and much more solidly entrenched in the legislative and bureaucratic institutions. Kerner's failure to grasp this reality in 1961 was a failure of vision, which produced his characteristic unwillingness to make free use of the authority available to him. His many proposals for reform thus hung in the air like balloons, lacking the ballast of understanding to bring them down to solid accomplishment. Other budgetary actors, who knew very well what they wanted and what others wanted from them, cartwheeled around each other, seeking and achieving their separate goals undisciplined by gubernatorial participation.

Not surprisingly, many of the decisions made between January and June, 1961, had to be undone in the interim between the 72nd and 73rd General Assemblies. An impending financial crisis forced Kerner to exercise his authority and, stimulated by its use, the Governor began to realize its potential. Moreover the Governor by now had learned enough about the orientations of his various colleagues to understand the lack of compatibility between his and their goals. Instead of working with them, therefore, he determined (on the strength of his advisor's recommendations) to ignore them. But ignoring them meant that he was precluded from changing the terms of the system within which they worked. His budgetary task force could not improve the information available to him; it could only rearrange it. The Governor could, and did, make more use of his budgetary authority in 1963 than he did in 1961, but the motivation for his increased activity was his own (and his advisor's) determination to decide, rather than more or better information. The Governor, let it be clear, wanted to be Governor again.

If this shift from a less to a more active decision-making role by a single governor thus symbolizes the difficulty of establishing generalizations concerning gubernatorial role orientations, the essential similarity of the actions performed by Governor Kerner in both 1961 and 1963 may stand symbolically for the permanence of "the system." In neither year was the Governor actively involved in the process of putting together any given agency budget from the inside out, nor was he even involved in hearings designed to review requests. Instead, he entered the process much later, after preliminary decisions were already made, and was asked for nothing more than approval or disapproval. In both years the Governor's problem was to eliminate a sufficient amount from agency requests to bring them into line with anticipated revenues. And in both years he did this, not by close examination of the total cost of every program run by each and every agency, but by cutting what he could from the *increases* requested by the various agencies, leaving the bulk of the budget unexamined and untouched. In this respect the budget document may be compared to a huge mountain, which is constantly being pushed higher and higher by underground geologic convulsions. On top of the mountain is a single man, blindfolded, seeking to reduce the height of the mountain by dislodging pebbles with a teaspoon. That man is the Governor.

CHAPTER SIX

THE LEGISLATURE: STRUCTURAL CONSENSUS

From a Constitutional point of view the legislature is the most important of all the agencies involved in decisions to utilize state resources. Departments can request, and the Governor can recommend, but only the legislative can authorize expenditures through its decisions to appropriate funds. This heavy responsibility is met in a fashion which suggests the existence of a relatively autonomous legislature culture with regard to state appropriations. That culture finds its expression in legislative behavior that appears to have a single purpose: to pass appropriation bills.

THE ORIENTATION OF THE UNINFORMED

In order to understand the unidimensional nature of legislative behavior in this area, it is necessary to bear in mind the obstacles which limit the possibilities of legislative action. Both the House and the Senate are relatively large bodies, containing 177 and 58 members, respectively, virtually all of whom look upon legislative service as a part-time activity at best. Indeed, legislative attention to state finance is a decidedly part-time activity. Regular sessions of the General Assembly meet for only six months out of every twenty-four, and within this relatively brief period, concern for state revenue and expenditures tends to be concentrated in the final eight weeks of the session. The state budget, due on April 1, typically is not presented until mid- or late April, while appropriation bills reflecting budget policies of necessity arrive at an even later date. To further complicate matters, the bulk of the important legislation introduced in each biennial session generally is not taken up until after the budget is presented. Caught in this last minute rush of activity, appropriation measures must compete for, and be satisfied with, whatever attention they can get.

However unfortunate these conditions may be, they are aggravated even further by the almost total absence of usable information for legislative decision-making. Many members, perhaps a large majority, are not particularly concerned with the details of state finance, preferring to allow their more expert colleagues to assume responsibility for such matters. The few legislators who do become concerned quickly discover the discrepancy between the decisions they must make and the information available to them. Unlike other organizational actors, who deal with requests for appropriations, which normally include at least some supporting information, the legislature deals with appropriation bills, which authorize the expenditure of specific sums of money without presenting supporting information of any kind.

For many appropriation bills, of course, information is not especially relevant. Considerable numbers of so-called "stray" bills (i.e., bills unrelated to the budget) are introduced in each session, usually providing funds to construct lakes, drainage ditches, buildings, or other capital items in a single legislative district. Legislators from unaffected districts accordingly feel little concern for the details of such appropriations. Other "strays" create commissions to investigate an endless variety of subjects of interest to individual legislators. Since it is understood that the chief sponsors of such bills will become chairmen of the commission so created, the funds appropriated become, in effect, appropriations made to a given legislator to be expended by his commission as he sees fit. The purpose of the commission is thus of less importance than the identity of the sponsor, and the amount to be appropriated.

Stray bills have two principal characteristics, the first being that they rarely receive anything but overwhelming approval. As one former Chairman of the House Appropriations Committee once explained, "That's a sort of comradeship that goes on here in the legislature. You know, it's the sort of thing where you roll my log and I'll roll yours." The second characteristic of strays is the anticipation of ultimate disapproval which frequently colors attempts to pass such bills through the legislature. Legislators vote for such bills less because they desire to finance the activities involved than because they wish to avoid an affront to a colleague who might, after all, provide a needed vote on a future bill. They are encouraged to vote affirmatively by the knowledge that many of these bills will be vetoed by the Governor, discreetly dropped from consideration in the other house, or otherwise prevented from becoming law. Such knowledge enables legislators to act as champions for causes they may not really support without creating consequences that tax the financial capabilities of the state. Such proposals are also occasionally useful to the Governor, who can use the promise of approval as an inducement for legislative cooperation. Detailed information about the contents of legislation is clearly not the most relevant quality of such games.

Bills appropriating funds to support the principal activities of the various state agencies, while providing no supporting information in and of themselves, nevertheless are presumed to rest on the details presented in the budget document—a presumption neatly expressed in the phrase "budget bills." The legislator who looks to the budget for an explanation of the bills he must consider, however, is likely to find little more than further confusion, for budget figures frequently have little or no relationship to the figures contained in the various appropriation bills. One reason for this is that bills are drafted by a number of different persons. While the Department of Finance does the drafting for most of the small- and medium-sized agencies, the larger agencies sometimes perform this chore for themselves, as do the elected state officers. Opportunities for last minute changes in earlier budget figures, either to correct omissions or to insert additional sums, are thereby increased. Moreover, agencies drafting their own bills are in a position to tailor the provisions of their bills to suit their own special needs. The requirements imposed by existing statutes which dictate the procedures to be followed in spending state money presumably are meant to bring uniformity to the expenditure of state appropriations. Yet if close examination is given to the sections of appropriation bills which follow the sections that specify appropriated sums, a considerable agency-by-agency variation in provisions governing expenditures can be discerned.[1] Thus, quite apart from differences between budget sums and appropriation bill sums, there is considerable variation in the spending authority granted by individual appropriation bills.

Variations of this kind are perhaps too subtle to be appreciated by most legislators who, it must be emphasized, are hard-pressed to look at, let alone examine, the bills they must deal with in an exceedingly brief period of time. Other difficulties in matching the budget with appropriation bills are less subtle, but equally confusing. Last minute gubernatorial decisions, coupled with the inability of the Department of Finance to incorporate those decisions in the budget book have been troublesome for at least the last two biennia. In 1963, as in 1961, the sum budgeted for salary increases was not distributed among the various agency budget requests, but rather was included as one lump sum. Agency appropriation bills, which included the salary increase provisions, were thus necessarily different from agency budget requests, in one case (Mental Health) by as much as $10 million. Or again, the Secretary of State's request for the 73rd biennium included a sum to pay for installation of a central telephone exchange for the state house, thus requiring a reduction in the amounts requested by other agencies for telephone services whose costs were to be assumed by the Secretary of State. However, the budget book, which already had been made up, contained the

---

[1] There is tremendous variety, for example, in the extent to which agencies apply the rule which limits expenditures in the first eighteen months of the biennium to not more than 75 per cent of the appropriation. Virtually every agency has its own formula for application of this rule and this formula can only be discovered by reading the appropriation bill all the way to its final paragraphs. While a detailed analysis of these variations would be tedious, readers who recall the nature of the major-object categories used in appropriating state money will perhaps appreciate the following illustration, drawn from pages 219 and 220 of the *Appropriations* book. The principal appropriation bill for the Department of Mental Health comes to a conclusion on these pages, and Section 17 of the bill begins by stating that the 75 per cent limitation will apply to the bulk of the operating appropriations, contained in Sections 1, 3, and 10 of the bill. Section 17 goes on further, however, to provide "that this limitation shall not apply to appropriations made in said sections for the following objects and purposes: personal services, contractual services, commodities, stationery, printing and office supplies, equipment . . . contingencies. . . ." I have left out of this quotation the bulk of a long paragraph indicating the variety of additional purposes to which this particular limitation does not apply for the 73rd biennium.

normal amounts for telephone services for the various agencies. To correct this situation reductions were made in the appropriation bills, to the great consternation of legislators who tried in vain to match agency budget requests against agency appropriation bills.

Even the format of appropriation measures appears to be designed to sow confusion. In point of fact, there is no standard format which is used by all agencies and, as a result, bills differ from budgets not only in amounts but sometimes in categories as well. Budget book figures for the elected state officers and a variety of other agencies include requests for state officers' salaries. Such salaries, however, are grouped together in a single appropriation bill, which thus coincides with no single agency request but affects all of them. Other forms of "grouping together" result in omnibus bills such as House Bill 1244 (1963) which in a single bill provided appropriations for twenty-nine separate agencies totaling in excess of $22 million. Just to read the data provided in the budget on these agencies would have required legislators to thumb through 130 of the 586 pages of the budget. Had they done so, of course, they would have discovered different figures in each place for many of the agencies involved. At the other extreme, many agencies submit several different bills each of which appropriates only a portion of the total sum to be expended by the agency in the coming biennium. Sometimes this is done purposefully by agencies which receive support from two or more funds, whose records are easier to keep in this fashion. Sometimes it is done to remedy errors in drafting or to attempt to gain legislative approval for some project not included in the budget. In such cases legislators are faced with the problem of reconciling many individual bills with a total sum in the budget that almost surely will be different from the total of the individual bills, for reasons that almost surely will be apparent to no one.

What these kinds of problems mean to the individual legislator can be illustrated easily enough by reference to a representative agency appropriation measure, in this case Senate Bill 823, providing for the "ordinary and contingent expenses of the Office of the Superintendent of Public Instruction." This bill, one of thirteen separate bills which appropriated funds to the superintendent in the 1963 session, provided some $5,318,352 from the General Revenue Fund for the superintendent's General Office appropriation out of a total appropriation in the bill of $10.9 million. Let us assume that we wish to have more detailed information about this $5.3 million General Office appropriation and that we turn to the budget document to find out. There we note immediately, on page 69, that neither the $5.3 million nor the $10.9 million figures are to be found, and we note also that the total figure recommended for the 73rd biennium is $516.9 million, or roughly 100 times the General Office appropriation. Most of this ($433 million), according to page 69, is to be supported by the Common School Fund, which obviously refers to state aid distributions to local school districts. In checking through the other twelve bills appropriating funds for the superintendent, however, we find nothing which comes close to that amount—though there are bills which appropriate another $57 million in general revenue for distributive programs, $7 million from the Driver Education Fund, and just under $13 million from various federal funds. Impelled by curiosity we make certain inquiries and learn that the $433 million which appears in the superintendent's budget is actually appropriated to the Auditor of Public Accounts in one of the seven bills appropriating funds for his office. Depending on the extent of our curiosity, we might also learn that the $433 million figure is developed by neither the superintendent nor the Auditor. It is the School Problems Commission which recommends the amount budgeted to the superintendent and appropriated to the Auditor. That commission, incidentally, appears in the budget book on page 11, where a $50,000 appropriation is recommended.

Returning, then, to our original interest in the General Office appropriation, a closer examination of the bill reveals that some $801,000 of the general revenue appropriation is assigned as the state share in administration of the National Defense Education Act, leaving a net general office appropriation of $4,517,400. The budget book figure, however, is $4,484,900, which puts the bill some $32,500 above the budget book. But wait—the budget contains $40,000 for the superintendent's salary which is not in the bill and this might account for the difference. No, on second thought, that only aggravates the problem, for now the bill is $72,500 above the budget. Perhaps a comparison of the object detail contained in both places will supply an answer. Yes, the appropriation for Contractual Services is $17,500 below the budget figure—very likely a result of the central telephone exchange installation. And look! the bill contains a $50,000 item "For Administration and Supervision of a Research Program" that was not in the budget. Plus 50 minus 17.5 means a net increase of exactly 32.5—we can now explain why the bill is $32,500 above the budget. But what about that other $40,000 for salaries? Retracing we see that the salary item was not included in the budget figure of $4,484,900 and should not have entered into our calculations. Thus if we add $32,500 to the budget figures of $4,484,900 and $800,952, we get exactly the total general revenue appropriation contained in the bill: $5,318,-352.

Except for the somewhat unusual successful reconciliation between the sums contained in the bill and those contained in the budget, the above example symbolizes the tortuous path legislators (or anyone else, for that matter) must follow if they attempt to utilize the budget as an aid to understanding appropriation bills. Consider the difficulties presented by this case alone: more than a dozen bills appropriating funds to a single agency, sums budgeted by one agency but appropriated to another, discrepancies between figures in the budget and figures in appropriation bills, items in the budget that are not in the bills, items in bills that are not in the budget. And note that, having taken considerable pain simply to match a portion of Senate Bill 823 to a portion of the budget document, we are still in no position to explain the differences between them. We have assumed, but we do not know, that a Contractual Services reduction reflected a changed estimate of telephone costs. And we literally have no idea of what is involved in a $50,000 research program. Furthermore, short of asking the superintendent, there is no way to get such information. There are no generally available documents analyzing the bill, and there are no regularized procedures followed by the legislature to inform itself either of the contents of appropriation bills or of their relationship, if any, to the budget document. Taken together, these several difficulties create obstacles to legislature knowledge which are virtually impossible to overcome.

Legislators typically respond to this situation by ignoring the budget book altogether as a device for informing themselves about appropriations. A few, whose attempts to utilize the budget have ended in frustration, are openly critical, referring to the budget as a document that is obsolete the day it is published. Most legislators, however, seldom make an effort to learn enough about the budget to justify either criticism or praise: it is simply regarded as irrevelant. In debate, occasional references to the budget are tolerated and even used occasionally as a rationale for supporting a particular appropriation measure. Too many references, however, are regarded as a nuisance, and those who make such repeated references are frowned upon as trouble-makers who slow up legislative action on appropriations. As one veteran legislator remarked on the floor of the House when asked if a bill for which he requested approval was in the budget, "Hell, I don't know—and I couldn't care less."

By generally ignoring the budget, of course, legislators cast aside the only source of information they have, other than the bills themselves. Appropriations bills thus stand alone, free from explanatory data of any sort, almost as if the bills constitute their own justification. Curiously enough, appropriations do appear to justify themselves. In a legislative system which accords individual legislators almost complete control over bills they introduce, it is well understood that nonbudget bills (i.e., strays) which arouse strong opposition or which are found to be otherwise defective will be allowed to die quietly by their sponsors. If such bills find their way through the entire appropriations process, it is because there is no outside opposition and because their sponsors desire to have them passed. That desire, in terms of the "comradeship" ethos, is normally enough to induce other legislators to give their approval. In such circumstances the lack of supporting information does little more than discourage any tampering with bills; it does not inhibit their ultimate approval.

Major appropriation bills are viewed with equal favor, largely because of the assumption that the legislative duty already has been carried out by the Budgetary Commission. Few legislators know what the commission does, or how, since the commission does not tell them, but virtually all are aware that commission hearings have been held. More significantly, other legislators recognize the commission to be composed of powerful and experienced members of the House and Senate leadership. Less experienced members are thus easily led to impute to the commission a specialized expertise, partly to justify the commission's presumed power and partly to rationalize their own lack of it. Without real knowledge of commission activity, legislators are free to believe anything they like about it; aware of their own inability to comprehend or control appropriations, legislators justify their own inattention by assigning this responsibility to a commission to which is imputed both power and expertise. Having created this creature of their own insufficiencies, legislators proceed to use it by giving rapid approval to any bill whose provisions can claim to have been heard by the Budgetary Commission.[2]

The legislature has thus earned a reputation for unwavering hospitality toward appropriation bills. Occasionally, to be sure, some political or financial crisis will give rise to legislative demands for economy, and "blocs" composed of economy-minded legislators will sometimes come into being. But, at least through the 1963 legislative session, such organizations have demonstrated little capacity to survive, largely because the idea of economy for the sake of economy is too fragile a rationale to motivate widespread and permanent legislative participation. As we shall see below, there was indeed an economy bloc in operation during the 1963 session, but its activities were considered to be virtually irrelevant with the submission of a balanced budget.

For most of the time, then, most legislators are content to give favorable consideration to appropriation bills about which they know very little, and to which they give little or no attention. Unwilling to risk offending colleagues whose votes on other matters may be important to them, legislators cheerfully approve nonbudget bills as a favor to their sponsors. Certainly a vote is a small enough price to pay for maintaining good collegial relations, particularly when risks are eliminated by the frequent expectation of gubernatorial veto at a later date. And budget bills are approved because there is really no alternative to approval. With little time and no information, what else can be done, par-

---

[2] The assumption that the Budgetary Commission has "made its cut" means that references to the commission on the floor of either chamber are almost always designed to expedite passage of a bill. A statement such as "this bill was approved by the Budgetary Commission" thus encourages legislators to vote in favor precisely because "review," in the form of a cut, has already been achieved.

ticularly since the Budgetary Commission presumably has asserted legislative responsibility. As legislators put it, "We've got to support state government."

Behind such statements there appears to lie a rationale of purpose which, though rarely verbalized, may account for the high level of legislative support for appropriation bills. Appropriations, it must be remembered, do not direct that expenditures be made; they merely authorize expenditures up to, but not exceeding, the sums specified in the various appropriation bills. If funds are not available, expenditures cannot be made, regardless of the amount appropriated. In this sense appropriation bills can be viewed as merely authorization bills, which are intended to (a) express legislative sentiment in favor of supporting specified activities up to stated monetary levels and (b) to leave actual decisions on when and how to expend money up to someone else, namely, the Governor. By depending on individual sponsors to weed out stray bills to which there is strong opposition and on the Budgetary Commission to keep budget bills under control, other legislators can feel free to approve appropriations, not as legislative decisions to determine expenditures, but rather as statements expressing what the legislature will support—to be transmitted to the Governor and dealt with according to his discretion.

Consider the following exchange between Representatives John C. Parkhurst, a young, economy-minded lawyer serving his third term, and Joe Russell, a farmer who was first elected to the House in 1932. The exchange occurred in the House Appropriations Committee, on which both men serve, over a nonbudget bill appropriating some $663,000 for various flood control projects in another legislator's district.

Parkhurst [explaining his vote]: Mr. Chairman, once again this committee is playing a kind of game. Everyone knows that when legislators come up before this committee with bills of this kind, the committee will generally tend to approve such measures partly out of courtesy to the sponsor and partly because the committee realizes that the bill may never be implemented due to lack of money, but mostly because the Committee likes to be able to allow legislators the opportunity of saying that they have gotten something for their home districts. When the Committee does this sort of thing we are, in effect, fomenting a fraud. We know the money is not available, we know that the chances are that the Governor will be forced to freeze any appropriation of this kind that we make, and yet we continue to vote these bills favorably. I say this is wrong and I say that it should stop and I vote no.

Russell [explaining his vote]: Mr. Chairman, I am supporting this bill because we don't operate on a hard budget here. We know that if we pass bills here which are not approved later on by the Governor, that is no reason for us not to indicate that we think that these projects are good projects and ought to be implemented. I think this bill accomplishes a good and worthwhile purpose and I think it ought to be supported on that basis.

The bill, which had been discussed for less than three minutes prior to the above exchange, was approved by a vote of 21 to 4.

Parkhurst's statement represented the view of a vocal, but very small, minority, interested in changing the nature and quality of legislative participation in financial decision-making. In its terms, legislative decisions on appropriations would be designed to have a direct impact on expenditures. But Russell's view, treating legislative decisions not so much as devices to control expenditures as advisory expressions of legislative sentiment, commanded the support of the overwhelming majority of committeemen, just as it appears to enjoy the support of the overwhelming majority of other legislators. In its terms, any bill that has not provoked strong opposition or is not otherwise defective, is treated as a "good thing to do," and dealt with accordingly, in deference either to a sponsor or to the need to support state operations. Budgets, revenues, or total expenditures are all essentially peripheral matters to a body more concerned with expressing opinions than with making decisions. That the opinions are almost always favorable is probably due more to the absence of grounds for alternative opinions than to an unusual degree of legislative good nature.

THE APPROPRIATIONS PROCESS

These collective orientations are reflected in the consideration given to appropriation bills, first by the Senate and House Appropriations committees, and later on the floor of each house. Some bills appropriating state funds, of course, are not referred to the Appropriations committees, particularly if they are introduced late in the session when the need for speedy action encourages consideration of many bills without committee reference. Many of these, however, are relatively unimportant from a financial point of view and in many cases are never brought to a vote. The great bulk of the bills which appropriate state funds are assigned to the Appropriations committees which, accordingly, are among the busiest committees of the legislature. During the 73rd session 175 bills were referred to the Senate Appropriations Committee, a total exceeded by just two other committees of the Senate. In the House only three committees handled more bills than the 195 measures referred to the Appropriations Committee.[3]

Committee consideration takes the form of hearings, in which bills are taken up one-by-one and, typically after listening to one or more witnesses, disposed of by voting on a motion to report the bill out with a "do pass" recommendation. Terms such as "committee" or "hearing," however, tend to evoke mental images which have very little to do with the activity stimulated by committees of the Illinois legislature. Writing in 1960, on the basis of more than two decades of combined experience in observing Illinois legislators at work, Steiner and Gove argued that committees were "of scant importance" to the decision-making process, which is generally carried out quite independently of committee action. They offered this analysis of the Appropriations committees:

. . . in the appropriations process, hearings before the standing committees of House and Senate are in the nature of necessary obstacles that must be overcome. They are not obstacles in the sense of dangers. Rather, the hearing can appropriately be compared to the constitutional requirement that a bill be read on three different days in each house. An obstacle to passage is the need for a minimum of five days to get a bill through both houses, but this represents no danger to the bill unless it is not introduced until the very end of the session. Similarly, the need for a committee hearing on appropriations bills

---

[3] The reader should be cautioned against the assumption that such figures are completely accurate. The Illinois legislature is not particularly concerned to exercise great care in keeping its records, as a result of which figures such as these can differ, depending on their source. My figures were compiled from the *Final Legislative Synopsis and Digest* for 1963 published by the Legislative Reference Bureau. They differ slightly from a memorandum prepared by the Illinois Legislative Council entitled "Final Status of Bills, 73rd General Assembly, 1963 Regular Session" (File 5-028, Mimeo., April 24, 1964), which reports that 174 bills were assigned to the Senate committee and 192 to the House committee. These differences are not great enough, however, to affect the conclusions offered in the above text.

is a nuisance requirement to be acknowledged and disposed of before proceeding to focus attention on other problems.[4]

To appreciate how little danger is involved in committee action one need only consider the figures presented in Table 8,

Table 8. SENATE AND HOUSE APPROPRIATIONS COMMITTEE ACTION, 73RD GENERAL ASSEMBLY

	Total Bills Referred	Recommended Do Pass	Recommended Do Not Pass	Tabled	Discharged
Senate	175	145	6	5	19
House	195	188	0	4	3
Totals	370	333	6	9	22

which presents a summary of the Senate and House Appropriations committees' activity during the 1963 regular session. Of the 370 bills originally referred to these committees, twenty-two were removed (discharged) from committee consideration by vote of the respective houses and nine were tabled by their sponsors, leaving a total of 339 bills for committee action. Only six of this number were reported out with a "do not pass" recommendation, all from the Senate committee, while 333 were reported with a favorable recommendation. But even the six is misleading, since four of the six unfavorably reported bills were companion measures, sponsored by Democrats, designed to initiate a tourist promotion program (Senate bills 887, 888, 889, and 890). Three other bills sponsored by Republicans did precisely the same thing, but with different jurisdictional arrangements (Senate bills 624, 625, and 626). A compromise was ultimately worked out, as a result of which the Democratic bills were given a negative report and the Republican bills voted out favorably in accordance with the compromise agreement that had been reached.[5] Thus only two

---

[4] Steiner and Gove, *Legislative Politics in Illinois, op. cit.*, p. 81.

[5] Members of the committee did not themselves work out the terms of the compromise arrangement. Instead, the two major contending lobbies, the hotel and motel associations, were instructed by the committees to "get together" on a program acceptable to both. While the groups were able to agree on a program acceptable to both, the committee could not agree on

bills (House Bill 1359 and Senate Bill 291) were actually reported unfavorably by the Senate committee. However, the Senate later passed a bill (House Bill 1578) without committee
reference that was substantially identical to one of the two unfavorably reported bills.[6] On this record, it would be difficult not
to be impressed by the friendly attitude taken by both committees to virtually all of the bills they are asked to consider.

It seems apparent, then, that the Appropriations committees
act as little more than way stations that must be visited by each
bill as it proceeds along the well-marked route which leads to a
final floor vote. Occasionally, of course, a bill is amended in
committee before it is voted out. But committee amendments are
infrequently made—only one of every ten bills considered was
amended by these committees during the 1963 session[7]—and
typically are proposed either by the sponsor of the bill or by the
agency affected by the bill, rather than by the committees. Moreover, committee amendments rarely have a major impact upon
agency dollars or agency programs. Normally committeemen operate on the assumption that bills assigned to them will be favorably reported and proceed to implement this assumption with
as much dispatch as they can muster.

As a rule, both committees are able to dispatch the bills
brought before them with remarkable speed, for the assumption
that the bills will be passed permits them to avoid several time-
consuming activities that, under different circumstances, might

which series of bills to report out for amendment on the floor. This disagreement caused the negative vote on the Democratic bills, though the
program as finally approved contained many of the provisions contained in
the Democratic bills.

[6] Both H.B. 1578 and S.B. 291 provided for state administration of a
mental health test for newborn infants, but the former bill appropriated
$50,000 for the program instead of the $100,000 provided in S.B. 291.
H.B. 1359, the only bill actually "killed" by the committee, authorized a
temporary loan of $32 million from highway funds to the Common School
Fund for the purpose of increasing state school aid. As I have noted earlier,
however, the Senate passed the bill which appropriated (read: authorized
the expenditure of) $32 million for the same purpose. By failing to pass
H.B. 1359, which provided the funds for the appropriation authorized in
H.B. 1097, which was passed, the Senate virtually guaranteed a gubernatorial veto for H.B. 1097.

[7] The Senate committee amended seventeen bills and the House committee amended nineteen for a total of thirty-six bills amended by both
committees during the 1963 session.

be considered essential to decision-making. Knowledge of the content of appropriation bills, for example, is not required in great detail. All that either committee really needs to know about any given bill is the amount of appropriation and the sponsor. Since the bill will be approved anyway, there is little point in going beyond the kind of information needed to maintain a ledger on committee action. Thus neither committee employs any staff personnel, except for clerk-secretaries who keep track of bills and record votes.[8] During committee hearings members seldom have anything more in front of them than copies of the bills under review—and frequently even these are nowhere in evidence.[9] Nor is it necessary for witnesses to offer anything more than a perfunctory statement in support of any given bill. Indeed, witnesses typically are interrupted by a "do pass" motion if they attempt to do more than indicate the sums involved and the general purposes to be served. If these sums and purposes are already fairly well understood—as in the case of bills to support the major state agencies—statements from witnesses are commonly eliminated altogether. Thus during the Senate committee's hearing of May 9, 1963 (to take a typical case in point), bills appropriating funds for the operation of six different departments (among a variety of other bills) were all reported out without a word from the departmental representatives who were present.

General lack of committee interest in the detailed content of appropriation bills results in hearings which normally run for no more than two or three minutes for any given bill, though five-

---

[8] During the 1951 session the House committee actually hired a man for fact-finding work. His activities were supplemented by the full-time assistance of the Director of State Government Research of the Taxpayers' Federation of Illinois. This experiment was not repeated. See Henn, *op. cit.*, p. 36.

[9] At the request of the "Economy Bloc" members of the House Appropriations Committee, the Budgetary Commission made available copies of the memoranda prepared by its executive director in 1963. The same documents were made available to members of the Senate committee. This was a significant "first" for both the commission and the legislative committees. On the other hand there is no evidence that these documents contributed significantly to committee deliberations. Few members made use of them, and those who did found them to be of limited relevance, since their analyses were focused on budget requests rather than appropriation bills. See *ibid.* for a report on earlier relationships between the commission and the two committees.

to-ten minute discussions sometimes occur and very rarely, a twenty-to-thirty minute discussion will take place. But the time spent in discussing bills is essentially irrelevant to members of the committees, for whom the issue of "pass or not pass" already has been decided. That legislators look upon committee hearings as occasions to record, rather than make, decisions is evident from the frequency with which they resort to proxy voting. Committee members who are unable to attend hearings will typically leave their votes on the scheduled bills with the chairman, who is empowered to announce the position taken by the absent members on each "do pass" motion. Frequently legislators will attend a portion of a hearing and leave proxies on bills to be discussed after they leave, or before they arrive. There is nothing particularly devious about this practice, much of which stems from the multiple committee membership held by Appropriations Committee members,[10] but it does emphasize the irrelevance of committee discussion to decisions that are made in other settings. In effect, the decisions which the Appropriations committees are asked to make have been made already, leaving the committees no task other than the production of a record to prove it. Such a task makes few demands upon information, time, or, thanks to proxy voting, the physical presence of committee members—as few as five members have reported bills out of the Senate Appropriations Committee.

At best, then, activities of the two appropriations committees are ritualistic in nature, conducted more for their own sake than for any impact they may have. Hearings are held and exchanges take place, not so much to make decisions as to mask the fact that neither committee has the knowledge, time, or interest to make decisions. As long as the ritual is continued, committee members and others have grounds for the belief that committee action is important—just because it takes place. Moreover, the continued performance of the ritual helps to maintain a potential source of considerable power—there is always the chance, after all, that

---

[10] On the average, members of the 1963 Senate committee belonged to four committees in addition to Appropriations, while members of the 1963 House Appropriations Committee belonged to three additional committees. Since some of these other committees met at the same hour as the Appropriations committees, it was frequently physically impossible for some members to be present at the meetings.

the committees will decide to do more than approve appropriation bills.[11] In the meantime, committee hearings continue to be uninformed by knowledge of the bills, frequently unattended by committeemen, and indiscriminate in the approval given to proposals to spend money.

STYLES

But if the results achieved by the two committees are similar their styles of behavior are noticeably different. Speed and informality are the chief characteristics of the sixteen-man Senate Appropriations Committee. It is not at all unusual for this committee to consider and dispose of a bill in less than ten seconds—a circumstance which imposes certain hardships on witnesses, researchers, and other outsiders. Appropriations to the major state agencies, in particular, are given little attention, largely because committeemen accept the need to provide support and are in no position to raise questions anyway. A commonly used technique for handling such bills, therefore, is a simple announcement by the chairman of the number of the bill, its purpose, and the sum appropriated, followed by a rhetorical inquiry: "Any objections?" Objections, of course, are rare, so that the chairman can simply turn to his secretary and indicate the vote by which the committee has recommended that the bill "do pass." By eliminating parts of this procedure, such as the statement of purpose or the number of the bill, the chairman can—and frequently does—dispose of a bill in literally no time at all.[12]

---

[11] The Senate Appropriations Committee actually made two amendments on its own initiative during its 1963 meetings. Both were offered by Senators Peters and Dwight P. Friedrich and both were punitive in nature. One reduced the appropriation for the Human Relations Commission to its 1961 level and the other imposed a similar reduction on the appropriation for the Board of Economic Development. In the former case senators did not appreciate the need for a state agency active in the field of race relations, while in the latter case, senators appeared to take an unfavorable view toward the board's chief executive, who was known to be close to a Chicago industrialist who had charged that some senators were racists. These were the only examples of amendments initiated by committee members encountered by the author.

[12] On one occasion, for example, the chairman had actually adjourned the hearing when he noticed another bill that he had forgotten to call. "Wait a minute, wait a minute," he called to his colleagues, who were already leaving the chamber, "we've got another bill here." Senator Bidwill,

How, then, does the chairman determine the vote to be dictated to the secretary? Normally it is sufficient for him to utter three words—"same roll call"—which permits the vote on the previous bill to be applied to the bill then being passed. Since opposition to bills is seldom recorded, there is little chance that anyone will object to the application of the same roll call. Indeed, committee unanimity is so firmly established that it has become customary for the committee to actually voice its vote only once during any given hearing. At the beginning of each hearing the chairman calls for a voice vote on the first bill in order to "establish a roll call." With a count of the yeas and nays so established the chairman is in a position to expedite consideration of other bills by ordering his secretary to record the "same roll call" on each succeeding bill instead of ordering a new vote for every one. The established roll call is unanimous, of course, so that virtually every bill is reported out by the same 12 to 0 or 14 to 0 vote which reflects the number of members present at the start of the hearing. Members who wish to challenge the assumption of unanimity do so by simply telling the secretary to "count me 'No' on that"—a procedure which officially records the infrequent opposition while preserving the established roll call intact. By eliminating the necessity for separate votes on every bill, the "same roll call" device makes it possible for the committee to record an official position on dozens of bills within a very short period of time.[13] That such records are largely inaccurate—since members come and go without any change in the established roll call count—is less important to committeemen than the opportunity provided by this technique to discharge their obligations in very short order.

---

who happened to be the member closest to the chairman, asked, "What bill is that?" "The aid bill for the superintendent," Chairman Peters responded. "Oh, that," said Bidwill, who waved his hand and added, "do pass." As Bidwill turned to continue his exit, Peters simply told his secretary to record the same roll call on this particular bill and prepared to leave himself. Meanwhile, the representative from the superintendent's office, who had observed this interchange as he moved forward to the witness table, made an abrupt ninety-degree turn to make his way toward the door. The bill, incidentally, made an appropriation of some $57 million.

[13] The committee met on twenty-two separate days during the 1963 session and considered as many as twenty-two bills at one meeting. Nevertheless, these meetings normally were completed within one hour. See Henn, *op. cit.*, for similar evidence.

The speed with which the "same roll call" device can be utilized to determine committee recommendations is largely a function of the informality of its application. Members seldom permit
a witness to conclude a presentation to the committee, particularly if the presentation concerns a budget bill, or a bill sponsored by a well-liked colleague, or a bill appropriating a small
amount, or a bill brought up at a time when committeemen are
anxious to conclude the hearing. On such occasions, the witness
will normally be permitted to begin his presentation, but after a
sentence or two some member will simply shout "same roll call"
in a voice loud enough to interrupt the presentation. The interruption is a signal for the chairman to ask "Any objection to the
same roll call?" and, unless some objection is made, to dismiss
the witness and order his secretary to record the same roll call.
A similar degree of informality is apparent in the utilization of
proxy votes. Though it is widely suspected that the chairman and
others who cast proxies frequently do so without the written authorization of the absent members, no effort is made to stop this
practice, or even to challenge it. Proxies are simply accepted as
a very useful device for expediting the committee's work, espe-
cally when a quorum is not present.

The sources of such practiced informality can be readily understood by reference to committee membership. In the 1963
session ten of the sixteen committee members were Republicans,
whose average length of service on the committee was ten years.
The most experienced in terms of service, and most important in
terms of committee decisions, was the chairman, Senator Everett
R. Peters. Peters had first joined the committee in 1945, had
served three terms as vice-chairman beginning in 1953, and had
become chairman in 1959. Through this entire period, of course,
Peters served as chairman of the Budgetary Commission and at
the same time was firmly established as chief spokesman for Senate Republicans on matters regarding state finance. Other Republican members included the core of the Senate leadership: the
President Pro Tem (Majority Leader), the Assistant Majority
Leader, the Chairman of the Republican Caucus, and the Chairman of the influential Committee on Committees, who was also
Vice-Chairman of the Appropriations Committee. The Democratic Senate Minority Leader was also a member of the committee, as were the remaining Senate members (three Republicans

and two Democrats) of the Budgetary Commission. Thus, the membership of this committee embraced virtually all of the most important Senate leadership positions and the entire Senate representation on the Budgetary Commission.

Since most of the men holding these positions were, like Senator Peters, veterans of many years in the Senate and on this particular committee, a certain looseness of procedure, based on years of doing the same things together, was inevitable. Beyond that, the nature of the positions themselves discouraged a rigorously formal approach to committee business. The chairman and five other members, after all, already had heard explanations of the major expenditure items before the Budgetary Commission. Given this fact, and given the long experience of Senator Peters in dealing with these matters, other members were inclined to go along with whatever decisions he made and whatever procedures he followed to achieve the principal committee goal of reporting out the bills as quickly as possible. Moreover, other committeemen were confident that decisions made by them under Peters' firm and speedy hand would produce no consequences likely to be embarrassing for, while the committee had no staff, Senator Peters did, again in the form of assistance from Budget Superintendent Leth. Sitting adjacent to Peters at the committee table, Leth was able to refresh the chairman's mind concerning the contents of bills, or give him technical advice, or explain the differences between the budget document and the bills themselves. The latter service was particularly important because of the many changes in agency requests made in the process of drafting bills and because only the Budget Superintendent was in a position to know what those changes were. These services enhanced the ability of Senator Peters to handle the committee's work—a result which simultaneously encouraged other members to use committee meetings as intervals of relaxation in which they, as well as persons on the other side of the committee table, acted as spectators to a game being played by someone else.

The whole committee, of course, might have attempted to develop staff services for all of the members, but that would have implied dissatisfaction on the part of the membership with the existing pattern of operations. Such dissatisfaction did not exist. For other Republican members, to whom Peters had been colleague and leader for twenty-four years, Peters was both expert and trustworthy, and thoroughly unlikely to take any actions that would be contrary to the desires of his associates who were themselves leaders. Disagreements, if any, were worked out in the caucus, permitting the Republicans to maintain their public unity in committee, as on the floor of the Senate. Presumably, other members who are Democrats were less satisfied with the activities of the chairman but such dissatisfaction as existed was seldom expressed. Democrats understood perfectly well that nothing they did would affect the absolute control available to a unified committee majority, which needed no help from the weak minority either to pass or to kill bills. Open opposition by the minority in this situation would have been pointless. Rather than risk the antagonism of the majority, therefore, Democrats for the most part participated in the informal maintenance of committee harmony. Indeed, this harmony was so striking that Democrats frequently rushed to make motions which produced favorable reports on Republican-sponsored bills, while Senator Peters occasionally cast proxy votes not only for his fellow Republicans, but for Democratic senators as well.[14]

The Senate Appropriations Committee in 1963 was thus a small and friendly group of men which issued favorable reports on appropriation bills with great speed and greater informality. Though the group had little or no information concerning the content of the bills it considered, it seldom engaged in lengthy interrogation of witnesses, in part because it was not interested and in part because it lacked an informational base upon which to formulate questions. Such questions as were raised tended to focus on the stray bills about which members had no knowledge or on particular aspects of major appropriation bills. Exchanges which took place were essentially ritualistic, however, for the committee seldom changed bills and rarely opposed them. The chairman, aided by Budget Superintendent Leth, did virtually all the work of the committee, a situation that permitted other members to relax and thereby contribute to the atmosphere of easy informality that characterized committee activity. As a final summary comment on this committee we may consider the more or less "typical" treatment given to the bill appropriating funds for the Department of Mental Health.

---

[14] Compare Steiner and Gove, *Legislative Politics in Illinois, op. cit.,* p. 78.

168

The date was June 12, 1963, a day on which the Senate's regular morning session ran slightly overtime. As a result, the Appropriations Committee meeting did not begin until 1:45 P.M., at which time a $100,000 appropriation bill was used to establish a 14 to 0 roll call vote in favor of a "do pass" recommendation. By 2:13 P.M., when Mental Health Director Gerty and Deputy Director Merten seated themselves at the witness table, eight other bills had been approved, each by the same roll call. House Bill 1242 embodied the departmental request prepared in December and reviewed by the Budgetary Commission in February. The Governor had reduced the original General Revenue Fund request by some $17 million, from $254 to $237 million, but also had earmarked almost $10 million in salary increases for this department. In place of the $237 million budget figure, therefore, the bill before the committee appropriated $247 million from general revenue to the Department of Mental Health.

Senator Peters began consideration of the bill by noting the existence of a minor amendment, which was immediately adopted without discussion. He then asked Director Gerty to explain the bill. Obviously well coached, Gerty responded by indicating only that his bill contained a sizable increase, but that his department was doing a sizable job. His concluding offer to answer any questions from committee members was immediately met with a loud shout from a Republican senator seated behind Chairman Peters: "I move do pass, Mr. Chairman." Democratic Senator Morgan M. Finley interrupted, however, to ask whether or not there was a "Healy School" in Chicago and if so, what the nature of its programs were. The question was prompted, he said severely, by one of his constituents, whose attempts to enroll a relative in the school had repeatedly failed. Director Gerty responded by explaining that this hospital was designed to develop new methods of treatment for retarded children and, while admittedly experimental in nature, was a very important part of the department's program and one to which he gave his strongest support. Apparently satisfied by this response, Senator Finley sat back in his chair while another member repeated the "do pass" motion. At this, Senator Peters turned to his secretary and ordered her to record the same roll call on the bill. A 14 to 0 vote was duly recorded, some three minutes after Director Gerty and Deputy Director Merten had seated themselves.

The same bill was treated quite differently by the House Appropriations Committee, in accordance with its own distinctive style. This committee considered the bill on May 28, 1963. Gerty and Merten again represented the department and Leth was again seated at the committee table, in a position to offer his help to Committee Chairman Peter C. Granata. Representative Harris, himself a member and former chairman of the committee, acted as sponsor and indicated that he had an amendment to offer to the bill which, he explained to his colleagues, was the biennial departmental appropriation. Harris explained the nature of his amendment by reading a three-minute statement that had been prepared by departmental representatives and then moved the adoption of his amendment. After a question from another member had been answered at some length by Deputy Director Merten, the amendment was adopted by voice vote. Representative G. William Horsley, a long-time member of the House "Economy Bloc" who had devoted the previous evening to studying the bill for Mental Health, then requested an explanation of the additional $10 million which was in the bill but not in the budget. Budget Superintendent Leth responded to Horsley by explaining that the increase was a result of the Governor's decision to include $11 million in salary increases in the budget. Some $9.8 million of that increase, he said, had been allocated to Mental Health in keeping with its status as one of the largest departments. Leth added that an additional $4.8 million in salary increases was also recommended to take care of a one-step across-the-board adjustment made when the Governor's "freeze" order was rescinded. "Do you mean to say that you actually had a $15 million increase in salaries in the budget?" Horsley asked. "That's right," was Leth's response.

Horsley then turned to Gerty and Merten to inquire about the salary scale for psychiatric aides in the state hospitals. Merten referred briefly to documents he had brought with him and replied that the current range was $245 to $325 per month. The following exchange then took place:

Horsley: What will the new salary scales be for these psychiatric aides?
Merten: I don't have that information, Mr. Horsley.
Horsley: Who does?
Merten: It hasn't been determined yet.

Horsley: Well now, how do you get to this $9,882,480 figure if you haven't even determined what the new salary scales will be?

Merten: We didn't provide that figure, sir.

Horsley: Well, who did?

Merten: The Department of Personnel determined the initial amount and then transmitted it to the Department of Finance which in turn distributed our portion of the over-all pay increase in the budget.

Harris: Bill [referring to Horsley], I think the real trouble here is not so much in this department as in the Department of Personnel. I think that if the legislature wants to make some changes in some of these things, maybe it ought to consider changing some things in the Department of Personnel.

This somewhat inconclusive exchange, which offered further evidence of the complications involved in budget preparation, was followed by a variety of other questions. Representative Parkhurst, another member of the Economy Bloc, asked for a clarification of the relationship between this bill and the functions to be performed by the new Department of Children and Family Services and debated Merten's response for several minutes with Representative Bernard M. Peskin, a strong supporter of the new department. Representative Rae C. Heiple, a third member of the Economy Bloc, then took turns with Representative Horsley in raising questions about large increases (compared to the current appropriation) in Travel and Contractual Services items. Both Merten and Gerty responded to these inquiries, frequently citing detailed figures to explain the bases of departmental increases. But again, these exchanges were inconclusive, for once the "explanations" had been made there was little more the questioners could say, unless they wished to propose reductions. Such proposals were not made, perhaps because the questioners had no grounds by which they could be justified. No further questions were raised, in any event, and on the roll call ordered by Chairman Granata, all members of the committee voted to recommend that the bill "do pass." Some thirty-five minutes had been consumed in considering this bill.

Compared to the Senate committee, then, the House Appropriations Committee took much more time, and was much more formal in its consideration of House Bill 1242. Though thirty-five minutes was an unusually long period to devote to a single bill, it did represent the general tendency of the House committee to give some attention, at least, to the detailed content of most bills brought before it. Similarly, the formal call of the roll to determine the committee recommendation represented typical procedure in a group that made relatively little use of the "same roll call" technique. These essentially superficial differences reflected more basic contrasts in the membership of the two committees. For one thing, neither the chairman nor the vice-chairman of the House committee could claim any special expertise, or indeed, experience, in dealing with state appropriations. Chairman Granata had served three terms as a member of the Appropriations Committee in the period 1945-49, but had not served on the committee since that time until his selection as chairman in 1963. Vice-Chairman Peter G. Miller was even more inexperienced, with no record of service on this committee during his tenure in the House. Clearly neither man was equipped to do more than see to it that meetings were held and bills were dealt with in the proper manner. For the chairman, who actually conducted the meetings, relatively close adherence to formal procedures (including roll call votes) simply reflected the absence of an alternative conception of purpose.[15]

Quite apart from the qualifications of the committee leadership, however, the large number of members made a relatively high level of formality difficult to avoid. Unlike the cozy sixteen-man Senate Committee, the House committee of thirty-nine members was one of the largest in the lower chamber. Moreover the committee was neither a very experienced nor a very homogeneous group. Only seven of its members had as much as ten years of experience on the committee, while eleven were without any experience at all, leaving twenty-one other members whose average length of committee service was less than five years. All of the House members of the Budgetary Commission were *not* included as members of the Appropriations Committee and, in sharp contrast to the Senate practice, the House committee was

---

[15] Perhaps it would be more accurate to say that Chairman Granata simply followed the course expected of most committee chairmen in the Illinois legislature. Thus Steiner and Gove write: "Committee chairmen do not kill bills, do not delay bills, do not ignore bills, and rarely make a parliamentary ruling that will have an important effect on the future of a bill. The major legislative role of the chairman is to receive requests and act in accord with those requests." *Ibid.*, p. 61.

divided almost evenly along party lines: twenty Republicans and nineteen Democrats.

The lack of firmly established committee leadership, coupled with the heterogeneity of the membership, resulted in far greater participation by more members, who took more time and frequently developed detailed information concerning the bills under consideration. While this was generally true for all members, it was particularly true for the small group on the committee who felt themselves to be members of the Economy Bloc. This group, which was bipartisan and therefore not susceptible to party controls, frequently led the questioning done by the committee, as in the case of House Bill 1242 discussed earlier, and had been known to force the extension of committee hearings well into the evening hours, to the great displeasure of their committee colleagues.

The principal basis of such displeasure, nicely illustrated in the treatment accorded the Mental Health appropriation, is the general inability of the questioning to produce changes in the bills. If questioned items are given satisfactory explanations—in the sense of providing detailed explications of the method by which dollar totals were calculated—the ground is cut from any attempt to propose changes. If answers are not considered satisfactory the problem becomes one of justifying a proposal for a change. But no committee member, including the Economy Bloc representatives, has sufficient knowledge of agency programs to justify amendments to bills. Thus, while bloc members sometimes voted against bills because the expenditures they authorized were not budgeted or because they were opposed to increases in general, they rarely proposed amendments. To other members of the committee, meanwhile, both the detailed questioning and the occasional opposition to bills appeared to be little more than futile and time-consuming expressions of a negativist attitude.

No better example of the frustrations implicit in the position of the legislature with regard to control over state finance can be offered than the activities of the so-called Economy Bloc. These activities will be explored in some depth in the following chapter but it may be useful here to emphasize once again the severe obstacles to usable knowledge encountered by even so diligent a group as the Economy Bloc. If we recall for a moment the interaction which occurred over the Mental Health appropriation bill, we can note that the bulk of the questioning was done by (a) a sixteen-year veteran legislator who had spent a large part of his legislative energy during this period on financial legislation, (b) a six-year legislator who had made governmental economy his principal interest and who, in addition, had obtained the services of a public affairs consultant in his examinations of state expenditures, and (c) a young lawyer-legislator who, like his two colleagues was concerned about economy, but who was serving on the Appropriations Committee for the first time. Each of these men, moreover, had spent the previous evening in the company of their Economy Bloc associates poring over the bills to be brought before the Appropriations Committee on the following day, attempting to match them with the relevant pages of the budget book. Yet despite their experience and despite their homework, these men were not aware of the impact of budgeted salary increases on the Mental Health appropriation, they did not understand the relationship between this department and the proposed new Department of Children and Family Services, and they had no satisfactory explanation of a variety of appropriation increases contained in the bill brought before the committee. By the time they obtained information on these matters, of course, it was too late to make use of it, for the impending committee vote prohibited the development of a policy framework that might have posed an alternative to committee approval of the appropriation.

FLOOR VOTES

The difficulty of obtaining information in time for use in Appropriations Committee hearings sometimes led members of the Economy Bloc—and occasionally other members of both committees as well—to support committee approval of certain bills while at the same time reserving the right to withhold approval when such bills are called for a final floor vote in either chamber. Such protestations are rarely effective, for once a bill is reported out of a committee the chances are overwhelmingly in favor of its passage by both houses. During the 1963 session, for example the House voted on a total of 252 bills appropriating funds for the support of state activities (Table 9). Only three of these bills

Table 9. House and Senate Action on Appropriation Bills, 1963 Session

House		Senate
252	Total Bills Voted	242
128 [a]	Senate Bills	136
124	House Bills	106 [b]
3	Failed to Pass	2
0	Senate Bills	1
3	House Bills	1
249	Total Bills Passed	240
128	Senate Bills	135
121	House Bills	105

[a] Seven Senate bills tabled in House committees.
[b] Fifteen House bills tabled in Senate committees.

failed to receive the eighty-nine votes required to pass in the House. Similarly, just 2 of the 242 bills voted on by the Senate were unable to secure the thirty votes necessary for Senate approval. Thus, of 494 votes on appropriation bills in both houses, there were only 5 on which a favorable majority was not recorded.[16] And it is of some interest to note the relatively small number of bills (twenty-two) which failed to come to a vote in the second chamber after having passed in their house of origin.

It seems abundantly clear, then, that both houses in 1963 were characterized by a substantially identical measure of affection for bills appropriating state funds. Unwilling to risk offense to legislative colleagues, aware of the need to carry on state activities, and generally uninformed with regard to either the nature of existing state activities or to alternative activities that might be necessary or desirable, most legislators treated virtually all appropriation bills as "good things" and voted accordingly. The few legislators who adopted a different orientation to their responsibilities found themselves frustrated not only by an absence of information, but also by a lack of time. Although final votes

---

[16] The difference between the number of bills referred to the two appropriations committees and the number of appropriation bills which came to a floor vote in each chamber can be attributed to the practice of assigning bills appropriating funds to committees other than appropriations or to the failure to refer such bills to committee.

on some appropriation bills were recorded as early as March, major bills generally did not come up for consideration until late May or early June, when the General Assembly was in session four or five days and two or three evenings every week, when the daily legislative calendar reached lengths of two, three, and four feet, and when the press of other business was so great that the time available for floor consideration could hardly be used for anything but the approval of bills on third reading.[17]

In such circumstances not only approval, but approval essentially without serious dissent, was perhaps unavoidable. Almost half (45 per cent) of the appropriation bills passed by the Senate in 1963 received no opposing votes at all, while slightly more than one-third of the bills passed by the House were in the same category. Many of these, of course, were major budget bills which typically pass without opposition—the Mental Health bill discussed earlier, for example, passed the House by 155 to 0 and the Senate by 49 to 0. To be sure, opposition votes were sometimes cast, particularly by advocates of economy who wished to record themselves as opposed in principle to many of the unbudgeted expenditures favored by their colleagues. However, such opposition seldom reached significant levels. Of every ten bills voted on by either chamber in 1963 roughly eight received, on the one hand, only trivial opposition and, on the other hand, the support of at least two-thirds of the members of both houses. On the floor, as in their committee chambers, senators and representatives appeared determined to live up to a characterization once made by a veteran bureaucrat: "They'll pass any bill you give them up there."

CONCLUSION: THROUGH A LEGISLATURE, DARKLY

The budget presented to the General Assembly by the Governor in April, 1963, requested appropriations totaling some $3.89 billion to operate the state government during the 73rd biennium. Eager, as ever, to "support state government," legislators passed all of the Governor's budget bills and went on to demonstrate the value they placed upon "comradeship" by passing 143 additional bills authorizing the expenditure of an additional $102.5

---

[17] Henn, *op. cit.*, pp. 28-63, provides detailed data for the 1951 session which leads to virtually identical conclusions.

million. Not all of this unbudgeted sum was inspired by legislators, of course. Indeed, an important part of the Governor's plan to balance his budget was implemented through a $7 million appropriation that was not in his budget (see Chapter 5). But the bulk of this money reflected a legislative determination that many things not in the Governor's budget were good things to do and that he should be so informed. Built into this orientation is the expectation that the Governor will not be able to do all of the good things desired by legislators.[18] In keeping with this expectation the Governor made liberal use of his veto power, producing the results summarized in Table 10. Close to $72 mil-

Table 10. FINAL LEGISLATIVE AND GUBERNATORIAL ACTION
ON APPROPRIATIONS: 73RD GENERAL ASSEMBLY [a]

	Total All Funds	General Revenue and Common School Funds	All Other Funds
Appropriations Passed by General Assembly	$3,992.7	$2,026.7	$1,966.0
Less: Vetoes	71.7	57.3	14.4
Total 73rd Appropriation	3,921.0	1,969.4	1,951.6
Amount Budgeted	3,890.2	1,943.4	1,946.8
Appropriations Exceeding Budget	$ 30.8	$ 26.0	$ 4.8

[a] In millions.

lion in nonbudgeted appropriations were vetoed, largely from bills authorizing General Revenue Fund expenditures. On the other hand, just under $31 million in additional appropriations ultimately were approved by the Governor, adding considerably to the burden carried by the General Revenue Fund. Legislative action on expenditures, then, cannot be said to be entirely without effect, though the effect is to do little more than add another source of pressure for increasing the level of state spending.

In the context within which appropriation bills are considered, legislative pressure for higher spending levels can hardly be sur-

---

[18] Further evidence of the legislature's disposition to let the Governor decide which good things to accomplish is offered in Steiner and Gove, *op. cit.*, p. 71.

prising, for the only realistic alternative is to take no action at all with regard to state expenditures. Without detailed knowledge of major budget bills, legislators are precluded from tampering with them: they do not know *what* to cut and are equally unaware of *how* increases can be achieved. Budget bills are thus given short shrift. They are not examined; they are not analyzed; they are simply passed, and with them passes the opportunity to reduce expenditures or modify programs. Under these conditions the legislature becomes irrelevant to major expenditure decisions, which are made in other places, by other men, who expect the legislature to do nothing more than provide legal authority for spending state money. Only by dealing with items not in the budget bills can legislators hope to have any impact on expenditure decisions. To the extent that such an impact is felt, therefore, it can only be felt as pressure for expenditures *in addition to* budgeted expenditures.

From a legislative point of view stray or nonbudget bills are the perfect vehicle for expressing this pressure for higher expenditures. Normally strays are very simple, in the sense that they provide one sum for one particular project or activity. Because they are not part of some over-all financial framework, moreover, they can be fully comprehended without reference to other programs or to the question of revenue—in short, little knowledge is required for their interpretation. And, most important, they are normally associated with some individual legislator who is chief sponsor. Such an association, as part of a system in which every legislator is expected to shepherd his own bills through to final passage, helps other legislators to establish their own relationship to any given bill, and in fact serves as a substitute for knowledge of a bill's contents. The strays which are approved by the legislature, therefore, do not represent a collective legislative judgment on "good things" that ought to be done so much as they represent a collection of individual judgments that have been ratified by the two houses. Indeed, under the conditions which prevailed in 1963 as in previous years, a collective judgment could not be made, for the legislature as an institution lacked the ability—in the form of knowledge and mechanisms for its application—to develop such a judgment. As far as state expenditures were concerned, the legislative role was confined to passing appropriation bills.

CHAPTER SEVEN

THE SYSTEM
AND ITS
CONSEQUENCES

Legally and constitutionally, the roles analyzed in the preceding chapters are bound to interact with one another to deal with a problem of utmost importance: the allocation of financial resources available to the state organization. It is precisely this *interaction between roles* which constitutes the system of action through which allocative decisions are made. Various aspects of this system have been discussed separately in earlier chapters. The purpose here is to pull together these several statements into a description of the whole system as it operated in 1963. Presented in this fashion, the system will necessarily appear to be static. To some extent such a presentation represents a conscious falsification for, while the system in 1963 appeared to possess extraordinary stability, the presence of a number of internal and external pressures for change was equally apparent. Nevertheless, a description that treats the system *as though it were* stable is useful, chiefly because it permits the constituent parts of the system to be delineated sharply. Having done this much we will be in a better position to examine the manner in which the system is both maintained and changed.

THE DECISIONAL SITUATION

In the process of analyzing the manner in which decisions are made to allocate state resources it is difficult to avoid the implication that nothing else is of much concern to the actors involved. The fact is, however, that each of these actors deals with this problem as only one among a host of other problems which must be dealt with at the same time. The clerks and administrative assistants who prepare budget request forms in the agencies must interrupt their normal clerical or administrative activities in order to get the job done, while the Governor and the legislature must wrestle with a variety of other policy problems, not all of which are relevant to budgets and appropriations, as they seek to shape a financial policy. Even the Department of Finance cannot avoid its numerous day-to-day responsibilities during the period in which it supervises the shaping of allocative decisions. Only the Budgetary Commission can claim a relatively unimpaired focus, but the legislative composition of this body coupled with its practice of dealing with budget requests while the legislature is in session are enough to guarantee commission interest in a variety of problems of a nonfinancial nature.

Decisions about expenditures, in short, represent only one of many sets of decisions which the relevant actors must make within a relatively brief period of time. The motivation for making them, furthermore, is not derived from a rationalized financial or administrative policy but from a legal system which requires attention to specified objects (i.e., budget requests and appropriation bills) at specified points in time (i.e., prior to July 1 of every odd-numbered year). Once made, these determinations can be ignored until the next decision period, some fifteen months away, when similar determinations will have to be made again. This is not to say that what happens in between one series of decisions and the next series of decisions is inconsequential, but merely to point out that there is no centrally organized effort to link decisions to consequences until the following decision period. In the interim, decisions which have erred on the side of generosity can be transformed into "accurate" decisions simply by spending more than is necessary. Decisions which have erred in the opposite direction, meanwhile, can always be corrected by submitting a request for supplemental appropriations to make up for an inadequate original grant.[1] There is thus no reward for accuracy and no particularly strin-

---

[1] The number of supplemental appropriations approved by the 71st, 72nd, and 73rd General Assemblies was 32, 31, and 30, respectively. Taken together with the numerous bills authorizing the transfer of funds between accounts which are introduced early in each session, these figures suggest that decisions are thought to be something less than binding.

gent penalty for inaccuracy.[2] In this sense the determinations made during any given decision period for the next fiscal period are divorced from their consequences and therefore among the least important financial decisions that are made. They are not made because anyone wants to make them but simply because they have to be made. And they are made by men who are quite busy with other matters and who become increasingly busy with other matters as the legislative session approaches its end.

Many of these decisions are made without any explicit perception of alternatives. In general it is assumed that what the state organization is now doing will continue to be done because there is no other choice: some of the most important state activities (e.g., school aid or highways) are in effect "guaranteed" by statutory formulae while others (e.g., mental health or higher education) are so large that abandonment is literally unthinkable. And the more knowledgeable the actors are about the total financial situation, the more impressed they are likely to be by the limitations which bind state action. Only when impositions are made by external actors (i.e., a bond issue referendum or the federal government) is there anything at all problematic about the actions to be taken, which otherwise remain the same from one biennium to the next. The situation is therefore one of relative certainty, in which busy men take time from their other concerns to do a job that has to be done, according to well-known and standardized procedures, with little expectation that the consequences of their actions will either have independent significance or be related to the acts themselves.

ROLES

The terms in which the various actors orient themselves to this situation are provided by a shared set of informational

---

[2] This point probably deserves stronger emphasis, since the "eighteen-month budget" is an Illinois tradition. Though always denied officially, the record shows a consistent pattern of under-appropriating for certain agencies in order to maintain a balance between projected expenditures and revenues. The consistency and magnitude (sometimes exceeding $100 million) of the supplementals required to finance the remaining portion of the biennium indicate that the original inaccurate decisions were planned, in order to achieve the "reward" of a balanced budget. See my earlier article, "Some Budgetary Aspects of the Illinois Fiscal Crisis," *op. cit.*

categories which structures a common universe of discourse. Within its terms, categories of objects are identified, criteria of relevance and significance are established, and relationships between objects are structured. Each actor, of course, selects certain categories for special emphasis, in keeping with the requirements of his particular role. But this is done within a framework of thought shared by all participants in allocative decisions. Such sharing is extremely significant, for it provides the foundation upon which each actor develops a more or less stable set of expectations regarding the actions of other participants in the system. It is precisely this anticipation of the behavior of other actors which enables any given actor to structure his own behavior into a relatively consistent and stable pattern—in short, a role. Thus roles do not "spring from" anything internal to the individual actor but rather from his perceptions of and expectations about himself in relation to objects and actors external to himself. Since roles are defined according to this complementarity of expectations, a review of each of the roles previously analyzed, emphasizing the perceptions and expectations of each actor, should provide a clarification of the system of action by which the state organization allocates its resources.

Agency Officials

Agency officials typically focus their attention on two classes of objects: the budget request forms and, later, appropriation bills. Normally they attach greater significance to their budget requests for, while major changes are frequently made in appropriation bills, such changes usually are beyond their control. Salary increases, for example, are typically determined by the Governor after the bulk of the budget is made upon the basis of a formula worked out by the Governor and the Department of Personnel. This kind of increase is important to agencies, of course, but there is little they can do about it except to make known their desires for the highest possible amount. Since it is understood that *some* increase will be granted, but that only the Governor can determine the specific amount, at least for the code departments, agency officials can put aside their problem in determining how much to request. Nonbudget bills which affect agency operations are also introduced and passed with some frequency. But strays normally provide marginal increases at best and seldom have a crucial impact on major agency operations. What really matters to agency officials, therefore, are their budget bills, which are based upon the budget request forms. Once their bills are introduced they are carefully followed, but it is the content of the requests which is given most attention prior to the submission of the Governor's budget.

The kind of attention given to the budget request forms differs considerably from agency to agency. The clerks and secretaries who fill in the forms for the smaller agencies handle the job as a routine matter, typically using figures provided by the Finance Department, and typically producing requests which do little more than fill in the blanks on the forms. In some of the larger agencies, on the other hand, considerable care is given to these forms, usually by relatively high-ranking administrative officials, who sometimes prepare mimeographed explanations of their request in addition to the completed forms. At the same time, the nature of the forms encourages a noteworthy consistency of interpretation among those who fill them out. Since the forms emphasize dollars expended, or to be expended, officials conceive their task to involve manipulation of dollar-expenditure categories. And since the forms require a sharp distinction between the current level of expenditure and some alternative level (in the form of "basic" and "supplemental" requests), much of this manipulation focuses on methods of dealing with this distinction.

The manner in which agency officials deal with these objects is determined to a large extent by their expectations regarding the behavior of other actors. Two actors are perceived to be especially relevant by agency officials. One is the Finance Department—frequently seen in personal terms as Budget Superintendent Leth—which initiates the process of budget preparation by means of a written communication sent in July or August of each even-numbered year. This communication, supplemented by detailed instructions on budget preparation (written) and normally by a meeting of agency officials, performs a number of important services in addition to providing instructions on how to fill out the budget request forms. Explicitly, it identifies the intellectual categories according to which decisions will be made, and also identifies other actors who will be involved in a significant capacity. Implicitly, it suggests the priority of values that will guide decisions and thus structures some rules which, if followed, will ensure agency success in budgeting. While agency officials do not expect the Finance Department to make any changes in their requests, Budget Superintendent Leth is viewed as an important means of communication and technical guidance. Thus Leth receives the completed budget forms and, several weeks or months later, contacts agency representatives to arrange for their appearance before the Budgetary Commission. Actions taken by the Governor will also be communicated by Leth and, later still, he will supervise and coordinate the drafting of many appropriations bills.

The second significant actor, from the agency point of view, is the Budgetary Commission. To a man, agency officials identify the commission as the agency which will cut their budget requests. They recognize, however, that such cuts will typically fall on their supplemental requests, leaving their basic budgets largely intact. Other actors, such as the House and Senate, or the Governor, are viewed as essentially unimportant. Thus the legislature as an actor is expected to approve whatever is in the budget, making few changes or none at all, while the Governor's actions are only dimly perceived. One veteran agency official was "not sure" when the Governor would see his request or what action he would take. Another less experienced official, meanwhile, who was upset at the harsh treatment the commission had given to his request, telephoned the commission's executive director to ask "What do I do now?" He was told to contact the Governor.[3]

In preparing budget request forms, therefore, agency officials anticipate the probable actions of the Budgetary Commission, using both the clues provided by Finance Department instructions and their own past experience (which in most cases is considerable) in presenting requests to the commission. Anticipating little or no trouble in securing approval of their basic

---

[3] This vagueness over the Governor's role was, in my judgment, a result of the peculiarities of the incumbent Governor's method of operation (see Chapter 5). The same officials who were uncertain about Kerner had no difficulty in recalling the actions of Governor Stratton, who preceded Kerner.

budgets, most agency representatives fill them out mechanically, and sometimes carelessly. A few of the larger agencies, on the other hand, exercise great care in completing their basic requests, seeking to put as much as they can into their basic budgets, precisely because they expect unquestioning approval.

And, expecting the commission to cut, agencies normally are careful to submit supplemental requests that can be cut. This is not to say that agencies lack grounds to support their requests for increases. Indeed, there is a sense in which, because of the basic-supplemental scheme, with its assumption that present expenditures are beyond question, increases are the *only* proposals that can be defended by the agencies. But requests for increases have an important political meaning quite apart from the rationale that may be used to support them. As one experienced agency official responded, when asked why he continued to request increases if he knew they would be cut, "I do it to protect myself." Requests for increases help to divert attention away from the basic budget and, more significantly, enable the commission to play its expected role without harming essential agency programs. Failure to ask for more money in this context represents a serious challenge to existing role definitions and, as a result, occurs only infrequently. Agencies continue to request increases, in short, because cuts have to be made.

The Budgetary Commission

The objects to which the Budgetary Commission orients itself are the basic and supplemental budget requests prepared by individual agencies and summarized in one page or less by the commission's executive director. These are taken up one at a time and decisions are made either immediately, before the next request is taken up, or at the end of the meeting in which a given request is considered. No attempt is made to relate decisions about expenditures for individual agencies to total state expenditures, in part because the total figure is unknown at the time decisions are made. Nor is any attempt made to relate individual requests to total state revenue. Once determined, recommendations for individual agency requests are largely forgotten by individual commissioners. The commission seldom, if ever, attempts to maintain the integrity of its recommendations during later stages of the decision process. Instead, the collective identity of the commission as an actor ceases at the conclusion of its hearings.

In deciding what to recommend the commission is oriented, first of all, to Budget Superintendent Leth, who is instrumental in initiating commission hearings and who provides the information which structures hearing activity. Leth is expected to act as both technician and participant in decision-making. As technician, he provides information not only about what is contained in the request forms but also about organizational and accounting changes made since the previous hearing period. As participant Leth is expected to offer advice on dealing with such changes, including his own preferences with regard to how much to recommend. The expectation that Leth will participate is founded on the knowledge, gained through years of working together, that Leth and the commission share essentially identical expectations regarding the actions of the various agencies. Both expect agencies "to ask for the moon," to borrow a phrase from Commission Chairman Peters, and both consequently understand the "How much to recommend?" question to boil down to another, more simple, query: "How much to cut?" The "how much" phrases are not accidental, of course, for they reflect commission acceptance of the dollars-and-cents definition of budget requests.

The third actor whose expected behavior helps to shape commission activity is the Governor. Implicitly recognizing the Governor's responsibility for keeping expenditures in line with revenues, the commission defers to his judgment on requests submitted by the largest agencies, on most requests for capital expenditures, on new requests, and on salary increases. Moreover, the commission makes no effort to deal with the whole structure of state finance and is thus in no position to offer any alternatives to the complex structure of revenue laws, special funds, and basic expenditure policies presided over, presumably, by the Governor. In this sense, the commission's expectations regarding the Governor determines a range of actions that it does not take, while its view of the likely behavior of numerous small-to-medium stage agencies determines the characteristic response to such agencies. Finally, it should be pointed out that the commission carries on its activities quite independently of the legislature, which is not considered to be relevant to what the commission does.

The Legislature

Legislators are oriented to one class of objects only: appropriation bills. It is true, of course, that legislators have access to the budget book, annual reports of the Finance Department, and a variety of other documents of potential relevance, at least, to the contents of appropriation bills. Apart from a very few exceptions, however, legislators make no attempt to familiarize themselves with these additional documents.

In deciding what action to take on appropriations, legislators are oriented primarily to the Budgetary Commission with regard to budget bills, and primarily to the Governor with regard to "stray," or nonbudget, bills. Unaware of the nature of commission activities, legislators nevertheless assume the commission review has been achieved and that further investigation of major appropriations is unnecessary. Close analysis of stray bills is thought to be equally unnecessary, since the Governor is expected to determine which of the strays will be implemented. On such assumptions, the legislature gives its approval to the great bulk of the appropriation bills it considers. To some extent certain members of the legislature—e.g., chairmen of the Appropriations committees—are also sensitive to the activities of Budget Superintendent Leth. At this stage of the process, though, Leth's participation is expected to be primarily technical in nature.

The Governor

Legal responsibilities, if nothing else, require the Governor to orient himself to all of the objects relevant to the allocation of state resources. At the outset he must concern himself with budget requests, and only he can authorize the sums which appear in the budget book. Later he must keep informed on the progress of appropriation bills, over which, because of his unassailable veto, he has considerable influence. Meanwhile the Governor cannot avoid the problem of revenue, and must concern himself throughout this period with estimates of the revenue likely to be available during the next fiscal biennium. To say that none of these objects can be avoided, however, is not to say that they must be given a like amount of attention. The nature of the process itself tends to organize the Governor's attention around two peak periods. One occurs just after all of the budget requests have come in, at which time the Governor must compare his estimates of total revenue against total requests. Normally requests exceed anticipated revenues—a circumstance that tends to concentrate the Governor's attention on the largest or most easily expendable (e.g., new capital requests) proposals. The second peak period occurs just after the legislature has adjourned, at which time the Governor must sift through the large pile of appropriation bills passed by both houses to determine which bills to approve. At this point the chief problem is not the largest bills, which are administration budget bills, but the myriad of stray bills of less fiscal significance which require careful screening.

In determining his actions during these peak periods the Governor is guided, first of all, by his expectation that agencies are likely to be "energetic" in their requests for funds. Depending on what he knows about the operations of individual agencies, this expectation will be more or less strong, but whatever its strength, its existence can hardly be avoided. By the time the Governor makes his final budget recommendations, it will be recalled, he has already seen the original requests, and also the recommendations for cuts made by the Budgetary Commission. The knowledge that other, presumably knowledgeable, actors have seen fit to cut considerable sums from original requests can only encourage a skeptical attitude toward expenditure proposals—particularly when such cuts are seldom appealed.[4] If such an attitude did not exist, it would probably have to be created, for the Governor normally faces a predicament in which he must find some way to eliminate millions of dollars from budget requests in order to bring those requests into line with anticipated revenues. He can, of course, be generous in his estimate of revenues and thus ease his burden somewhat. But this sort of gamble is discouraged by (a) the difficulty of accurately predicting revenues for a period that will not come to an end for twenty-seven months and (b) the gravity of the consequences, particularly for the large state institutions, if such optimistic predictions are not borne out. Pressures of this kind almost force the Governor to lean in the direction of conservative revenue estimates and thus aggravate his predicament.

---

[4] According to Governor Kerner, appeals from department heads were made only "occasionally" in preparing the 73rd budget. Interview, February 18, 1963.

From experience and from the difficulties of his unique position as the only actor concerned with balancing revenues and expenditures, the Governor is led to take a somewhat skeptical view of agency requests for money. As suggested above, moreover, this view is to some extent a product of the Governor's expectations of another actor: the Budgetary Commission. While the commission recommends cuts, the Governor knows that it does not do this within a context of an over-all financial policy framework. The Governor thus expects commission recommendations to be no more than a first step toward the budget book figure.[5] Typically the Governor will make his own decisions on most agencies, adjusting commission figures downward, and occasionally upward, as need be. To do this the Governor requires much technical assistance, which he expects to get from Budget Superintendent Leth, and much policy assistance, which he expects to get from political associates in whom he has confidence— in the case of Kerner the latter role was played by Revenue Director Isaacs. Because many decisions made on technical grounds have important political consequences the Budget Superintendent is sometimes a source of important political advice for the Governor. And finally, the Governor anticipates legislative approval of many stray bills which nobody expects to be implemented. Liberal use of the veto power after the legislature has adjourned is a reflection of this expectation.

One additional and significant aspect of the gubernatorial role is that it can be—and frequently is—oriented to the expectations of actors external to the state organization itself. Particularly in matters regarding state finance, the Governor acts as a mediator between the state organization and the more or less undifferentiated mass public, which is affected by actions of the organization and which occasionally affects the organization by its own actions (e.g., voting). The newspapers and other media which report the activities of the state for their mass audiences assume that state finance is the Governor's job and focus largely on his proposals and activities, while giving little attention—or, what is often worse, inaccurate attention—to other actors. Since this

---

[5] I believe this is a reasonably fair summary of Governor Kerner's expectation in 1963, though in 1961 he appeared to be more inclined to accept commission recommendations as the final word.

focus is always interpreted within the framework of media commitment to the twin symbols of support for governmental economy and opposition to new or expanded taxes, gubernatorial action is frequently designed to assert or exploit the virtues of these symbols. And since these same symbols are accepted by the party organizations which seek to mobilize the public in support of a governor's candidacy, he is led to act in a fashion designed to accommodate the perceptions of the persons whose business it is to keep the Governor in office. Thus it was that Governor Kerner in 1963 repeatedly referred to his efforts to achieve economy and a "business-like" government. Thus it was, too, that the Governor's budget, with reelection in view, subsumed other goals under the principal goal of avoiding new taxes. Significantly, the actions which resulted from this orientation to external actors—further budget cuts—were precisely the actions which were called for on the basis of a knowledgeable orientation to other actors in the system.

The Department of Finance: Superintendent of Budgets

For reasons which will become clear, this role was the most active single role in the system of action that allocated state resources for the 1963-65 biennium. In effect the role was, and is, so closely associated with a single individual that other actors almost automatically think "Ted Leth" when the budget or the Department of Finance is mentioned. Thus the role of the Budget Superintendent is all but indistinguishable from the individual who has performed it for so long.

Of necessity, the Budget Superintendent is oriented to all of the objects relevant to state financial decisions. Indeed, as a veteran of twenty-years incumbency in this role, during which time he has not only used these objects but originated some of them as well, Budget Superintendent Leth is the chief custodian and interpreter of the system of informational objects upon which allocative decisions are founded. Like the Governor, Leth deals initially with request forms, moves on to the budget book, and later has a great deal to do with appropriation bills. But Leth's involvement begins before, and continues long after, that of the Governor. Thus Leth's attention to these objects does not end with the compilation of the appropriations book; between legislative sessions his daily responsibilities enable him to observe and record the disposition made of appropriation bills. When the next decision period arrives, he is in a position to supplement his knowledge of the informational categories with considerable additional knowledge concerning the use made of these categories by the various agencies. For the Budget Superintendent, then, the objects used in resource allocation are not unfamiliar items presented from the outside, but items he has nurtured and whose utilization he has carefully watched. Oriented to all objects, and in a position to know historical as well as current details of their use, the Budget Superintendent embodies within his person an organizationally unique combination of financial information.

Awareness of his superior knowledge relative to other actors colors the Budget Superintendent's orientation to them. To be sure, Leth's long experience has led him to develop rather definite expectations regarding the actions of other participants: he expects agencies to present inflated requests, the Budgetary Commission to cut these requests (with his help), and the Governor to make further reductions or not as he sees fit (again with his help). But to a large extent these expectations are less important than his assumption that no other actor will know as much as he knows or possess a technical ability which can match his own. Located at the center of the communications network, Leth receives information from every actor. At any given time, therefore, he not only possesses a great fund of information about any other actor, but he may also have a variety of different funds of information from several different sources. Since Leth is the sole possessor of such knowledge, he is free to pick and choose how much of what kinds of information to release to other actors. And since he typically deals with only one actor at a time, he is free to change his choices with regard to any given object from one actor to the next. This is not to say that there is anything particularly devious about the Budget Superintendent's selection of information to be released to other actors. In a situation which offers limited informational access to most actors but virtually total access to one actor, this one actor cannot avoid selectivity if he is to play his expected role in the decision-making system. Nevertheless, Leth does select information for release and thereby exerts considerable control over the information available to other actors.

By controlling the flow of information, of course, Leth is frequently able to control the premises upon which decisions are made and thus is able to influence decisions. Whether or not he encourages an agency to include some ambiguous item in the basic request, rather than a supplemental, can make the difference between approval or rejection of the item. Whether or not he chooses to call the Budgetary Commission's attention to a lapse in one object account and a supplemental request for the same account can determine which decisional rule the commission will apply. Whether or not he chooses to tell the Governor about an item which has been overlooked or which he disapproves can determine what goes into the budget document or what appropriation bills are approved. All other actors in this system thus depend upon Leth, not solely for the information which permits them to do what they are expected to do, but also for the particular combination of informational items that can—and frequently does—determine whether final expenditure decisions are favorable or unfavorable from their special points of view.

In a position to know more than other actors, Leth can choose the information he releases to them; having chosen, he is frequently able to see his choices reflected in final appropriation decisions. Inevitably, then, the Budget Superintendent comes to view such decisions as *his* decisions made by *him,* according to an informational system which *he* dominates and which to some extent *he* has created. A considerable personal attachment is thus generated, not so much to the content of the decisions themselves, but to the informational system which permits him to exercise such influence. Actors who accept the system without question and who defer to his judgment within it are granted rewards which only he can grant—typically in the form of additional information that can either enhance status or improve the chances of success in obtaining appropriations. Actors who criticize the system or attempt to circumvent it are punished, when possible, typically by the withholding of information or the withdrawal of access to information. Such rewards and punishments are sometimes nothing more than accidental by-products of a process which forces Leth to limit the amount of information released. However, they can also be administered consciously, making use of techniques carefully designed to maintain Leth's control over information. Within the Budget Division itself, the budget analysis unit is physically separated from the revenue analysis unit by Leth's office, and internal communication between units is discouraged. Moreover, in dealing with other actors Leth, and only Leth, speaks for the Finance Department, unless the director is present.

Long tenure in working with familiar objects, considerable control over the flow of information, and decision-making influence commensurate with that control all combine to give the Budget Superintendent a deep personal stake in existing procedures according to which state resources are allocated. Though Leth thinks of himself as nothing more than a technician and tries to avoid imposing his own policy preferences on other actors, he is also fully aware of his own abilities to influence their decisions. Indeed, since he realizes that he will bear much of the responsibility for implementing the expenditure decisions of the politicians long after they have departed from Springfield, he does whatever he can to use his knowledge to produce determinations that he can live with. For the most part this means acting to ensure reductions from requests in amounts sufficient to enable the state to meet its obligations. Such action is, of course, "political," in the sense of influencing decisional outcomes, but Leth's informational control allows him to take such action on purely "technical" grounds. And because he can so easily exert such influence, other actors are viewed somewhat cynically as largely disinterested or unknowledgeable men whose concerns are confined to "just politics." It is he, Leth, who must act responsibly to see that the right decisions are made and who must bear the consequences if decisions are wrong. Such a heavy personal burden requires and justifies a highly personalized system of information. That system, inseparable from the personalized role of Budget Director, is the linchpin of the action system through which resource allocations are made.

CHARACTERISTICS AND VALUES OF THE SYSTEM

Viewed as a whole, the system reflects characteristic operating traits and general value orientations. To begin with, actors in the system are not guided by norms relevant to anything other than the particular context within which budgeting and appropriating are accomplished in the Illinois state organization. Although the common culture shared by the various actors encourages the organization of behavior along consistent and predictable lines, the culture itself cannot be generalized beyond the specific situation around which it has developed. Thus there are no "theories of organization" or "principles of administration" from which actors have derived the rules governing their behavior. Nor are there any abstract principles, such as efficiency, rationality, or consistency, which are used by actors to organize their activities. Instead the system is organized according to expectations regarding a thoroughly specific set of objects and actors, held together by symbols which are peculiar to this system and to no other. The "rules" that are followed are not deductions from principles to be imposed on behavior but habitual and largely unrationalized outgrowths of years of doing the same thing in the same way with the same men. In such a system appeals to principle or program, sometimes made by new administrators or "Young Turk" legislators, ring a false note, for the system does not recognize any principles or programs to which appeals can be made. Experienced actors instinctively recognize this and refrain from such appeals.

Complementing and reinforcing this absence of generalized abstract norms to guide action is a heavy reliance on ascriptive rather than achievement criteria in the definition of roles. In orienting themselves to other participants, actors normally pay far more attention to the attributes of other actors than to the performance characteristics of their roles. To a considerable extent this is a direct consequence of the predictability of role behavior. Thus from the agency point of view there is rarely any doubt that the Budgetary Commission will cut, that the Governor will adjust as he sees fit and that the legislature will approve. Or from the commission's point of view there is scarcely any doubt that agencies will exaggerate their needs, that the Governor will make all big decisions, and that the legislature will approve almost all appropriations. The actions of these various roles are seen as so mechanical in nature that they are removed from the realm of probability: they are virtual certainties. Since *what* the various actors do is seen to be so largely predetermined, *how* they do it becomes essentially irrelevant. Budget requests may be described as "loose" or "tight," but there is no such thing as a "good" or a "bad" budget request, for there are no performance standards which would sustain such judgments. Whether or not budget requests and appropriation bills are fully documented or undocumented, and the nature of the documentation, where it exists, are therefore matters which are essentially immaterial to decisions—provided only that the proper forms are completed. By the same token, whether or not the commission, the legislature, or the Governor can justify their actions is beside the point, for there are no achievement criteria by which to measure their accomplishments. The criteria which are applied—the amount cut by the commission, the amount approved by the legislature, and the ability of the Governor to balance expenditures against revenues—are specific to these particular roles rather than deductions from generalized achievement standards (e.g., quantities of service per unit of expenditure, quality of service per unit of expenditure, or accuracy of financial calculations).

Implicit in this argument is the notion that the actions of the various roles, being largely mechanical and predetermined, are beyond influence, i.e., not susceptible to alteration. There is a sense in which this proposition is false, for none of the roles which comprise this system are so precisely defined as to determine the exact nature of their actions. For example, while the expectation that the Budgetary Commission will cut is generally borne out in practice, *how much* it will cut from any individual request is subject to a wide variety of unpredictable factors. Or again, while the expectation that the Governor will veto many appropriation bills approved by the General Assembly is generally fulfilled in practice, the individual bills he will choose to veto cannot be predicted on the basis of any generalized rules. It is precisely for this reason, of course, that ascriptive criteria are so important in the definition of roles, for if the broad outlines of the system are largely predetermined by mechanical formulae, variations within it are not. Such variations typically are determined by the qualities inherent in the actors rather than by any performance expected of them. Thus an agency official who is a close personal acquaintance of the Budgetary Commission Chairman, say, will very likely suffer a less drastic cut at the hands of the commission than would be justified by his budget request forms. Or a legislator who is close to the Governor will very likely get a favorable response to a stray appropriation he has sponsored, whether or not the Governor is persuaded that the activity involved is worthwhile. In all such cases the relevant question is not "What is to be done?" but rather "Who wants to do it?"

Yet in its broader outlines the proposition that role behavior is beyond influence is valid, though it requires a more precise formulation. More accurately, the point is not that the actions of these roles cannot be altered, but that they cannot be altered within the framework of existing orientations to the system. Thus within the confines of an intellectual universe composed of major-object and basic and supplemental money budgets, there is no way to persuade the Budgetary Commission, say, to forego a cut if a cut is implied by the rules governing action in this universe. Without achievement or performance criteria, appeals to documentation (of whatever kind) or program needs are of little avail, for the cut is not evaluated with reference to programs or documentation. Nor is it possible, to take a different kind of example, to persuade the legislature to defeat an appropriation which has come out of committee without serious opposition. Evidence to prove that a particular appropriation is achieving no purpose or is duplicating something financed by another appropriation normally will not shake the legislative will to pass the bill. It is an appropriation, after all, and as such the question of what purpose it is designed to achieve is of distinctly secondary relevance to legislators. This inability to alter the actions of these roles means that actors whose goals cannot be accommodated by the system must somehow get outside its confines (in a social-psychological sense) to gain their ends. Agencies seeking to expand typically face this problem in its most serious form, since the systematic assumption that only current activities are legitimate virtually guarantees the failure of expansionist efforts unsupported by external pressure.

From a slightly different point of view, the absence of achievement criteria is reflected in the lack of specialization in the role structure. None of the actors in this structure do things which require any particular skills or which cannot be done just as well by anyone else who can add and subtract. There are no certified public accountants here, nor computer technicians, nor management consultants, nor, indeed, are there many budget specialists: the same actors who perform roles in this system perform

roles in a variety of other systems. Only the Budget Superintendent plays a role that is at all specialized, but again, his specialization is specific to the system. He is not specialized because he can
do things that no one else can do; he is specialized only because
he is in a position to gather greater quantities of the very same
information than is available to other actors in the system. His
specialization, in short, is related to position and power, rather
than skill. Such specialization, related as it is to a specific activity and a specific set of actors, can be neither generalized nor
taught to other individuals; of necessity it will come to an end
when this particular system is changed.

None of this should be taken to mean that other systems within
the state organization do not make use of specialist roles. As previously indicated, some of the larger departments make considerable use of program planners and accounting specialists to
coordinate and keep track of their internal affairs, frequently on
a highly automated basis. But the information generated by such
specialists is seldom utilized by the actors who make expenditure
decisions for the over-all state organization, since it is not thought
to be necessary. Moreover, representatives of some of the larger
state agencies purposely keep more sophisticated information
summaries away from actors in this system, lest the availability of such information encourage actions harmful to such
agencies. This "what-they-don't-know-can't-hurt-us" orientation
reflects still a third general characteristic of this role structure, which may be summarized as a lack of loyalty to the abstraction known as "the state." For most of the actors whose role
performance helps to determine expenditures the term "state"
has little practical meaning and even less effect on their actions.
What matters most in determining their behavior is membership
in a smaller and less abstract unit: the agency or the commission
or even, in the case of some legislators, the individual person.
Only the Governor consistently takes this abstraction seriously as
a guide to action, largely because the nature of his position forces
him to do so. In taking this abstraction seriously, of course, the
Governor cannot avoid at least some conflict with roles organized
around loyalties to less comprehensive organizational units.

These several characteristics of system activities are nourished
by the principal values around which the system is built. From
an operating point of view, one goal stands out: to get the job

of allocating resources done as quickly and with as little friction as possible. This value may be expressed, somewhat more elegantly, as the desire of the various actors to fulfill the obligations imposed upon them by custom, statute, and Constitution. In practice this means little more than the completion of various documents used in determining expenditures (i.e., the budget book or appropriation bills) according to the standard formulae implicit in the shared system of informational categories. Attempts to consciously manipulate these categories for strategic purposes are relatively rare, in part because certain strategies are understood to be built into the categories themselves, and in part because actors in the system rarely have great—or even different—causes to champion. Within the framework of this system things are expected to go along as they always have. The principal problem, accordingly, is to see to it that budgets and appropriation bills are pushed through the executive and legislative mill in time to meet the July 1 deadline. Actors within the system are far too busy, in the relatively short time available to them, checking figures and legal forms to worry about any larger purposes or broader goals.

Pressure to get the job done leads inevitably to an emphasis on the virtues of existing relationships. All of the actors in this system are busy men with much to do and, given the customs of legislative politics, little time in which to do it. The existing system does get the job done in the time allotted and is vigorously defended on that basis. On the one hand, actors defend current practices as not only adequate but better than most alternatives with which they are familiar. On the other hand, proposals for change are either dismissed as impractical within the Illinois context or, if certain changes are admitted to be potentially useful, they are discarded as being impossible to implement. Changes, it is argued, would have to be at least approved by the legislature. Since the legislature meets for only six months of every twenty-four, however, and since it must cope with allocative decisions framed in terms of procedures already well under way by the time it meets, any changes attempted would necessarily create great confusion and possibly do great harm. As long as the budgetary and appropriating job is accomplished, such a risk is hardly worth taking. Preservation of the status quo, in both the present role structure and the organizational environ-

198

ment which gives it support, is thus a subsidiary operating value of some significance.

Getting the job done is an important operational value. Far more important is the substantive value represented by the concept of the balanced budget. The overriding importance of this value stems chiefly from its ability to legitimize the actions taken by the system. As long as the Governor's estimate of revenue matches his recommendations for expenditure there is little or no inclination to question the process by which expenditure determinations are made. Lacking any other rationalized criteria to judge the propriety of proposed expenditures, members of the state organization as well as outside commentators assume expenditures to be justified by a budget which provides a method for financing them. To a considerable extent this assumption is focused on the budget proposal itself, perhaps because the hectic chaos of later changes in the financial plan are too difficult to follow. Thus the legislature's consistent pattern of appropriating more money than recommended in the Governor's budget arouses little comment, just as the Governor's veto of many excess appropriations is scarcely noticed. Both patterns are thought to be quite normal and fully expected. Only when budgeted expenditures fail to generate sufficient revenue support—as occurred in 1961—is there any inclination to challenge either the expenditures or the system of roles through which they are determined.

The legitimizing quality of the balanced budget and of its powerful associated symbols—such as "fiscal responsibility" or "financial integrity"—gives virtually everyone who participates in the system a stake in seeing to it that the budget is, in fact, balanced. Only the most disaffected agency head or utopian legislator would think of opposing a goal whose achievement is a guarantee against any challenge to the existing order. But while every actor has a stake in the balanced budget, the responsibility and the authority to bring it into existence are confined to a single actor: the Governor. Other actors, realizing that the Governor's failure to match revenues with anticipated expenditures can have unfavorable consequences for them, are strongly motivated to accept gubernatorial decisions which have the effect of balancing the budget. It is largely for this reason that agencies normally do not press for increases once the Governor has turned them down. Similarly, disputes between the Governor and the legislature over the substance of expenditures rarely occur, for disputes over expenditures represent a challenge to the system that nobody wants to make. Arguments which do occur tend to focus heavily on the problem of revenue, which can be solved without affecting either the budgetary system or the organizational environment within which it works. As the predominant substantive value of the system, then, the balanced budget provides both a legitimating symbol and an important power resource for the one actor who can bring that symbol into existence.

CONSEQUENCES

Most of the financial decisions made by this system of action involve an essentially mechanical response to informational objects that contain built-in criteria for decision. The systematic assumption that current expenditures will be continued removes such expenditures from further consideration, while the great bulk of the increases approved in any given biennium are dealt with by an essentially automatic process. Existing statutes determine the level of highway, welfare, or school aid expenditure with little need for discussion unless changes are sought in the statutory formulae. Minor upward adjustments for many of the small-to-medium agencies are not automatic, of course, but neither are they very significant from an over-all point of view. Major adjustments are thus confined to a very small number of agencies which, though few in number, typically account for the greatest portion of any given biennial increase. Significantly, such major adjustments—whether increases or occasional decreases—are not generated by the roles analyzed here. Normally they are initiated through different systems of roles and merely reflected in this system, frequently through the actions of the Governor.

Thus the Mental Health expansion was triggered initially by popular approval of a bond issue to finance new buildings. With the support of a newly elected governor a new department director then formulated plans for the expansion which were reflected in enlarged requests for financial support. Action by this system came after these plans had been formulated and approved, and took the form of a ratification of proposals conceived and implemented by others. Or, to take a different kind of adjustment, the large reduction imposed on the 1963 request for the public aid program was fought out as a partisan matter between a Republican Senate majority and the Democratic administration. Budgeting and appropriating roles played no part in this struggle until the terms of its resolution had been worked out, at which time those terms were simply recorded on the proper financial forms. Or again, the important change in the state's approach to financing capital expenditures worked out in 1963 was initiated by actors only peripherally connected to this system, and in securing ratification from the system some of its roles (e.g., the Budgetary Commission or the Appropriations committees) were bypassed completely. In each of these cases, involving major adjustments in existing expenditure patterns, the budgeting and appropriating system was only formally involved: it did not initiate, it did not plan, it did not negotiate; it merely ratified actions taken by other roles.

Since most of the decisions made by the system are arrived at mechanically, and since major adjustments are left to other roles, there is seldom any occasion for actors in this system to probe into detailed records of agency expenditures. The single exception in this respect is the Governor, who may occasionally require detailed information in order to balance the budget. But even for the Governor such probing is relatively infrequent and, as in the case of the incumbent (see Chapter 5), often fruitless. As a result, detailed information on how money is actually spent rarely goes beyond the confines of the individual agency—a situation which leaves agency officials free to exercise as much discretion as they can in using their appropriations. In this sense the system represents no threat to any unit of the state organization. Both current levels of appropriation and the manner in which they are disposed of are left relatively untouched. From a financial point of view this means that the actions of the system cannot operate to reduce expenditures. And from a political point of view, this means that the existing decentralized structure of organizational authority is subject to no challenge from actions of the system.

What, then, is to be made of the emphasis on budget cuts and opposition to appropriation increases which characterize the statements made by many actors in the system? To begin with, it is necessary to recall that such statements have little bearing on the course of financial events: large-scale appropriation increases have been recorded in virtually every biennium since the close of World War II. In this situation, verbalized opposition to increases has become largely a mechanical ritual, built upon existing informational categories, and meant to apply primarily to the smaller agencies rather than to the largest spenders. Precisely because these responses are now mechanical, rather than instrumental, there are no criteria to sustain their use. When increases are eliminated, they are not eliminated for purposes of efficiency or because of opposition to programs; they are eliminated because that is what actors dealing with these forms have always done. Expressions of hostility to increases thus are not so much purposive as symbolic. They are meant to express the power thought to be attached to certain roles rather than to assert a generalized and rationalized statement of policy. The absence of such a policy means that both cuts and increases can be and are accommodated with equal ease. In this sense the system is operationally neutral on the question of increases, despite the symbolic rhetoric practiced by some of its actors.

None of this should be taken to mean that the rhetoric is unimportant. On the contrary, constant repetition of the symbolism of "cuts," not solely by actors in the system but also by outsiders such as newspapers or chambers of commerce, provides a useful source of justification for the system itself. It demonstrates that the system has "done something" and, in the absence of information to show otherwise, presumably for "good" reasons. Such a demonstration undermines the validity of criticism aimed at the system and casts doubt upon the motivation of critics. Because the system is active and doing something, other actors and other models of what to do are denied participation. In addition there is a more subtle psychological effect on the actors, who can point to the cuts that are administered as justification for whatever actions they take, or fail to take. In this sense the rhetoric is self-justifying as well as system-justifying. Acting as though they are seeking a verbalized goal, actors come to believe that they are in fact achieving that goal, whether or not the evidence presented to their senses can sustain such a conclusion.

To suggest the absence of rationalized criteria is not to assert the absence of all standards but rather to point out that the operative criteria for determining increases are related more to status and power than to purpose. This is reflected in many of the marginal increases allowed to smaller agencies, which frequently turn on factors such as friendship or partisan position. It is similarly—and much more significantly—reflected in the largest increases, which normally turn on the ability of the agencies involved to develop massive support from the Governor, the legislature, the public (i.e., newspapers), organized groups, or other governments (local and federal). In such a context the conspicuous failure of the smaller agencies to achieve a rapid expansion in appropriations becomes understandable: lacking the capabilities which are implicit in big money and big payrolls they are unable to withstand the cuts that are automatically applied against their requests for additional funds. Larger agencies, on the other hand, with many dollars, many people, and well-structured relationships with external governments, are sometimes able to generate the "clout" necessary to achieve rapid expansion of their programs. But note that "clout" is not generated through the system of action which acts upon budget requests and appropriation bills. Without criteria of action which differentiate this system from other power-generating systems there is little to be gained from bringing it into play, particularly since there is no question that "clout" decisions will be easily accommodated by the system. The system thus represents a form of holding operation, which acts to maintain a current level of expenditure until sufficient power is mobilized through other roles to establish a new, and higher, level.

This conclusion helps to clarify the significance of financial information to the system. The cardinal fact about current expenditure levels, of course, is that maintenance of such levels has nothing to do with information that may or may not be available: it is simply assumed that current expenditures will continue. And since changes from current levels are dependent upon the mobilization of influence, information with regard to such changes is of distinctly secondary importance. That is, it is safe to assert that every agency can develop a persuasive case in support of a change in its level of support. Failure to achieve such a change is thus due less to an absence of information than to a lack of sufficient power to bring it about. To the extent that increases are within the control of the state organization, lack of power means inability to persuade the Governor to include a proposal for change within his budget.

The relative unimportance of information, either to the activities of the system or to the adjustments made by other systems, does not encourage the exercise of great care in maintaining financial records. Indeed, the looseness of control over expenditures guarantees the inaccuracy of most financial statements. Consider, for example, the typical small-to-medium agency, whose expenditures from appropriations must be authorized by the agency's chief executive officer. During the course of the biennium this officer may be faced with a number of crises which lead him to approve payments from one object account for purchases that more properly should be charged against another account. Perhaps he has used almost 75 per cent of his Commodities appropriation prior to the expiration of the eighteenth month of the biennium and does not wish to run afoul of his legal obligations just to purchase an additional item; or perhaps the clerk who keeps his agency's books has made an inadvertent mistake in record-keeping which must be corrected. For these or other equally innocuous reasons he may decide to purchase something from an account that normally would not be used for such a purchase. Crises of this kind are not unusual and can be resolved by charging some expenditure against an account which can easily bear the charge, whether or not it is the proper account. So long as an object appropriation is not exceeded or consistently used for improper purchases, there is no particular difficulty in receiving approval for such purchases. Having achieved such resolutions according to his own discretion rather than prescribed rules, the chief officer of the agency will in all probability be hard put to recall the nature of his discretionary judgments within weeks after they have been exercised. And he almost certainly will have no way of recalling them months later, when his budget request is being prepared and defended.

Now consider what this situation implies for the process of determining expenditures. First of all it is clear that in agencies which have felt compelled to juggle their accounts in the fashion described above, the chances are that no one in the agency will be in a position to give an accurate representation of the disposition of agency appropriations. To be sure, quarterly—and sometimes monthly—statements of expenditures from object accounts will exist. But if accounts have been juggled, these statements may well range from slightly to highly inaccurate and in any case will report dollar sums without reporting the nature of the purchases made. Second, since it is these same summaries of expenditures from object accounts which provide the most important basis for calculating budget requests, their inaccuracies are carried over, as it were, to the processes of budgeting and appropriating, where they serve to trigger the series of responses which constitute the various decision-making roles. Ultimately, therefore, the extent to which actors external to the agencies familiarize themselves with budget requests may be of little consequence, for the responses they make may be based upon inaccurate accounts. In short, the agencies themselves may not know how they are spending their appropriations, in which event the system of determining state expenditures takes on the character of a time-consuming, but essentially frivolous, game.

Completely accurate records of agency expenditures, of course, may be impossible to attain, particularly under the present accounting system. But the fact that agency officials are sometimes uncertain about the exact disposition of their funds encourages them to submit requests for appropriations which provide a "margin of safety" over and above the amounts they feel are necessary to maintain agency operations. Failure to provide such a margin would create the risk of running short of funds before the biennium is completed. This is not a very dangerous risk, since deficiency appropriations can always be requested, but it is nevertheless an area of uncertainty that most agencies feel it best to avoid. For their part, reviewing officials who understand the ambiguities inherent in agency expenditure records are provided an additional incentive to interpret appropriation requests in terms of people and money rather than policies and programs. In the absence of reliable accounts, program or policy review is exceedingly difficult to achieve. People, however, can be required to explain the expenditures they make or want to make. Whether or not the explanations offered can be made to square with financial accounts is less important than the personal relationships which define agency officials as "trustworthy" and reviewing officials as "responsible."

SUMMARY

The budget game in Illinois, then, is an intensely human and personal game which makes important contributions to an organization in which both formal authority and decision-making power are highly decentralized. As long as actors play their roles according to the rules discussed above, the budget game will neither threaten the present distribution of power and resources nor prevent changes in it. Meanwhile, expenditures will continue to increase—gradually for most agencies but drastically for any agency or program which can mobilize sufficient pressure to implement a rapid increase. From the agency point of view the advantages of the game are evident; a guaranteed minimal level of funds, relative freedom in the disposition of those funds, and the possibility of achieving a large expansion under the right circumstances. If the system lacks any discernible point of view or purpose of its own, it merely reflects an organization in which "point of view" and "purpose" are not structured around the abstraction called "state," but around smaller concrete units called departments or commissions or universities. An organizational revolution would be required before the system could determine expenditures on the basis of a rationalized point of view centering on the concept "state." The occurrence of such a revolution, of course, would necessarily alter the system.

These considerations help to explain why the system continues to exist: a game which guarantees no interference with existing statuses while increasing expenditures is not likely to arouse opposition from officials enjoying either or both benefits. But what about officials who are dissatisfied, or persons and groups outside the organization who object to financial procedures or outcomes? Dissatisfaction has been voiced with increasing frequency in recent years, yet there is little evidence to show that such opposition has had any discernible effect on the system. Indeed, the role orientations and the actions of the system appear to have remained essentially the same for the best part of two decades. In view of the rapid growth in expenditures and the many new organizational statuses created during the same period, such stability is striking. A closer examination of the manner in which the system is maintained is obviously in order.

CHAPTER EIGHT

STABILITY
AND CHANGE

Any answer to the question "How is a social system maintained?" necessarily must come in two parts, for it is impossible to analyze system maintenance without also analyzing system change. Semantically there is no difference between the above question and its equivalent, "How is a social system not changed?" By the same token there is no difference between the two questions (1) "How is a social system changed?" and (2) "How is a social system not maintained?" Whether one phrases the question positively or negatively, in terms of either change or maintenance, therefore makes very little difference. In each case the focus of interest is the empirical referent of the concept "social system," and in each case the issue is whether the properties of the system remain the same over time, and if so, how, or whether the system takes on new properties over time, and if so, how.

It has already been suggested here that the social system through which the Illinois state government determines the allocation of its financial resources has remained essentially unchanged for the better part of two decades. In accounting for this stability it will be particularly important to bear in mind the distinction between the "system" and the "organization," as well as the distinction between "change" and "growth." References to the "system" are references to the roles analyzed in preceding chapters and the orientations and rules which guide the actions of those roles. This particular system is just one of many systems which together make up the larger state organization. Such a system "changes" when the role orientations and rules of action become something other than what they now are; it "grows" merely by adding more members, or by spending more money, or by increasing the number of actions it takes. It is thus possible for either the system or the organization to grow without being changed, or to change without experiencing growth. Our principal focus here is the "system" (i.e., role orientations and rules) and our principal concern is to account for "change" or the lack of change.

Scattered throughout the preceding chapters the reader can find a variety of passing references to actors who, implicitly or explicitly, challenge the system: a bureaucrat who questions basic-supplemental budgeting, a legislator who would like to do more than simply approve appropriation bills, a governor who hopes to alter the entire system of information upon which budget forms and appropriation bills are fashioned. Such cases of role strain indicate the extent to which the system embodies within itself a considerable potentiality for change. I have also suggested earlier that environmental conditions external to both the state organization and its financial subsystem have been important in shaping the pattern of state spending and, by implication at least, the pattern of role orientations. As we begin this discussion of stability and change, therefore, it will be useful to anticipate the possibility of change or maintenance arising from sources both internal and external to the system and its parent organization. What some of these sources might be can be illustrated in terms of two sequences of events which occurred during the period of this study. One concerns the activities of the so-called "Economy Bloc." The other concerns the attempt to implement a "program" or "functional" budget.

THE RISE AND FALL OF THE ECONOMY BLOC

The idea of governmental economy is a powerful, pervasive, yet peculiarly ephemeral, symbol in Illinois finance. Virtually everyone involved in the determination of state expenditures trades on this idea in one fashion or another, perhaps to justify the uses they make of what is conceived to be "other people's" money. As a guide to action, however, it is most commonly used by legislators, especially legislators of a different political persuasion from that of the administration in power. From time to time in the past, groups of legislators have mobilized themselves to promote economy by imposing across-the-board percentage reductions on all appropriation measures proposed by a Governor. While occasionally successful in reducing appropriated amounts, such meat-axe cuts arose more out of ignorance than detailed knowledge, and more out of partisan bickering than out of purposive goals. Reductions were sometimes achieved, but the power to determine where and how these reductions were to be made remained in the hands of the various agencies, which were thus permitted to exercise all the discretion they had exercised previously—except at somewhat lower expenditure levels. Meat-axe economy drives, in short, were part of the game. They presented the appearance of change, but they changed nothing. And since they changed nothing they disappeared almost as quickly as they appeared. There was nothing to hold these economy movements together from one session to the next, or indeed, from one month to another within the same session.

Though owing something to this tradition, the Economy Bloc which arose during the first years of the Kerner administration was different in several important respects. For one thing it began as an essentially bipartisan group and to a large extent continued to exist as a bipartisan group. For another thing, the bloc was not interested in wielding a meat-axe. It sought reductions that could be defended on grounds of inefficiency or duplication, rather than any reductions at all. And finally, the very existence of the bloc represented a direct challenge to one of the cardinal rules of the existing system. The idea that reductions could not be made unless there was some reason for making them necessarily implied that expenditures could not be approved without reason, from which it followed that existing expenditure levels were not to be taken as automatically justified. For the Economy Bloc, all expenditure requests, for the support of current levels as well as new levels, were fair game for investigation and criticism.

The bloc came into being, it will be recalled, during the final weeks of the 1961 legislative session, when it became apparent that the legislature and the Governor would not be able to reach agreement on a balanced budget. A joint Senate-House Economy Committee was hurriedly created, composed of both Democrats and Republicans, but including none of the leaders of the Budgetary Commission.[1] Working long hours behind closed doors, the committee met with representatives from a variety of state agencies and managed to find some $14 million that could be removed from various appropriation bills.[2] This was considerably short of the $90 million that was needed to balance appropriations with revenues but it nevertheless represented an important accomplishment for a group which began from scratch and which was forced to complete its work within five days. For some of the newer legislators in this group, at least, this activity demonstrated that a variety of opportunities to reduce expenditures did in fact exist, provided someone or some agency wished to take advantage of them. Moreover the work of the joint committee generated a powerful motivation to continue. As one of its members said later, "That was the most rewarding thing I've done since I first came to the legislature."

An opportunity to continue was provided by the legislature's acceptance of Governor Kerner's proposal to create a Revenue Commission. Approved in the special session of November, 1961, the Revenue Commission was given broad authority to investigate state revenue requirements. In addition, it was authorized to "investigate and make recommendations where economies in state government may be achieved. . . ." To implement this responsibility a six-member Subcommittee on Economy Measures was created. Republican Representative John C. Parkhurst served as chairman of this group, whose other members included Democratic Representative Paul Elward of Chicago and Republican Senator Russell Arrington of Evanston. All of these men had been active members of the 1961 economy group in the legislature.

During the late spring and early summer of 1962 the subcommittee held a series of meetings at which a variety of persons from public and semipublic organizations offered suggestions for reducing state spending. The subcommittee also sent ques-

---

[1] Representative Lloyd (Curly) Harris was the only Budgetary Commission member included in this group. It should be noted, however, that the commission's executive director did participate in the work of the Economy Committee.

[2] At this point in the bloc's existence, reductions were largely arbitrary and based primarily on evidence of lapsed funds. This very arbitrariness emphasized to many bloc members the need for additional information.

tionnaires to some sixty state agencies asking for their ideas on potential economy targets.[3] As a result of these efforts the subcommittee was able to release a preliminary report in September, 1962, which recommended reductions totaling some $32 million for the next and succeeding biennia. Some of these suggestions were immediate and specific: abolish the Illinois Veterans' Commission, eliminate the Department of Aeronautics, curtail or abolish the State Fair. Others called for the merger and consolidation of various state agencies and for reexamination of the state's school aid formula, printing regulations, and minimum wage laws. And from a long-term point of view, the subcommittee urged that a management consultant be obtained to do a thorough analysis of state operations. In a covering statement Chairman Parkhurst suggested that savings far in excess of $32 million could be expected if these and other economies were implemented. Parkhurst claimed neither infallibility nor comprehensiveness for his committee's labors: "Some of these recommendations are admittedly the opinions of knowledgeable individuals. Since this is so, they are of course subject to challenge. In this sense, we do not claim this list is 'perfect' . . . any more than it can be called exhaustive or complete. But we do believe it is a major step in the right direction—specific recommendations in the direction of huge economies and huge savings for Illinois taxpayers." [4]

Issued *when* it was—just before the start of the next budgeting period—and *how* it was—as a series of preliminary suggestions rather than carefully researched proposals—the subcommittee report was as much an invitation for discussion as anything else. But who would accept the invitation? Wittingly or unwittingly the subcommittee had rather strongly suggested that the state organization was a mess—it was not only wasteful, but badly organized to boot. Whatever the merits of this position, it was hardly likely to find favor with the Governor, who was facing a legislative session in which a record would have to be made for

---

[3] The work of the subcommittee is summarized in "Appendix A: Report of Subcommittee on Economy Measures," in *Report of the Commission on Revenue* (Springfield, 1963), pp. 45-46.

[4] "Introduction" to "Report No. 1" of the Subcommittee on Economy Measures, p. 2.

the next campaign, and even less likely to be warmly received by the bureaucrats whose activities were alleged to be wasteful or unnecessary. Nor was the legislature a likely candidate for economy discussions, in view of the subcommittee's pointed references to legislative inadequacy. Indeed, the report reopened the question of the adequacy of the Budgetary Commission: "According to law, the Illinois Budgetary Commission is supposed to submit to legislators and the Governor by March 1 a report on its meetings with state agencies concerning the agencies' budget requests. This report is supposed to provide legislators the *reasons behind various requests* as well as the Commission's recommendations on such. . . . However, the Commission has never submitted a report of its budget recommendations and analysis to legislators; it should be required to do so, in accordance with existing statutes." [5] While the subcommittee's invitation to discuss economy was thus something less than appealing to potential discussants, it was an invitation nevertheless, and bound to be handled as such. Accordingly, arrangements were made for Subcommittee Chairman Parkhurst to appear before the Budgetary Commission when it opened its hearings on 1963-65 budget requests.

The Budgetary Commission meeting of October 23, 1962, was the first commission meeting of the new budget period; as such it was devoted to a general discussion of financial prospects for the 73rd biennium rather than to review of agency budget requests. Governor Kerner, Arnold Maremont, then Chairman of the Public Aid Commission, and Revenue Director Isaacs all presented statements to the commission which were purposely ambiguous. Though the commission sought specific figures, Kerner refused to predict what his total budget would be, Maremont declined to speculate on the total public aid request, and Isaacs asserted the impossibility of predicting, at that time, the total revenue the state might expect for the 73rd biennium. These rather inconclusive exchanges did not appear to disturb commissioners, partly because Budget Superintendent Leth provided some very specific figures on public aid expenditures in the course of a half-hour discourse. At the conclusion of Leth's

---

[5] *Ibid.*, p. 6. Italics in original.

statement, Representative Parkhurst, who had been listening to the discussion, was invited to take a place at the table around which members of the commission were seated.

"Now, Mr. Parkhurst," Senator Peters began, "I understand that you have some recommendations here that you think will save the state a lot of money." Parkhurst responded by asserting his feeling that his subcommittee's recommendations could indeed save a great deal of money, but he pointed out that the proposals were not to be understood as official proposals of the Revenue Commission. He went on to stress that as yet his proposals had not been adopted by the Revenue Study group, that he did not know which of them, if any, would be adopted, and that they could only be considered as advisory proposals at this point. Nevertheless, he concluded, he did feel that their implementation could introduce a great deal of economy and efficiency into the operations of state government.

Senator Peters' response to this statement began to clarify the nature of the interaction which was to follow. "You know, Mr. Parkhurst," he said, "most of these ideas you have here have been presented to us many times before and I'm wondering whether you have given any thought to the problem of how you're going to get all of these things done." So challenged, Parkhurst admitted that many of his recommendations had been offered before, and continued: "But that's just my point, Senator. As far as I'm concerned, what has been lacking in the past has not been ideas for economy, but the will to economize."

"Well, that may be, Mr. Parkhurst," Peters retorted, "but you've also made some statements that are critical of the Budgetary Commission. We try to do a good job here but we don't have a big staff and we probably don't do the kind of job we could do. But all things considered we do as well as we can. Now if you think we can do our job better you ought to come to some of our meetings. You're welcome to come down and tell us what we ought to be doing." As this emphasis on Parkhurst's inexperience was being absorbed by other commissioners, Peters turned to the subcommittee recommendation that the Budgetary Commission submit a report of its deliberations to the legislature. "Why do you think that's necessary?" he asked. "Do you think anybody would read it?"

Parkhurst's response was to cite the statute which requires

such a report, but Peters repeated his feeling that most legislators would not read such a report even if they had it. "We'd
have to spend a lot of money to make such a report and the
money would be wasted. Most legislators would throw the report in the wastebasket." At this, Minority Leader Paul Powell
turned to Peters with mock horror and asked "Do you mean to
say, Pete, that you don't read any of the mail you get?"

"Well of course, Paul, if it's got your name on it I read it,"
said Peters, as other commissioners chuckled. By this time it had
become clear that Parkhurst was in for a difficult time. Far from
joining with Parkhurst in a discussion of potential state economies, the commission seemed interested in discrediting both Parkhurst and the recommendations he had made. Having already
suggested that Parkhurst was inexperienced and thus an illegit-
imate critic of the experienced budgetary group, it remained
only to show that his recommendations were the impractical
products of a naive mind. Unfortunately for Parkhurst, such a
showing was all too easy within the context of the hearing
situation.

Powell now assumed leadership of the interrogation. "I've
been around here some twenty-nine years," he began, "and at
one time or another all of these ideas have come up before us
but they've never been passed by the legislature. Every time
we consider one or more of these proposals people come down
here and tell us that we can't do it because they want the programs that you want to cut out here." After reciting some of the
proposals that had been defeated in past sessions, Powell continued. "Now what we're interested in here is not ideas that
you want to come up with that don't stand any chance of acceptance but rather with specific proposals that we can implement. Do you, for example, have any specific information as to
how we could cut down on the use of state cars? Do you know
which people are using these cars for their personal use, in which
departments, and how great the extent of the use is?" Parkhurst
was forced to admit that he had no such information, that this
idea had come from a representative of the Taxpayers' Federation, and that the best he could do would be to develop such
information if he were given the opportunity. A series of similar
questions forced Parkhurst to repeat, again and again, what was
obvious: the subcommittee report was nothing more than a

series of preliminary suggestions tossed out for discussion and buttressed by little or no factual research. As a sort of coup de grâce, Powell concluded by asking "Do you really think that we can eliminate the State Fair?" Again Parkhurst had to back-track, though he continued to maintain that the fair certainly could be run more economically.

While Powell hammered away at the weaknesses in Parkhurst's report, when taken as a series of specific proposals, Senator Peters interrupted from time to time to complement Powell's attack. "Well now that's very good, Mr. Parkhurst," he repeat-edly interjected, "we want you to help us out all you can." When Powell was finished, other commissioners rushed to join the attack initiated by their leaders, concentrating on the imprac-ticality, from their point of view, of the Parkhurst proposals. Not surprisingly, Parkhurst became increasingly flustered and, when Powell humorously suggested that hundreds of veterans in uniform and with bayonets drawn had forced the legislature to maintain support for the Veterans' Commission, Parkhurst lost his patience. "Now Mr. Senator," he began, then quickly cor-rected himself, "I mean Mr. Speaker, you know that you are just trying to twit me a little bit here. That's not at all what I meant and you know it. Nobody ever suggested that these people weren't serious about their commission and of course it couldn't be true that they were trying to threaten you to influ-ence your decision on the matter."

"Well I don't know how serious they were," replied Powell, grinning, "but they sure convinced me not to get rid of that commission." Everyone in the room, except Parkhurst, laughed hard in response to Powell's well-timed joke. What had begun as hostility was rapidly developing into ridicule.

Senator Peters now began where Powell had ended. "I see here that you have a recommendation to introduce some econo-mies in the university," he noted. Parkhurst allowed that such a recommendation had been made. "Well I don't know about that, Mr. Parkhurst," said Peters. "It seems to me that we can't afford to cut down on any spending for education because education, I think, is our most important national asset—especially in these days. And if you want to cut down on the education of our children I don't know where this country is going to be."

"Senator Peters, you have been known as an advocate of education for a long time," Parkhurst replied, "and you have earned a good deal of respect for that. But I think that there comes a time when economies have to be considered and I also think that perhaps this is the time."

"Well again, Mr. Parkhurst," said Peters, "a lot of people have been telling us to cut down on the university for a long time. I can remember somebody from the Treasurer's office coming over here a few years ago to tell us we ought to make some big cuts in the university's budget. You know what I said to him? I said to him that a good watchdog never bites the home folks."

Laughter once more engulfed the hearing room, to the great discomfort of Representative Parkhurst. Several other less successful jokes were made at his expense before he was excused from what had become a difficult ordeal. Not only were his recommendations thoroughly discredited, but he himself had suffered considerable abuse from his legislative elders. Leaving the room, he turned back momentarily at the request of Representative Pollack, withdrew another copy of the subcommittee report from his briefcase, and angrily slammed it down on the table. Additional discussions between Parkhurst and the Budgetary Commission were clearly not likely to occur.

The meaning of this incident is worthy of further speculation. Although members of the commission were considerably less than enthusiastic about Parkhurst's economy proposals, just minutes earlier they had demonstrated an energetic concern for economy when questioning Public Aid Commission Chairman Maremont. Even granting the normal degree of legislative skepticism for welfare spending and the equally expected support for activities such as the State Fair, it is difficult to believe that members of the Budgetary Commission could not have found something in the great variety of proposals put forward by Parkhurst with which they could agree. But the commission did not want to agree with any of Parkhurst's ideas; indeed, it was not even prepared to discuss them as the preliminary recommendations they were intended to be. Instead the subcommittee report was treated as a finished product to be questioned, then attacked, and finally ridiculed. To have accepted Parkhurst's report as a basis for discussion would have implied commission acceptance of his right to participate in such discussions. By refusing to take the subcommittee report seriously, and by heaping ridicule on Parkhurst, the commission was rejecting Parkhurst's claim to participate in decisions which traditionally had been left to the commission. The point was not that the subcommittee proposals were good or bad, but simply that such matters were none of Parkhurst's or the economy subcommittee's business.

Refused access by the Budgetary Commission, advocates of economy were in difficult straits, for there was little more that could be done until the Governor's budget was submitted. Given the potentially explosive effects of premature disclosure of budget totals to a Republican-controlled legislature, the Governor was unlikely to encourage legislative economy investigations within departments, particularly since budget requests would be screened by the Budgetary Commission anyway. All that the economizers could do was to wait until the budget book and its resultant appropriation bills provided something tangible on which to work. During the first few months of the 1963 legislative session, therefore, the new version of the Economy Bloc necessarily contented itself with a series of informal weekly discussion meetings. While unproductive from an economy point of view, these discussions did accomplish some useful purposes. For one thing they enabled the bloc leaders to gauge the strength of their support. For another, they enabled advocates of economy to become acquainted with one another. In the process they established that members of the Senate were not interested in participation. The bloc in 1963 was to be a House Economy Bloc.

Although some thirty to forty House members indicated an interest in participation, most of these men were relative newcomers to the legislature and almost totally uninformed with regard to the details of state finance.[6] Leadership of the group accordingly fell into the hands of the few men who, through experience or special interest, had become familiar with the way things were done. These included Representatives Parkhurst, from Peoria, and William Horsley, from Springfield, who expressed the downstate Republican point of view. Representatives Abner J. Mikva, Anthony Scariano, and Bernard M. Peskin

---

[6] The Illinois State Chamber of Commerce listed the members of the Economy Bloc in its publication "Springfield Scene," dated June 8, 1963. The list included twenty-eight Republicans and eight Democrats, for a total of thirty-six legislators.

were Democrats from the Chicago area who had established reputations as the liberal and brainy "Young Turks" of their party. Another Chicago Democrat, Paul Elward, was in a more ambiguous position. Though he was to some extent identified with the "Young Turks," he was also serving as Assistant to the Democratic Minority Leader in the House. All of these men were lawyers and all were agreed that considerable economies in state expenditures could be achieved, despite wide disagreements on political values between the more liberal Democrats and the conservative downstate Republicans.

Since the bloc was not an official House committee, it had no funds with which to secure staff. However, it did have the services of an employee of the Tax Federation of Illinois who had worked with the 1961 Economy Committee, and Representative Parkhurst did have the help of an employee of the Caterpillar Tractor Company of Peoria who had also worked with Parkhust in 1961. The availability of these people made little difference during the first four months of the 1963 session as the bloc, waiting for the budget, remained essentially without organization. Groups of members, working together explored areas of interest to them and began to raise an occasional protest in committee hearings, but it was not until the evening of May 20 that a more or less formalized structure took shape with the selection of a bloc secretary. Horsley and Parkhurst, who appeared to be the most dedicated of the more knowledgeable members, assumed the responsibility of guiding discussions as informal co-chairmen. As the evening wore on, however, it became clear that bloc decisions, to the extent that there were any, would proceed from discussions in which all of the better-informed members participated.

The chief purpose of the meeting was to develop a strategy for dealing with the major appropriation bills which were beginning to move through the House. Horsley raised the issue and Parkhurst immediately took the floor to express his point of view. Noting that three-men bloc subcommittees had been set up to investigate various state agencies, Parkhurst argued that these subcommittees should personally appear before the Appropriations Committee to report their findings and propose amendments. This would impress the committee with the extent of legislative interest in economy measures and, more important to

Parkhurst, would relieve some of the pressure he and Horsley were beginning to feel from their committee colleagues, who looked upon economy proposals as nuisances. When Horsley pointed out that Appropriations Committee Chairman Granata would not accept amendments unless there were six copies, Parkhurst responded energetically: "All right, then, have six copies when you come, but come in and offer them and let us fight it out right then and there in the committee. We may not win," he recognized, "but I think what we ought to do is try to use the Appropriations Committee in order to implement economy. There would be nothing better," he concluded, "than to have the Appropriations Committee finally hear from other members of the legislature with ideas for reducing the cost of state government."

Horsley then opposed Parkhurst's proposal, principally, he said, "because if we fight the battle and lose it there it will then be very difficult for us to fight the same battle again on the floor of the House on second reading. Having fought it once, these people [referring to Appropriations Committee members] and others who control the House will be reluctant to take the time again to go into details that may have been heard already in the Appropriations Committee. All Granata [House Appropriations Committee Chairman] or someone else would have to do," he concluded, "would be to get up and say we went into all of this already, the committee voted you down by 36 to 2 or 32 to 6, and other members of the House would be reluctant to give us more time." Horsley's view was that information might be developed in committee but that amendments should wait until bills were out of committee and on second reading in the House.

The contest between these opposing points of view continued for some minutes, with Mikva supporting Parkhurst's view and Elward supporting Horsley. Ultimately, the other members were persuaded that a fight for amendments in committee was worth a try. If successful, a useful precedent would be set; if unsuccessful with the first few measures, there would remain the opportunity of fighting on the floor. With this understanding Horsley concluded the meeting by reminding the twenty-five legislators present that their activities in the next week would be crucial. Though no important bills were scheduled to come up on the following day, when the regular Tuesday committee meeting would be held, it was certain that many large bills would be scheduled for the next week. To make the bloc strategy work the various members would have to gather as much information as possible within the succeeding six days and have it ready for the May 28 Appropriations Committee hearing. Another Monday evening bloc meeting would be held on May 27, Horsley announced, at which time plans for the following day would be worked out. It remained only for the bloc members to get to work.

Considerable dedication and enthusiasm characterized this night's work by the Economy Bloc, but it was apparent that the road ahead would be difficult to travel for, despite the presence of two staff aides and a number of sophisticated and experienced legislators, the bloc remained largely ignorant of many fundamental details of state finance. This became clear at the outset of the meeting when one legislator asked whether appropriation bills followed the recommendations of the Budgetary Commission. Since no one knew what these recommendations were, the question could not be answered, but a staff aide stood up to explain that the bills were different from the budget because of the manner in which the salary increase was handled. He went on to point out that the installation of a centrex telephone exchange also affected the appropriation bills but when asked who would pay the telephone bill for the state office building in Chicago he was unable to answer, and he and another legislator could not agree later on which major-object category was utilized to support telephone expenditures. The same staff aide also spent some twenty to thirty minutes explaining a lengthy document he had prepared analyzing the State Treasurer's appropriation—at which point it was discovered that the House had already voted on the appropriation that very afternoon. Much additional time was devoted to lectures by the other staff aide and the experienced legislators on subjects such as "where to look for expense account records" or "what to look for in the budget book." Though unquestionably useful for the newcomers, such lectures did emphasize the financial innocence of most bloc members.

Lack of knowledge was even more noticeable during the bloc's next meeting on the evening of May 27. Although warned that this was to be a crucial discussion, many legislators failed to appear, perhaps because they had been unable to find time to conduct the investigations assigned to them. The fourteen who did appear, moreover, gave no indication that they had done any homework. Had bloc members begun with a more solid foundation, the absence of fact-gathering might have been less significant. As it turned out, the information gap was a severe handicap which undermined both the evening's discussion and the bloc's plans for future action. Early in the meeting one legislator wanted to know "What happens to an appropriation if it's not all spent?" Bloc leaders were able to explain what a lapse was, but the leaders themselves later fell to quarreling among themselves over other equally fundamental items of information. They were still confused over the centrex telephone installation, they were unable to make sense of the Mental Health appropriation which was supported by several funds, they did not know which lines of the budget to compare against which lines of the appropriation bill (again for Mental Health), and they literally threw up their hands in frustration over the variety of items included in the omnibus House Bill 1244. "We can't make sense out of this kind of thing," said one legislator, "without some full-time staff help. What we really need," he continued, "is a legislative committee with responsibility for developing information about budget requests that would work on a twenty-four month basis and get this information to us ahead of time so that we would know what we're doing."

"We've already got one of those," Parkhurst replied sarcastically. "It's called the Budgetary Commission."

Without any detailed information the bloc could hardly formulate a very sophisticated strategy for the following day, when a number of important bills were to be brought before the Appropriations Committee. It was now clear that the various bloc subcommittees had done little or no work and could not, therefore, appear before the Appropriations group. The ball would have to be carried by bloc members who were also members of the House committee. Since even these legislators had found it impossible to prepare themselves very thoroughly, the only course of action left was to raise questions and hope to gain support either for committee amendments or for later changes on the floor of the House. This was hardly an encouraging prospect, but the bloc could hope for nothing more as it prepared itself for the following day's activities.

The hearing room was crowded as the House Appropriations Committee began its work shortly after 4:00 P.M. on Tuesday, May 28, 1963. One of the bills on the calendar was House Bill 1097, to provide a substantial increase in state aid to local school districts, and a large number of officials from various school districts across the state had come to Springfield to lobby for the bill. They were joined, of course, by administrators and lobbyists interested in the seventeen other bills on the calendar for this meeting. Chairman Granata indicated that the first bill to be considered was House Bill 1244, which appropriated more than $22 million to twenty-nine different agencies. Representative Lloyd (Curly) Harris, former Appropriations Committee Chairman and sometime member of the Budgetary Commission, acted as sponsor for the bill and asked whether or not he should ask representatives from the several affected agencies to offer statements. Representative Clyde Choate, also a Budgetary Commission member, then asked Harris if the Budgetary Commission had approved these various appropriations and whether or not they were included in the Governor's budget. When Harris replied in the affirmative, Choate immediately moved that the bill be reported out with a "do pass" recommendation.

An amendment designed to halve the appropriation for the Veterans' Commission—one of the twenty-nine agencies included in the bill—was then offered by Representative Albert W. Hachmeister, a Chicago Republican sympathetic to the Economy Bloc. The amendment was quickly voted down, but Representative Rae C. Heiple, a participant in the Economy Bloc, indicated that he had other questions to ask about this agency if its representatives were present. Two men from the Veterans' Commission seated themselves at the witness table as Heiple challenged Choate's previous statement by pointing out that the figure for this agency contained in the bill was actually higher than the budget figure by well over $100,000. Mr. James P. Ringley from the veterans' agency attempted to explain that this was not an increase but merely a fund transfer. Heiple, who had nothing on which to rely except the budget book and the bill, did not understand, particularly since he had noted another increase in the Personal Services category. A good deal of confusion followed as a series of questions and attempted answers failed to clarify the issue to Heiple's satisfaction.

Through it all Chairman Granata became increasingly impatient until, noticing Budget Superintendent Leth standing behind him, he signaled Leth to join him. "Here is Ted Leth," Granata interrupted, "a man who we all have a great deal of trust in and who can explain this." Given this opportunity Leth explained that the Governor originally reduced the Veterans' Commission appropriation by $58,000 but later determined that the money could be restored. In restoring it, however, the Governor utilized the General Revenue Fund, rather than the Vocational Rehabilitation Fund and this change in funds accounted for the major difference between the budget and the bill. Pointing his finger at the witness who had attempted to make the same explanation, Leth concluded that "This gentleman is right." The clear implication of Leth's remarks, of course, was that Heiple's questioning was both uninformed and unnecessary. To underline this point Representative Miller angrily asserted that unless this kind of questioning was stopped, "we'll be here all night."

But Heiple was undeterred. In another series of questions he sought to contrast the case-loads carried by Veterans' Commission employees in Cook County against downstate case-loads to show considerable variation and to imply the need, at the very least, for some organizational consolidation. The witness again defended his request and Heiple again appeared to be less than satisfied with the defense. He was temporarily silenced, however, as Horsley, Mikva, and Parkhurst took turns in seeking clarification from Leth of the Veterans' Commission appropriation, the mechanics of the salary increase and the impact of the centrex telephone installation. When they had finished, Heiple resumed. Though he did not doubt the sincerity of the Veterans' Commission staff, he said, he remained dissatisfied with their explanations of their appropriation request. To clarify the matter Heiple offered a motion to replace the existing "do pass" motion: he moved that a subcommittee be created to look further into the Veterans' Commission and report the results of their investigations back to the full committee.

By this time close to an hour had elapsed in the consideration of just one segment of just one bill. Chairman Granata,

never very receptive to this turn of events, ruled Heiple's substitute motion out of order and ordered the clerk to call the
roll on the original "do pass" motion. Heiple responded by
shouting "Mr. Chairman" several times until Granata finally
turned to him again. "I want to appeal the decision of the chair,"
said Heiple. Now it was Granata's turn to shout. "You want to
appeal the decision of the chair?" he roared. "All right, you
can appeal. All those in favor of the decision of the chair say
aye." There was silence. "All those opposed?" Again there was
silence as Granata banged his gavel down hard and snapped,
"Appeal denied."

Apparently unable to recognize defeat, Heiple insisted that
he wanted a roll call on his appeal. Granata was now openly
angry. "You want a roll call? All right, I'll give you a roll call.
I'm going to cut this stuff out. I want everybody to talk who
wants to talk or who has something to say, but I'm not going
to let these obstructionists get on with this stuff. We are going
to cut it out." Granata ignored Parkhurst's attempt to clarify
the motion on which there was about to be a roll call by shouting "The secretary will call the roll. We are going to cut out
this noise." On the vote, Granata was upheld by 27 to 7 and
another legislator immediately moved the previous question.
Parkhurst again asked what the previous question was but this
time Granata explained it: a "do pass" motion was pending.
Learning this, Parkhurst indicated that he had some questions
concerning other parts of the bill. But Granata refused to listen.
"The clerk will call the roll," he shouted. "Mr. Chairman, Mr.
Chairman," Parkhurst shouted back. "The clerk will call the
roll," repeated Granata, once again slamming his gavel down.
Parkhurst, too, was now beaten, and settled back in his chair
as the secretary began calling the roll.

On the roll call several members of the Economy Bloc—Mikva,
Elward, and Scariano—decided to explain their votes. Once
again, they stated, they were faced with a bill containing appropriations for a great many agencies and were forced into
the position of having to vote for many bad items in order to
support the good ones. Mikva cited the Spanish-American War
Veterans Commission—for which an appropriation was made in
the bill—and asked "How many Spanish-American War veterans
are still around in 1963? I know one," he continued, "but he is

my congressman [81-year-old Barratt O'Hara of the Second District] and he doesn't need any help." Though he personally supported most of the agencies whose appropriations were contained in House Bill 1244, said Mikva, the presence of items such as this forced him to vote against it. Only a few other legislators shared these sentiments, however. When the tally was completed, it showed 30 for, and 7 opposed. House Bill 1244 was reported out with a recommendation that it "do pass."

The defeat on the omnibus bill signaled the failure of the bloc's strategy of "fighting it out" in the Appropriations Committee. Inadequate preparation on the part of the bloc obviously was part of this defeat—but a very small part. Far more significant was the reluctance of the committee to tolerate anything which might slow it down, such as detailed questioning. And most significant of all was the near-impossibility of developing, through channels outside the system, the kind of information that would have permitted bloc members to prepare themselves. Members of the bloc continued to raise occasional questions in committee and continued to oppose "do pass" motions, but these activities had no impact on the outcome of committee deliberations.[7]

In losing this battle the Economy Bloc had lost the war—though many of them did not seem to realize this. With the Appropriations Committee unavailable for bloc purposes, there was no way to develop what was most needed: detailed information upon which to base reductions in appropriations. The bloc's secondary strategy of proposing amendments to bills on second reading could still be attempted, but of what would proposed amendments consist? On what information could amendments be based and where and how would they be prepared? It was now the end of May. No more than three weeks remained in which to analyze the many appropriation bills, discuss them, prepare amendments for them and attempt to have them adopted on second reading. Could it be done without staff or time? Could it be done at all?

Amazingly enough, in view of the many rebuffs suffered, the bloc made a show of trying. Two more evening meetings were actually held on Tuesday and Wednesday of the following week,

---

[7] Evidence to support this conclusion is provided in Chapter 6.

with the second of the two devoted to presentations by representatives from several agencies. But the bloc still lacked usable information of its own and thus still lacked solid grounds for action. In frustration the bloc considered offering amendments for across-the-board reductions on all bills, though ultimately the idea was dropped as something that could not be rationalized. Ironically, the bloc determined a series of proposed cutting amendments on grounds that were essentially identical to the kind of criteria applied by the Budgetary Commission itself. Where expenditure records indicated lapses for various agencies, it was decided to propose reductions; where no information was available on several agencies, it was decided to propose reductions anyway, particularly if the administrators involved were not regarded very highly or if it was felt that an agency had nothing to do of any consequence. "We're not gonna win on these amendments anyway," said one legislator, "so we might as well make as much noise as we can."

Many of the proposals agreed to during the first week in June were offered on second reading in the House, but without organized staff work they came out as amendments offered by individual legislators rather than bloc amendments—and most were quickly defeated. Plans for additional evening meetings had to be canceled when the House, under the pressure of a mountain of last minute business, instituted evening sessions, thus eliminating any opportunity for further bloc activities. As it turned out, the bloc was not completely ineffective, for the legislature did approve a proposal to require a separate bill for each agency appropriation, and several thousand dollars were cut by second-reading amendments—including a reduction in the Spanish-American War Veterans Commission appropriation. For the most part, however, the meetings until midnight and the discussions and the investigations were a waste of time. Dejected, Parkhurst later admitted that "Nobody cares about economy as long as the budget is balanced."

THE LIFE AND DEATH OF THE PROGRAM BUDGET

If the history of the Economy Bloc is a history of great effort which met with little success, the story of the program or "functional" budget represents a contrasting case of great initial success arising from a minimal effort.[8] The effort was made by Governor Kerner, shortly after assuming office in 1961. Personally committed to a "public interest" view of his office, and pushed by his advisors in the direction of reform, Kerner used his first budget message to propose a performance budget for the state. What the Governor had in mind was clarified shortly afterward when the Democratic leadership in the Senate introduced Senate bills 643 and 644 on May 3, 1961.

Senate Bill 644 amended the Civil Administrative Code to require that agency budget requests be "formulated according to the various functions and activities for which the respective department, office or institution of the state government . . . is responsible." It further provided that all such requests were to be "accompanied by comparative performance data formulated according to the various functions and activities, and, whenever the nature of the work admits, according to the work units, for which the respective department, officer or institution . . . is responsible." Tabulations of personnel, by number, title, and, if possible, function, were also required. As a sort of capstone, the Governor was to follow this changed format in making his budget recommendations to the legislature, which would thus possess a great deal of new information centering on functions (or activities), performance data, and comprehensive tabulations of personnel employed by the state. The older format was not completely abandoned, however, for each function was required to be broken down further into the older object classification.

On the surface, at least, Senate Bill 644 represented a radical change, not so much because it did away with traditional informational categories, but because it sought to inject considerations of *purpose* into a system dominated entirely by considerations of *purchase*. Significantly enough, the attempt need not have been made through the vehicle of statutory reform. Existing provisions of the Civil Administrative Code granted ample authority to the Governor and the Department of Finance to have budget requests prepared according to whatever format was desired (see Chapter 1). Further administrative action could not be avoided

---

[8] No attempt was made by actors to distinguish between "functional," "program," or "performance" budgeting. The text therefore follows the usage of the actors in providing no distinctions between these several concepts.

in any case, for the concept of "functions" remained to be defined and until it was, the impact of this bill would remain unclear. But if the impact of Senate Bill 644, taken by itself, was problematic, the effect of the companion measure, Senate Bill 643, was not. Under existing provisions of the "Act in Relation to State Finance," agency appropriations were made according to the standard major-object categories only. Thus, for any given agency appropriation measure, the total amount appropriated was simply the sum of the dollars assigned to Personal Services, Travel, Commodities, etc. Senate Bill 643 proposed to amend the statute by requiring that appropriations be made for "functions and activities," with an object classification provided within each function. The effect of this proposal is illustrated in the figure below:

Figure 1. TYPICAL APPROPRIATION BILL FORMAT, EXISTING AND PROPOSED

Existing		Proposed		
Personal Services	$ 50,000	Function X		$ 50,000
		Personal Services	$ 10,000	
Contractual Services	40,000	Contractual Services	5,000	
Travel	10,000	Travel	5,000	
Commodities	30,000	Etc.	—	
Equipment	10,000	Etc.	—	
Contingencies	10,000			
Total	$150,000			
		Function Y		50,000
		Personal Services	40,000	
		Contractual Services	5,000	
		Etc.	—	
		Function Z		50,000
		—		
		—		
		Total		$150,000

Appropriating by function instead of by major object would have represented a radical change in thinking about the purpose of an appropriation. But again, how radical such a change might be would depend to a large extent on the definitions given to the notion of "functions." Since Senate Bill 643 made no attempt to provide such definitions the question remained ambiguous. What was crystal clear, however, was the necessity for a large-scale expansion of the accounting system to implement Senate Bill 643. Appropriations made to agencies by major objects required only one set of accounts, classified by object, for each agency. The new proposal required a set of accounts, classified by object, *for each function* performed by the agency receiving an appropriation. In Figure 1, for example, the number of accounts for the hypothetical agency is tripled. Depending on the number of functions finally determined for each agency, therefore, the total number of accounts might well be increased six, eight, or ten times. Quite apart from its other effects, then, Senate Bill 643 was certain to add to the burden of state bookkeepers.

This consideration was not lost upon the agency officials who maintained the books and prepared budgets. From their point of view neither bill was necessary, while Senate Bill 643 was both unnecessary and positively harmful, since it would require more work and increase the cost of doing it—perhaps by as much as several hundred thousand dollars. But administrative hostility, though real enough, had to be kept underground. These were administration bills, after all, and agency officials were not anxious to challenge the authority of the Governor, particularly since the Governor was still something of an unknown quantity. Only Budget Superintendent Leth felt secure enough to voice open opposition to the proposals from within the administration. In this case, however, his opposition was ineffective. By the end of May the two bills had moved through the Senate without a show of opposition. In the House Executive Director Whitney of the Budgetary Commission opposed the bills in committee, but the outcome was never in question. The bills had been listed as administration measures and on that basis many committee members had departed the hearing, leaving favorable proxy votes behind. Whitney's effort was thus a failure even before it began. Once out of committee, the bills passed the lower house as well, though not until the last day of the session, and not without a final attempt to block them brought about, apparently, by Leth's informal lobbying.[9]

Here, then, was a change of potentially major proportions, brought about by a Governor who had just assumed office and was required to do little more than announce that he wanted these bills passed. Though opposition to both bills was widespread among state agencies, uncertainty regarding the intentions of the new Governor combined with the turmoil of the final weeks of the legislative session to render such opposition ineffective. For their part, legislators paid very little attention to the bills, treating them as "something the Governor wants" and acting accordingly. Not until the final stages of legislative consideration did any semblance of opposition appear, by which time most actors were too concerned with completing the work of the session to worry about a pair of apparently innocuous administration bills. Like so many other bills, before and since, these two passed into law virtually unnoticed by most lawmakers.

Though the Governor had succeeded in amending the statutes, it was not clear that he knew why he had advocated the amendments or what they would accomplish. These matters became even less clear when the job of implementing the required changes was turned over to the man who had led the opposition to them: Budget Superintendent Leth. Leth could hardly be said to have been enthusiastic about his new task, but the law and the Governor's assignment left him no choice except to perform it. As a practical matter the new provisions would not seriously disturb Finance anyway—at least immediately. Since appropriating by function would not begin until the 1963 session, additional staff in the Accounting Division would not be required until after July 1, 1963. All that was required from Finance in the meantime was preparation of another budget form for use by agencies in making up their requests for the 73rd biennium. This was easily accomplished by the simple expedient of printing new forms which left a blank space for each function, followed by separate lines for each of the traditional major objects. Directions for use

---

[9] On the final day of the session a motion to reconsider passage of the two bills was made. The motion was tabled.

of this form had to be prepared as well, but this, too, was accomplished without unusual difficulty.[10]

The most pressing immediate problem was the creation of definitions for the notion of "functions." Characteristically, Leth chose to allow as much latitude as possible in defining agency functions to representatives of the agencies themselves, virtually all of whom also had opposed the functional budget idea. "Administration," it was determined, was a function performed by every agency and would therefore be included as a category to be filled in by each agency. Beyond that, however, the nature and number of functions was left for the agencies to decide. Once they reached their separate decisions Leth was contacted and problems, if any, were worked out in further discussions between Leth and the agencies. Approval by the Governor was the final step in the process. By the time the various agencies began preparing their requests for the 73rd biennium, each of them had worked out the functional categories which would guide their future budgetary activities.

The results of these activities were revealed in the budget document, which gave every evidence of the careful and painstaking work contributed by officials opposed to program budgeting. Apart from the concept "administration," which was commonly—but not comprehensively—used, the nature and number of functions varied greatly from agency to agency. Some agencies determined their functions simply by applying the name to existing organizational subunits. Others derived functional classifications for some portions of their program, leaving other portions without the legally required functional categories. Indeed, the Department of Finance itself demonstrated how seriously it took the new law by refusing to provide a program analysis for *any* of its activities or organizational subunits. But perhaps Finance was simply being more straightforward with regard to the potentialities of program budgeting in Illinois than other agencies. One wonders, for example, whether it was, or could be, of much use to anyone to learn that the $171.4 million requested for the University of Illinois would be allocated to just three functions: "Administration," "Instruction," and "Physical Plant."

That such generally meaningless categories were developed

---

[10] See Chapter 2, above, for a discussion of these directions.

was no surprise, in view of the persons involved and the procedures followed. That they were allowed to stand, and that
some agencies were allowed to ignore the new law altogether,
was yet another indication of a certain lack of firmness in gubernatorial leadership. Given the opportunity to take the sting out
of the "functions" concept, agency officials did just that and thus
guaranteed their immunity from any change in financial language.
Meanwhile, as this offensive was being carried to its successful
conclusion, another attack was in progress, this one designed to
ensure that functional categories—whatever their nature—would
not, as a practical matter, be utilized at all.

Leading this second offensive, as he led the first, was Budget
Superintendent Leth, again supported by virtually all of the
officials involved in maintaining the state's financial books. The
target this time was the idea—embodied in Senate Bill 643—that
appropriations were to be made by function rather than by object. Even more than the companion idea that "functions" could
and should be defined, this notion represented the essence of the
proposed change, for in the final analysis the definition adopted
for any given "function" was bound to be arbitrary. The utility
of such a category would therefore be less a matter of conceptual clarity than a matter of administrative consistency in
application. Appropriations made to functions would force administrators to record all expenditures for a given function under
the same functional category—however that category was defined. Maintained for a sufficient length of time, such records
would permit comparisons of program costs or work-unit costs
from one period to another. Thus instead of showing fluctuations
only in terms of expenditures from object accounts, functional
records would permit such fluctuations to be related to general
activities performed and even permit the measurement of unit
costs for particular kinds of activities. The only way to get such
records was to change the appropriations format which determined the categories used to account for expenditures. Unless
such a change were made, administrators would retain their
ability to use different combinations of object accounts in determining the "functions" they would apply to future budget
requests. If functional budgeting was to have any useful meaning
at all, therefore, this change would have to be made.

In acting against this proposed movement away from the

232

status quo, Leth was assured of widespread bureaucratic support. Concentrating his attention on the legislature, Leth made use of his customary access to the Budgetary Commission to press his case against functional appropriations. Given frequent opportunities to express himself on this subject by Senator Peters, Leth repeatedly made a threefold case. The change to functional appropriations, he argued first of all, would be expensive. Since the number of accounts to be maintained would be drastically increased with functional appropriations, many departments (including Finance) would be forced to hire many additional clerical workers at a cost of several hundred thousand dollars. Exact predictions were impossible to make, but Auditor of Public Accounts Howlett strengthened Leth's contention on January 28, 1963. Appearing before the Budgetary Commission that day, Howlett justified a portion of his requested appropriation by referring to his need for additional clerks to handle "an estimated 7,196 appropriation accounts, as compared to the 2,685 accounts now maintained." [11] Implying that he had given the matter a good deal of thought, Howlett offered the observation that the state might save roughly $190,000 if the performance budget act were repealed. Leth, of course, had been making similar comments for some months, and now took this further opportunity to make clear to commissioners that the expense would be caused by performance appropriations rather than mere performance budgeting.

Leth asserted, second, that functional appropriations would impose a financial straitjacket on state agencies. Since the idea had never been tried before, mistakes were bound to be made in the allocation of object accounts to functional categories. Some agencies would turn out to be overbudgeted while others would probably run out of spending authority before the end of the biennium. Under the existing system, Leth pointed out, problems of this kind were easily resolved simply by securing the Governor's approval to transfer funds from one account to another within the same appropriation or by amending the appropriation to divert funds between accounts. By chopping each agency appropriation into smaller functional portions, Leth argued, the

---

[11] The quote is taken from a press release issued by Howlett on January 28, 1963.

new law would simultaneously increase the probable need for adjustment while adding complexity to the mechanism for achieving it. "You fellows better get ready to pass more laws," Leth told the Budgetary Commission on several occasions, " 'cause we're sure going to need them."

Finally, Leth insisted that functional appropriations would add nothing to legislative understanding of the budget. Initially such categories would have to be created by rearranging existing object-account records. Since the old objects were to be retained under each functional category in any case, the change amounted to no more than a reshuffling of existing information—and an expensive reshuffling at that. Most legislators, he thought, would continue to make use of the object categories, even with functional appropriations.

These arguments were all perfectly valid as far as they went— which was far enough to impress legislators with the need to do away with functional appropriations. When a bill to achieve this goal was introduced into the Senate on March 5, it became clear that the Governor, too, had been persuaded, for one of the two sponsors was Senator O'Brien, the Senate Minority Leader (the other was Senator Peters). Senate Bill 421 (1963) simply deleted the language placed on the statutes by Senate Bill 643 of the 1961 session and, in its place, restored the language which had existed prior to the passage of the 1961 act. In order to give immediate effect to the restoration, Section 2 of Senate Bill 421 declared the existence of an emergency in the following revealing language: "Whereas, the provisions of existing law for minute and detailed itemization of appropriations of each State agency require much greater detailed itemization than is provided for by the constitution, and such provisions require that appropriation measures be so extensive that great administrative difficulties will be encountered in the drafting of such measures unless the language of the law prior to August 25, 1961, is restored; therefore, an emergency exists and this act shall take effect upon its becoming a law." Twenty-one days after it was introduced the bill had passed both chambers. It was signed by the Governor on April 9, 1963, well in advance of the day scheduled for release of the Governor's budget. The functional appropriation statute was thus eliminated before it ever had been used.

What, then, was left of the program budget? Virtually nothing

—other than a statutory requirement that agencies prepare budget requests in terms of functions or activities performed by them. Since that requirement already had been emasculated by the agencies themselves, partly by ignoring it altogether and partly by defining functions to suit their own purposes, its impact was certain to be minimal. But even if program budgeting were taken seriously by the various agencies, the absence of an accounting system to support a program budget would necessarily undermine its utility. The repeal of functional appropriations meant that state funds would continue to be appropriated for objects of purchase and that expenditures from those funds would continue to be recorded as subtractions from object accounts. Of necessity, budget requests would continue to be built on the categories for which historical records were available, namely, the object categories. For agencies which continued to pay attention to the program budget requirement, a translation— from object categories to program categories—would be necessary. Thus, expenditures charged against object accounts would have to be regrouped in terms of agency functions. Unless agencies were willing to maintain day-to-day functional accounts in addition to object accounts, any such regrouping would be completely arbitrary. Furthermore, changes in the arrangement of object acounts into functional accounts from one biennium to the next would be easily accomplished and almost impossible to detect. Any such changes, of course, would destroy the utility of historical comparisons by function, just as they would destroy the possibility of developing meaningful unit-cost data. The repeal of functional appropriations, in short, eliminated the basis for a usable program budget in Illinois.

It is of some significance to note that neither side in the program budget fight articulated the political issue involved. For his part, the Governor appeared to view the program budget as little more than a desirable change in format, useful primarily as a means of increasing the intelligibility of the budget. Such a change obviously did not require a change in the accounting system, particularly if an accounting change would be difficult to implement. It was the nature of the format, rather than the manner in which the format was filled, that was of predominant concern. Opponents of the program budget also viewed it in essentially technical terms. For them, as for the Governor, the proposal involved a change of format to rearrange existing information. The technical defects of such a proposal were considerable: it would require more work, more people, and more money; it would complicate spending procedures; it would be initially difficult to understand. These arguments were all true and, precisely because both sides accepted a technical view of the issue, were ultimately decisive in the settlement that was reached.

What the Governor seemed unable to see, and what his opponents were unwilling to state, was that implementation of the program budget—i.e., appropriating by function as well as budgeting by function—would have altered the existing structure of control over financial information, and thus would have affected the distribution of organizational power. With three, or five, or seven separate appropriations to guide his expenditures, the agency official would exercise far less discretion than before in spending agency funds. The recorded· basis of the agency budget request would, by the same token, be less amenable to discretionary usage. The contemplated change in appropriations, in short, would have narrowed the boundaries within which agencies could control the disposition of appropriations made to them and also would have reduced the techniques available for financial impression-management.[12] For agency personnel anxious to maintain organizational status, these were high stakes. The stakes were equally high for a governor interested in improving his ability to control a decentralized bureaucracy. Anything that reduced agency discretion would necessarily improve a governor's understanding of agency operations and would, therefore, enhance the effectiveness of gubernatorial authority. Failure to understand this cost the incumbent governor dearly. The program budget statute he had passed so easily was killed by his own hand.

FACTORS CONTRIBUTING TO MAINTENANCE AND CHANGE: SOME TENTATIVE GENERALIZATIONS

Two sequences of events, occurring largely within the period of a single biennium, hardly provide a solid foundation for gen-

---

[12] Functional appropriations would have greatly increased the difficulty, to agencies, of manipulating their accounts to present the desired financial image to reviewing officials.

eralization. Taken together with the material in previous chapters, however, these events do offer some bases for suggesting the conditions under which the system is maintained or changed.

Maintenance Factors

The Structure of Access to the System. Because the system provides very few points at which decisions can be made, only a very small proportion of the total organizational actors ever become involved in expenditure decisions. Those who do become involved, moreover, normally do so at the behest of their organizational superiors. Within the administrative agencies clerks and secretaries are instructed to fill out the budget request forms by their superior officers or, as in the case of some of the larger agencies, high-ranking administrative officials are assigned this responsibility by the agency head. Agency heads change frequently, of course, and are typically less familiar with budgeting procedures than their subordinates, most of whom have participated in budgeting for many years, under many superiors. Lacking familiarity with procedures, agency heads are not inclined to press for changes in them. Lacking responsibility for agency operations and uncertain as to the effects of changed procedures, the more knowledgeable subordinates are inclined to go along with the way things have always been done. The effect, as far as administrative agencies are concerned, is to encourage organizational satisfaction with things as they are and to encourage organizational opposition to any changes from the status quo (e.g., the program budget).

Within the legislature participation is confined to the leadership of both houses and such other legislators as the leadership cares to admit to participating positions. The experience of the Economy Bloc, discussed above, indicates quite clearly that the leadership grants the privilege of participation only to those legislators who accept (or do not object to) the orientation of the leaders themselves. Legislators who express a different orientation are passed over in the selection of new participants and, if they attempt to inject themselves into the system, are explicitly turned away. By confining access to those legislators who share (or do not oppose) their own views, the leadership guarantees stability in the legislative orientation to state expenditures, for the leadership itself is extraordinarily stable. Virtually complete control by Republicans elected from "safe" districts is firmly established in the Senate, while House membership and leadership are assured of lengthy tenure by virtue of cumulative voting to elect representatives from three-member representative districts. There is thus a close relationship between a decision-making system in which access is firmly controlled by legislative leaders and electoral mechanisms which serve to guarantee long tenure to leaders. This relationship is itself a powerful contributing factor to stability in legislator orientations to state expenditures.[13]

The Pattern of Informational Control. The information upon which expenditure decisions are based is confined exclusively to members of the system. Original budget requests submitted by the various agencies are carefully protected from outsider scrutiny prior to the submission of the Governor's budget, at which point (mid- to late April) the lack of time remaining in the legislative session prohibits such scrutiny. Adjustments by the Governor and the Budgetary Commission are also made before the budget is presented and are equally mysterious: the commission does not provide a record of its deliberations, since it keeps none, while the Governor's budget presents a record of his final decisions with little or no supporting rationale, other than general statements explaining what the various agencies do. At best, then, nonparticipants in the system are presented with a statement of sums allocated to each agency with no indication of why or how these sums were determined. The only actors who have any idea of the rationale behind budget recommendations and major appropriation bills are members of the system, who physically handle budget request forms and summaries associated with such forms.

The lack of publicly available information to rationalize the figures contained in the budget and in appropriation bills provides dual support for the system. On the one hand, challenges to the system are discouraged by the absence of a public rationale that can be attacked. If they are to attack at all, therefore, potential challengers must challenge the amounts presented to them, on grounds that such amounts are too high or, rarely, too

---

[13] The at-large election held in 1964 has altered this system but whether the alteration is temporary or permanent remains to be seen.

low. But this form of challenge represents an affront to the judgment of the actors who were involved in determining the amounts, rather than an attack on a policy position. Such an affront tends to be avoided precisely because the actors involved in decision-making enjoy such high status within the state organization. No legislator or administrator lightly challenges the Governor or the Budgetary Commission.

On the other hand, challenges which are made are easily defeated by simple application of the informational resources available to the system. Lacking knowledge of system operations, challengers are hard put to identify targets for attack and seriously handicapped in their efforts to formulate strategies for successful attack. If the attack is couched in terms of some general principle—such as economy—the attackers themselves can be challenged to produce evidence to support their general allegations (e.g., wasteful spending). Without access to financial comparisons, of course, such evidence is virtually impossible to obtain. If, alternatively, the attack focuses on some specific item or items, a variety of justifications can be offered by members of the system, based upon information available only to them. By demonstrating that outsiders are misinformed, uninformed, or both, members of the system undermine the status of challengers while simultaneously maintaining or enhancing their own. Thus actors in the system encourage outsider ignorance concerning the nature of their activities, and at the same time use that ignorance to ward off the challenges, to them, that are occasionally attempted.

The Pattern of Legislative Process. Cutting across both of the preceding factors is another which, for want of a better term, can be referred to as the pattern of legislative process. Since members of the system monopolize participation in financial decision-making until the Governor's budget is presented, there is nothing for nonparticipants to do until the budget is available. By the time the budget is presented, however, only eight to ten weeks of the legislative session remain. Nonparticipants are thus forced to gather whatever information they can get and act upon it within a relatively brief period of time. This would be difficult enough if state finance were the only problem to be dealt with in this period. The difficulty is immensely compounded by the long-standing legislative custom of deferring consideration of most important legislative matters until this very same period. As a result there is a pronounced reluctance to tamper with expenditure decisions or with the system of action through which such decisions are made.

The Availability of Adequate Revenue Resources. Less clearly revealed in the two cases presented above, but nevertheless important to the maintenance of the system, has been the availability of revenue in sufficient quantities to support the expenditure requirements of the state organization. In the preceding chapter I suggested that the principal goal of the system is a balanced budget and that success in achieving this goal—or in appearing to achieve it—legitimates the actions taken by the system. For most of the period since 1945 the state has been able to achieve an excess of revenues over expenditures. In part this has been due to a large revenue surplus built up during the war years 1941-45 and in part it has resulted from the relatively steady growth in the Illinois economy.[14] Thus even the technically "unbalanced" budget of the 1961-63 biennium was able to rely on sharply increased sales tax revenues in an expanding state economy to produce a revenue surplus at the end of that period. Adjustments made by the Kerner administration were extremely important in achieving this surplus, of course, but such adjustments were far less important than continued economic growth. Such growth, which is largely beyond the control of the state organization, has made an important contribution to the stability of the expenditure system.

The Availability and Use of Federal Funds. A major factor contributing to the "adequacy" of state revenue sources has been the availability of funds contributed by the federal government. Some 22.6 per cent of total revenues available to the state in the 1961-63 fiscal period came from the federal government, while 30.7 per cent of total revenue anticipated for the 1963-65 biennium was expected to come from the same source. The activities financed by such contributions—highway construction, a reasonably high level of welfare payments to needy persons, hospital construction, airport construction, and many others—are obviously important in and of themselves. More significantly,

---

[14] It is important to note here, too, that periodic increases in the sales tax have greatly increased available state revenues.

however, the use of federal money to support these programs has permitted the state organization to blunt the demand on its own resources and has thus aided the system in continuing to achieve its major goal: the balanced budget. To be sure, many of the federally financed programs will ultimately require higher levels of state support. Highways constructed with federal funds will have to be maintained and patrolled from state resources, to take one example. But this long-term problem has not yet had to be faced squarely by actors in the system. So far at least, federal money has been useful in helping to balance the budget, despite increasing service levels, and has in this way helped to maintain satisfaction with a system that "works."

Change Factors

"Crisis," or the Failure of Goal Achievement. In the Illinois context the test of whether or not the system "works" is its ability to balance revenues against expenditures. By relying upon a substantial revenue surplus generated in wartime, federal funds, and gimmicks such as the eighteen-month budget, the system has managed to work throughout the postwar period. On the other hand, the system failed to work in 1961 and, as a result, an economy bloc sprouted up to challenge its basic assumptions. Though the bloc had little success in 1963, when the system once again found a way to balance the budget, the experience of this group does suggest that failure to meet this goal does create an environment within which pressure for system change can develop. This is not to say that pressure for change *will* develop in such an environment: one plausible response to this kind of crisis is the meat-axe reduction which, for reasons stated in the preceding chapter, changes nothing. Unless the environment of crisis is present, however, the experience of the past two decades indicates that pressure for change is quite unlikely to develop. Crisis, in short, appears to be a necessary, but not sufficient, condition for system change.

It appears likely that this condition will characterize the state organization for the foreseeable future. By 1961 the war surplus had disappeared, and with it the ability to make use of eighteen-month budgets. Simultaneously the demand for higher levels of expenditure, particularly for education and welfare, was reaching a level which seemed certain to require new and expended taxes.

Economic growth and resort to debt-financing for capital expenditures temporized this problem through the 1963-65 fiscal period, but even with vastly greater use of debt-financing it hardly seems likely that expenditure demands can be put off indefinitely. Thus the prospects are for increasing difficulty in achieving the balanced budget and therefore increasing pressures for changing the expenditure system. The form which these pressures will take, and the effects they will have, remain to be seen.

The Structure of Gubernatorial Participation. Earlier it was pointed out that access to the few points at which decisions are made is controlled by actors occupying superordinate bureaucratic and legislative positions. These actors are thus able to use their positions to maintain existing orientations to the problem of determining state expenditures. The single exception to this conclusion is the Governor, who is elected to his position from outside the state organization and who is therefore less bound by the twin constraints of hierarchy and custom. As an outsider the Governor is likely to operate on the basis of assumptions which differ from those of other members of the system—that is, he will not take the same things for granted. Precisely because of this difference in viewpoint the Governor will be in a position to identify "problems" that do not occur to other actors. With no superior to whom he must report his ideas for approval, and with a Constitutionally guaranteed right to participate in decisions, the Governor is free to voice his ideas and to use whatever ability he has to bring about their implementation.

Gubernatorial opportunities to perceive problems and to offer proposals for change (recall Governor Kerner's program budget) are complemented by the considerable legal and political resources available to him. He can command administrative agencies to provide him with information (if he knows what information he wants); he can control the product of the legislature on financial matters; he alone is in a position to balance the budget and thus encourage the cooperation of other financial actors. Thus even a relatively uninformed Governor can bring about significant adjustments, such as a much greater use of debt-financing, or major changes in system orientation, such as a program budget. The eventual destruction of the latter innovation does not reduce the significance of the ease with which Governor Kerner brought it about in the first place, though it does suggest that innovation and implementation may require quite different forms of behavior.

In sum, the Governor is far and away the most powerful actor in the system. He is the one actor most likely to be sensitive to possible changes, and he is the actor who is most likely to achieve change, even when he has less than adequate knowledge of the system or the changes he may be seeking to implement. The Governor need not seek change, of course, but chances are that he will. As suggested in Chapter 5, one of the Governor's chief problems is to find some way to demonstrate that his presence has an impact on an organization which can easily function without anything more than formal gubernatorial participation. Change is a good method for providing such a demonstration.[15] Given the prospects for a more or less continuing financial crisis in the years ahead, the Governor will hardly be able to avoid a search for changes in the expenditure system. Like the crisis environment, gubernatorial action appears to be a necessary, and in some cases a sufficient, condition for system change.

Organizational Growth. In the present context, organizational growth refers to the creation of new units (boards, departments, commissions, etc.) or to increases in expenditure levels, or both. I have distinguished between such growth and system change— i.e., alteration in orientations and decisional rules—precisely because the state organization has demonstrated a considerable ability to tolerate growth without changing the expenditure system in any significant way. Beyond a certain point, however, organizational growth seems likely to provide additional pressure for changes in the expenditure system, for continued growth will necessarily complicate the problem of balancing revenues against expenditures. Obviously that point had not yet been reached through the end of the 1963 legislative session, but it was equally obvious, even then, that its arrival was close at hand.

---

[15] It is not the *only* method, however. The available evidence suggests that former Governor Stratton demonstrated his relevance by centralizing control in his own hands. Stratton did *not* seek to change the system, though he could easily have done so. For a partial confirmation of this view see Malcolm Moos and Francis E. Rourke, *The Campus and the State* (Baltimore: Johns Hopkins University Press, 1959), p. 238.

When it does arrive, the system will experience heightened demands to change its ways.

The Penetration of Outside Ideas. By preventing widespread dissemination of information concerning its activities, the system has been able to isolate itself from other action systems in the state organization. Such isolation has aided immeasurably in maintaining the system, but that very success has eroded the ability of the system to deal with changing organizational requirements. System survival has been due less to any actions of its own than to a set of favorable circumstances largely beyond its ability to control—the availability of federal money, or continued economic growth, for example. On occasions when these favorable circumstances have not prevailed the system has been bypassed completely, as it was during the final days of the 1961 session when a new set of actors assumed responsibility for reducing excessive budget requests. Even when favorable circumstances have prevailed, as in 1963, attempts to adjust to new realities have ignored the system. Thus the Governor in that year resorted to outside consultants in his attempt to establish a more adequate pattern of expenditure control, because he and his advisors were persuaded that actors in the existing system would be of no help.

Neither the Economy Bloc nor the Governor's consultants proved to be a match for the actors in the system, but their efforts nevertheless suggest the significance of ideas which differ from the orientations of the system as a potentially powerful force for change. The nearly successful attempt to implement a program budget, on the strength of new ideas imported by the Governor, provides additional support for this view. In theory, such new ideas could be developed by participants in the system. In practice, hierarchical control over access to the system discourages such a result and establishes outsiders as the principal source of different orientations. Structurally, the most important outsider is the Governor, who is in a position to generate new ideas and whose power to implement such ideas is limited primarily by his political skill. Of less importance historically, but nonetheless potentially important, are legislative outsiders such as the men who led the Economy Bloc. Elevation of men possessing such ideas to positions of legislative leadership, from which positions they could gain access to the system, would increase the probabilities for system change. Because different ideas are likely to be generated by the Governor and because they are likely to be found among at least some members of the legislature, outsider orientations are built into the structure of the state organization, where at any given time they exist as latent forces for system change.

SUMMARY

One way to summarize the preceding analysis is to suggest that system change requires (a) an agent or agents through which change can be implemented, (b) a socially acceptable motivation for change, and (c) some idea or set of ideas to provide the direction for change. In the absence of evidence to show that the system has, in fact, changed during the period for which this study is relevant, it is difficult to be clear about the significance of each of these requirements. From the author's point of view, however, they have been listed in order of increasing importance.

Agents for change already exist within the state organization, in the person of the Governor and in the persons of a number of more or less dissident legislators. These agents have been hampered, in the recent past, by the general absence of financial crisis. Given the characteristics and values of the system, crisis provides virtually the only motivation for change which is accepted by the majority of the actors involved. But a crisis does not guarantee that change will occur; it merely provides the environment within which change becomes palatable. Without ideas for directing change—i.e., without some model which specifies a different set of orientations and relationships—the problem presented by crisis is more than likely to be met by temporizing measures (such as meat-axe reductions) whose ultimate effect is to promote maintenance of the existing system. Perhaps the general absence of such ideas represents another, and more deep-seated, form of "crisis."

CHAPTER NINE

THE AMBIGUITY
OF "GOVERNMENT"
IN ILLINOIS

The data presented in the preceding pages will doubtless generate a variety of interpretations, depending upon the identity of the reader and the purposes for which he reads. For those who have been patient enough to come this far with me, I would like to offer some summary observations based upon my own sense of the significance of what I have written here. Conclusions regarding the power to determine state expenditures seem to me to have been firmly established for the 1963-65 fiscal period. These conclusions, together with the implications they may reasonably support, are clearly worth summarizing. Moreover, since my conclusions about power are based upon participation in decision-making, it seems appropriate to attempt to relate these conclusions to ideas about decision-making which are currently the focus of much discussion. Finally, I would like to offer some observations, growing out of the previous chapters, regarding the meaning of "state government" in Illinois.

THE POWER STRUCTURE OF STATE FINANCE

Operationally speaking, organizational influence is exerted through a social system within the state organization composed of five rather well-identified roles: agency official, Department of Finance, Budgetary Commission, Governor, and legislature. Together these roles determined the manner in which financial resources were distributed for the 1963-65 fiscal period. But the relative power of each of these roles, as measured by their decision-making ability, varied greatly, as the following summary suggests.

Legislature

Despite its formal authority over appropriations, the 1963 General Assembly was virtually powerless in the determination of state expenditures. Pressed for time, lacking usable information, and without leadership interest in examining appropriations, the legislature did nothing more than pass appropriation bills. The legislature had no criteria of its own to apply to such bills other than the fact that they were appropriations and therefore worthy of passage. In the absence of such criteria legislative behavior could only produce a stamp of acceptance for decisions made elsewhere. As an institution the legislature was incapable of doing more.

Budgetary Commission

Though generally regarded as an extremely powerful group, the 1963 Budgetary Commission was in fact only slightly less irrelevant to expenditure decisions than the legislature, for which the commission acted as financial surrogate. The commission possessed no authority to make decisions. All it could do was offer advice to the Governor and the legislature. But the commission chose to ignore the legislature completely and, in advising the Governor, made use of information which the Governor himself had supplied. Of necessity, such advice as the commission offered was of limited relevance—particularly since large portions of the total spending program failed to come under commission review. However, the commission did ease the political burden borne by the Governor by providing an agency to bear responsibility for unpleasant decisions the Governor was reluctant to make. The choice of which decisions to "blame on" the commission, of course, was entirely up to the Governor. It was nevertheless useful for the Governor to maintain the fiction that the commission, and not he, had made the choices. Maintaining the fiction was even more useful for the commission, since it created a public record to affirm the power attributed to the commission by others. Thus, despite the absence of commission-derived criteria for decision and despite the essentially mechanical procedures followed by the commission, expenditure "decisions" for a number of agencies appeared to be made by this group.

Agency Officials

In terms of actual determinations of what funds agencies would receive for what purposes, agency officials were unquestionably the most important actors during the 1963 decision-making period. By virtue of their ability to control expenditures from funds appropriated in the previous biennium, agency officials were in a position to control the information contained in documents submitted for review by external authorities. And since external review was predicated largely upon decision-making formulae implicit in the information summaries, agency control over information was largely decisive in determining the decisions that were made. For the most part, of course, this power was confined to current expenditure levels and the moderate changes from those levels that were made. But agency officials also were responsible for many proposals to increase expenditure levels and were thus able to structure the alternatives from which large increases were selected, even if someone else made those decisions.

Governor

Decisions with regard to large increases, and all other major decisions made in 1963 were determined by the Governor, or persons acting in his name. Deference to the Governor on all "big" decisions was in part a function of his control over a centralized budgetary mechanism and in part due to his unique ability to take the actions necessary to balance the budget. Had he desired to do so, of course, the incumbent easily could have imposed his own judgments on any or all of the more routine financial matters which came before him. His intervention in areas involving less than major adjustments in existing levels of expenditure was more active in 1963 than in 1961, but by and large the incumbent confined his decisions to the big changes that he could influence. The combination of decisions made by the Governor on all major and some routine matters entitles him to be described as the single most powerful actor in the system in 1963.

Budget Superintendent and the Department of Finance

The informational and technical glue which held the system together in 1963 was provided by Budget Superintendent Leth. Leth's technical competence was helpful to agencies; information provided by Leth was indispensable to the work of the Budgetary Commission and the legislature; his peculiar combination of skills greatly facilitated the Governor's work; in short, all other actors in the system relied upon Leth for information, technical advice, or both. Though Leth officially made no decisions of his own, those who did make decisions frequently did so on the basis of material provided by him. The Governor may have been more powerful—primarily because he developed other sources of advice—but Leth's activities were more pervasive, and therefore more indispensable to the continued operation of the system.

To the extent that expenditure decisions involved determinations concerning the utilization of presently available funds, or slight adjustments in the level of available funds, power was exercised in 1963 by persons acting in the role of agency administrator. To the extent that major adjustments in expenditure levels were determined in 1963, it was the Governor who determined them. Coordination of the actions of these two powerful roles was provided by the Budget Superintendent, who also exercised considerable influence over decisions in his own right. Legislative roles, meanwhile, were almost totally ineffective. These conclusions are meant to apply primarily to the 1963 decision-making period, but there are considerable grounds for the belief that they would apply equally well to some previous biennia.

DECISION-MAKING DYNAMICS: SOME MODEL COMPARISONS

Decisions to spend public money possess an objective importance which frequently seduces those who attempt to account for them. The seduction consists of imputing various kinds of significance to such decisions, usually on the basis of a posteriori or a priori judgments. One common form of seduction, for example, is the notion that the totality of expenditure decisions made by a government accurately represents the political values to which the government is devoted. The reasoning behind such a notion is something like this: to be active in any given area the government must be able to pay for such activity; but government activity is confined to a limited set of programs, which is to say that government chooses to do some things but not others; the choice of activities must be based on evaluations for and against government action; therefore expenditure decisions reflect the values held and applied by the government. Using such reasoning one can take an official document such as a budget, thumb through it, and conclude that if a government spends more money to build highways than to build hospitals, it is more interested in highways than in health. Or if it spends more money on welfare than on schools one can conclude that it is more concerned about the poor than about education. One can even deduce precise measurements regarding the relative importance (or scale) of different values. Thus, if the government spends $1 million to control diseases among race horses and only $100,000 on tuberculosis control, one can assert confidently that sick horses are considered by the government to be ten times more important than tubercular human beings.[1]

Now there is a sense in which such statements are generally true. Decisions to spend money could not be made unless some person or persons wanted to make them, and people do not "want" unless they possess values to identify the nature of the thing wanted. In the long run, at least, it is not unreasonable to read values into gross expenditure decisions. But expenditure decisions in Illinois are not made in the long run; they are made in the here and now, by people pursuing goals that have little or nothing to do with the kinds of values referred to above. The criteria applied by actors to 1963 expenditure decisions for the most part were mechanical rather than purposive, and grew out of organizational and situational constraints rather than policy or program preferences.

Another common seduction, not unrelated to the preceding example, is the idea that expenditure decisions, because of their crucial importance to government, must be subjectively (if not objectively) rational—that is, made by men pursuing carefully designed strategies to achieve self-conscious goals. Here the imputation is a priori, in the form of an assumption that all de-

---

[1] This example is not offered lightly: a prominant state senator frequently offers a similar argument in public speeches around the state.

cision-makers are cut out of the same rational mold and will therefore behave in such a way that their actions always have a goal and a rationale that is fully apparent to them. This, of course, is a reasonable assumption to make, since many actors do attempt a careful specification of their goals and do try to calculate the best methods of achieving their goals. But many other actors do none of these things. The goals of some agencies are relatively unchanging, with the result that nothing more than an habitual response to financial stimuli is required from agency personnel. Financial support for other agencies is so predetermined and guaranteed by devices such as special funds that anything more than formal compliance with budget regulations would be ludicrous. Actors in still other agencies are simply too busy with more pressing (to them) matters to become involved in detailed financial calculations. It is necessary to emphasize, moreover, that there is no such thing as rationality-in-the-abstract. To identify goals or to calculate strategies in Illinois finance is to become unavoidably involved in the forms and vocabularies through which expenditure decisions are expressed. For this reason the concept of "rationality" either has a contextual meaning or it has no meaning at all. Searching for the "reasons" behind particular expenditure decisions without first understanding the categories of thought that structure rationality is bound to be fruitless.

What is missing from both of these interpretations is a sense of the reality of organization as an intervening factor between individual orientation on the one hand, and social value on the other. Before an individual can hope to have an impact on expenditure decisions made by the State of Illinois he must learn how to play the budget game, according to assumptions and rules that have guided organizational behavior for years. Similarly, before a socially desired goal can receive financial support from the state organization, it must be filtered through the procedures established by the organization to determine expenditures. The organization, in short, is in a position to set the terms according to which both social and individual pressures are translated into state expenditure decisions.

A useful method of clarifying the procedures followed in making such translations is to compare them against a series of intellectual models which purport to describe the manner in which decisions are made, or the manner in which decisions ought to be made. Do the procedures I have described, for example, approximate a system of "budgeting"? In a formal sense, of course they do. Forms for estimating expenditure needs are prepared by a central fiscal agency, which distributes them to the various operating units. The completed forms are then returned to the central fiscal agency, where they are summarized and sent to a legislative commission and the Governor for review. Changes made by these officials are then incorporated into a more or less comprehensive budget, which is then submitted to the legislature where, after further review, appropriations are passed, more or less in accordance with the budget document. Apart from the interposition of a legislative screening agency prior to the submission of the budget, these procedures appear to possess all the required attributes of a formal budgetary system.

Formalities apart, however, there is virtually nothing in the behavior of the various actors which meets the requirements of our hypothetical budgetary process. Budgeting demands a clear specification of the objectives to be met by public expenditures; the forms used in Illinois frame alternatives in sums of money, allocated to agencies, whose programs and purposes are only imperfectly reflected in the forms. Budgeting requires a continuous reevaluation of all programs supported by public funds; actors in the Illinois system uniformly assume that activities supported by current levels of expenditure will be continued and thus require no reevaluation. Budgeting asserts the necessity of a comprehensive review of all items of proposed expenditure prior to deciding for or against any one item; in Illinois expenditure requests are taken up one-by-one, in no particular order, and decisions are made on each item without regard to the impact of any one decision on all other decisions. Budgeting requires that expenditure decisions be related to estimates of revenue; in Illinois such relationships are effectively considered only at the last minute, when most decisions already have been made, and when the principal concern is to establish the magnitude of the increases to be allowed. Budgeting assumes a hierarchy of substantive values, agreed upon by all participants, and applied as criteria to determine expenditures; actors in Illinois seek a variety of different substantive values, which in any case are seldom applied to the decisions they make. Budgeting requires consideration of a variety of means to achieve stated objectives in order to achieve those objectives at least cost; in Illinois such comparisons are rarely made: many decisions result from the application of purely mechanical criteria, many others are based upon considerations of political status, and still others are the product of habitual responses to familiar stimuli. Budgeting, in brief, is a rational process, whereas financial decision-making in Illinois is the result of a social process in which rationality is only sometimes apparent.[2]

However else it may be described, then, the process by which expenditures are determined in Illinois can hardly be called "budgeting." Are there alternative models against which the Illinois system can be matched? One such alternative has been developed recently, using the term "incrementalism." In essence, this model suggests that decisions are made through a process of "successive incremental comparisons," in which decision-makers exclude many important variables while concentrating only on those few variables that are "politically relevant."

According to this model, decision-makers approach their task with neither a fully developed scale of values nor a comprehensive knowledge of all the variables relevant to the decisions they make. Instead, decision-makers make choices in situations which typically present limited alternatives among policies that are only incrementally different from existing policies—i.e., the choice normally is not between this new program or that new program, but between additions to or subtractions from ongoing programs. In choosing the increments to be adopted or rejected, actors do not gather all the relevant facts, apply their values to those facts, and then choose. Nor do they compare one increment against all other increments before them at a given time. Rather they make successive comparisons in which facts and values are intermixed. Each incremental proposal is treated individually, as the latest in a series of decisions regarding this particular program. The

---

[2] I have not attempted to exhaust the hypothetical requirements of "budgeting." Readers are invited to compare my listing against requirements put forward in sources such as Jesse Burkhead, *Government Budgeting* (New York: John Wiley & Sons, Inc., 1962), or Arthur Smithies, *The Budgetary Process in the United States* (New York: McGraw-Hill Book Co., 1955).

past decisions are compared to the results achieved, taking cognizance of the changing objectives produced by past choices. On this basis another choice is made to add, or not add, another increment. Insofar as criteria of choice are related to program objectives, the objectives considered are those of this particular program, considered at this point in a time sequence which stretches back for a number of years. Insofar as choice criteria are related to the values of decision-makers, the operative values are less likely to reflect philosophic orientations than political and administrative desires structured by the decision-making environment.[3]

Even this rather brief summary of "incrementalism" is enough to suggest that this model provides a much closer approximation of the Illinois system than is provided by the "budgeting" model. Those who determine expenditures for the state organization do not possess anything like comprehensive information and rarely seek to structure decisions according to a well-ordered set of value priorities. They do begin with an implicit commitment to continue what is already being done; they do deal typically with proposals which are only incrementally different from current activities; and they do make choices in a fragmented manner, treating each expenditure proposal as something isolated from all other expenditure proposals and taking only a small number of variables into account. Moreover, while "incrementalism" as a model is too abstract to permit identification of the "politically relevant" variables in any given empirical system, the idea itself can be applied with profit to data that is available. Thus in Illinois, the "politically relevant" variable for agency officials is maintenance of *at least* the current appropriation. For the Budgetary Commission it is maintenance of the commission's "powerful" image, and for the Governor it is the balanced budget. One

---

[3] Charles E. Lindblom has been the chief proponent of "incrementalism." My summary of the argument is drawn chiefly from Lindblom's "Decision-Making in Taxation and Expenditures," in *Public Finances: Needs, Sources, and Utilization* (Princeton: National Bureau of Economic Research, 1961), pp. 295-329. But see also Charles E. Lindblom, "Policy Analysis," *The American Economic Review*, 48 (June, 1958), 298-312, and the more recent expansion of many of these arguments in David Braybrooke and Charles E. Lindblom, *A Strategy of Decision* (New York: Free Press of Glencoe, Inc., 1963).

need not assert the desirability of incrementalism as a method—
as its principal spokesmen do—to recognize its applicability to
Illinois.

Yet if the fit is close, it is by no means exact, for the incrementalism model does not accommodate a variety of actions
which are taken in Illinois. A mistake in addition, made by an
agency official as he fills in the budget request form, results in a
proposal for several thousand dollars more—or less—than the
agency has decided to request. The error is not noticed in the review and appropriation process, with the result that the agency
receives a considerably larger—or smaller—appropriation than
it has desired. Such errors, by testimony of the actors themselves,
are common, and occasionally of considerable magnitude: recall
the $11 million mistake in the school aid calculation that was
discovered largely by accident. Or, to take a different example,
legislative appropriation committees commonly practice the
habit of approving major appropriation bills without so much as
a question. Still a third example is provided by the Budgetary
Commission, which not only makes most of its decisions by applying a mechanical formula, but on one occasion gave blanket approval to a dozen requests from smaller agencies without even
looking at them, on grounds that "we can't waste time on that."
To the extent that erroneous calculation, application of habitual
and mechanical decision rules, or sheer lack of attention are accidental occurrences, they are not likely to be accommodated by
any decisional model. But in Illinois such behavior is a structured
aspect of the decision-making process for which some accounting
is required.

Incrementalism cannot provide such an accounting because it
imputes a form of rationality to decision-makers and thereby
avoids analysis of the structural bases of expenditure decisions.
To be sure, rationality in this model is incremental rather than
comprehensive, but it is rationality nonetheless, for decision-
makers are assumed to make calculations which successively
compare one incremental change against a series of past decisions. If such comparative calculations are not made—as they
frequently are not in Illinois—incrementalism loses its relevance.[4]

---

[4] Incrementalists might wish to argue that decision-makers who give no
attention whatever to items upon which they pass judgments ignore these

By imputing even this limited form of rationality to all decision-makers, incrementalism assumes more than it need assume to apply to Illinois, and gives less attention than it should to the structural conditions that give rise to the behavior patterns it seeks to describe. The structural conditions it does discuss—complexity of decision and limited human capacity to know—are imputations made necessary by the concern for rationality rather than derivations from a body of empirical data.

ENVIRONMENTAL PRESSURES AND ORGANIZATIONAL CHANGE

In Illinois the conditions which structure behavior along lines which closely resemble the incrementalism model are organizationally defined patterns of role orientations and decisional rules. Although the nature of these patterns and their operative effects should be clear enough for those who have read the previous material, they do possess a deeper meaning which deserves further comment. We can begin to appreciate this deeper significance by raising two related questions: (1) How are major changes made in current programs? and (2) How do completely new activities come into existence? Here again, these are questions for which incrementalism provides no answers, except to say that such actions typically do not occur. That is a fair enough answer, at least in Illinois, but it is hardly satisfactory, for such changes do take place. During the period in which this study was conducted, for example, Governor Kerner created a wholly new Board of Economic Development. This was not only a new organizational unit, but it conducted programs in state planning and tourist promotion that had not previously been carried on by the state. In the same period appropriations made to the Department of Mental Health were enormously increased and applied to a program whose fundamental premises were com-

---

items because they have calculated the costs of such action and decided that the costs, to them, were sufficiently low to encourage their lack of attention. For some of the actors in Illinois this argument would have some plausibility, though it destroys a distinction between positive action and lack of positive action that I consider useful. For the Budgetary Commission, however, the argument has little validity, since commissioners are frequently unaware of the items that they deal with in such fashion.

pletely changed. These were not mere increments; these were major changes which obviously require some kind of explanation.

Part of the explanation, of course, is the simple fact that the Governor wanted to bring these changes about. As I have suggested earlier, the Governor comes into the state organization as an outsider and is likely, for that reason, to be an innovator. This structural condition, coupled with the Governor's organizational authority and his power to make all final appropriation decisions, enables the Governor to make a variety of major changes if and when he desires to do so. Individuals or groups seeking to promote change would do well to begin by approaching the chief executive, for without his support, major changes are unlikely to occur.

It is foolish, however, to suppose that a governor can achieve any change he desires, and it is equally foolish to suppose that only the Governor can successfully initiate changes. Although the Governor is clearly the most important agent of change within the state system, a variety of other factors normally are involved. Gubernatorial support for the expansion and reorientation of the Mental Health Department, for example, would have been fruitless in the absence of expanded funds from a bond issue approved by popular referendum held before the incumbent Governor took office. Similarly, the new state planning program was predicated on the availability of federal funds for its support. However important the Governor may be in achieving major changes, then, he does not and cannot operate in a vacuum. Of necessity he operates in a context which structures both opportunities for and limitations against change.

These considerations suggest the relevance of an inquiry into the major changes that have actually taken place in the pattern of state expenditures over the past two decades. Steady growth, of course, has been obvious, but what is more significant than mere growth is the relationship between the various activities supported by state appropriations. Have there been changes in the proportion of total appropriations assigned to particular programs? If so, have these changes been of a magnitude sufficient to warrant their designation as "major" changes? And what, if anything, does evidence bearing on these questions suggest about the process by which such changes are effected, or about the development of new programs?

Table 11 summarizes data from which partial answers to these questions, at least, can be drawn. The data selected are designed to show 1945 and 1963 appropriations for the most costly state

Table 11. APPROPRIATIONS MADE TO MAJOR STATE FUNCTIONS, BY AGENCY, 1945 AND 1963 [a]

Agency and Function	1945 Appropriation	Per Cent of Total	1963 Appropriation	Per Cent of Total
Highways (Div. of) [b]	$ 72,190,858	11.1	$ 994,828,443	25.4
Education				
Common Schools[c]	44,187,300	6.8	433,090,000	11.1
Universities	46,223,715	7.1	445,960,534	11.4
Health and Welfare				
Mental Health	64,863,087	10.0	418,971,013	10.7
Public Health	4,212,955	.6	48,126,924	1.2
Public Aid	171,923,423	26.5	640,004,401	16.3
Selected Other Activities				
Public Saftey	19,679,539	3.0	76,692,885	2.0
Labor	3,067,370	.5	44,484,659	1.1
Revenue	20,244,178	3.1	47,954,310	1.2
Total, These Appropriations	446,592,425	68.7	3,150,113,169	80.3
Total, All Other	202,863,131	31.3	770,703,745	19.7
Total, All Appropriations	$649,455,556	100.0	$3,920,816,914	100.0

[a] Federal aid included, in keeping with Illinois practice. Figures include reappropriations, but do not include supplemental appropriations made in either 1945 or 1963 to complete the previous biennium.
[b] Does not include Motor Fuel Tax distribution to cities and counties.
[c] Does not include appropriation for special educational programs or transportation.

functions (Highways, Education, and Health and Welfare) and for three agencies which are more or less representative of the typical, but not major, state agency. Perhaps the first thing to note about these figures, apart from the sixfold increase in appropriations which occurred within the space of two decades, is the growing share of total allocations assigned to agencies included in Table 11. In 1945 these agencies accounted for 68.7 per cent of total appropriations; by 1963 the percentage had increased to 80.3. Appropriations for all other state agencies, meanwhile, decreased from 31.3 per cent in 1945 to less than 20 per cent in 1963. If we eliminate from Table 11 the three agencies not involved in major state functions it becomes possible to see the increasing share of total appropriations allocated to Highways, Education, and Health and Welfare alone. These functions received 62.1 per cent of the appropriations pie in 1945, but more than 76 per cent in 1963.

Apart from the agencies involved in the major state functions, then, it would appear that other agencies have been declining in their relative financial importance. Despite nearly a fourfold increase in the dollars appropriated to the Department of Public Safety (prisons, state police), for example, the department suffered a one-third decline in its share of total appropriations between 1945 and 1963. Similarly, the dollars appropriated to the Department of Revenue more than doubled in this period, yet its relative share was more than halved. Within this context the Department of Labor appears to constitute an exception, for the fourteen-fold increase in its dollar appropriation permitted Labor to double its relative share of total appropriations. A closer look at this extraordinary increase, however, reveals that appropriations to Labor from state funds have actually decreased, from $3.1 million in 1945 to $2.4 million in 1963. Thus almost all of the $44.5 million appropriated in 1963 is supported by federal, rather than state, funds. Significantly enough, no federal money is used to support appropriations made to Public Safety or to Revenue. While these data are hardly conclusive, they do suggest that access to federal funds is one method of improving the relative financial standing of an agency or program and they do suggest that such improvement is unlikely to occur without such access, or without access to some other external source of funds.

Such conclusions are both affirmed and qualified by the record of appropriations made for the major state functions, particularly Health and Welfare and Highways. Far and away the most significant increase, in dollars and in relative share of total appropriations, has been recorded by the Division of Highways, which jumped from 11.1 per cent of all appropriations in 1945 to 25.4 per cent in 1963, largely as a result of funds made available by the federal government. Federal highway grants have been important to Illinois finance, of course, for a half-century, but their magnitude recently has assumed new dimensions with the passage of the interstate highway program in 1956.[5] The impact of

---

[5] For a useful analysis of federal participation in Illinois finance see Phillip Monypenny, *The Impact of Federal Grants in Illinois* (Urbana: Institute of Government and Public Affairs, 1958).

this and other federal programs is evident in the fact that federal funds supported more than 65 per cent of the 1963 highway appropriation. In the Health and Welfare area, the doubling of the proportion of all appropriations allocated to the Department of Public Health (from .6 per cent to 1.2 per cent) can also be attributed to federal contributions, amounting to some 57 per cent of the department's total 1963 appropriation. Conversely, the Department of Mental Health, which receives relatively little federal aid, has not significantly improved its relative share of total appropriations since 1945, despite large-scale increases in appropriations from state sources in that period.

On the other hand, the Department of Public Aid has lost considerable ground to other agencies in spite of heavy reliance on federal support. Almost half (48 per cent) of the 1963 Public Aid appropriation was supported by anticipated federal money, but such aid was unable to prevent a decline in the Public Aid share of total appropriations to 16.3 per cent. The activities carried out by this department, of course, are rather unusual, in that they are primarily concerned with the distribution of money to dependent families and/or individuals. The magnitude of total payments made and the size of the federal contribution thus depend more upon social conditions which create dependency than on the real or imagined requirements of an administrative organization. Nevertheless, the experience of the Public Aid Department suggests that federal money alone is not sufficient to improve the relative importance of an agency or activity. For some agencies, large quantities of federal money may even prove inadequate to permit these agencies to maintain themselves against the more rapidly improving statuses of their expansionist sister agencies. Federal money is assuredly of great significance, and can improve agency status, but such a result is by no means guaranteed.

Apart from highways the only other relative increase of major proportions to occur in the past two decades has taken place in the field of education. Since 1945 state contributions to local school districts and to the support of the three university systems together have jumped from 13.9 per cent to 22.5 per cent of total state appropriations. As far as the university systems are concerned some of this increase is probably attributable to federal funds made available to the universities and retained by them outside of the state treasury. While such funds are not appropriated by the state, the additional personnel and equipment made possible by such grants has created an indirect pressure for higher levels of state support to accommodate enlarged programs. This sort of pressure aside, however, it is clear that the most significant source of pressure for higher university appropriations has been the rapid increase in the number of students seeking admission to the state-supported institutions. A bond issue for new buildings at the state universities was approved by referendum in 1960, thus providing a large share of the resources to support growing appropriations. At a lower educational level the correlate to this pressure has been the vast increase in numbers of children attending the public schools. This increase is clearly reflected in the expansion of state aid from the Common School Fund, which is entirely supported by state revenue.

From this record it seems clear enough that major changes in the relative level of support available to the various state agencies and programs have, in fact, occurred. The principal proportionate increases have been recorded by agencies involved in highway construction and the educational enterprise, while most other agencies, except for a few with access to federal money, appear to have declined in relative importance. The manner in which these major changes occurred is significant. A one-shot, $70 million supplemental request initiated by the Governor in 1957 opened the door to the expansion of federal highway grants to support state participation in the interstate highway program. Referenda approved by popular vote in 1960 paved the way for expansion of university and mental health appropriations, though only the universities significantly improved their relative standing as a result of these referenda. Expansion of state aid to local schools has also occurred, in part due to increasing numbers and in part due to changes in the state aid formula. Formula changes, however, have generally required gubernatorial consent, if not leadership. Thus the absence of such consent defeated a proposed formula change in 1963, despite considerable legislative and popular support.

Major increases occur, then, when (a) some external source of funds (in addition to state tax revenues) is available, (b) there is considerable popular support or pressure for such increases, and (c) the Governor supports such increases. Once adopted, these higher levels are assimilated by actors involved in the budget game as assumptions about the minimum level of appropriations to be made in the succeeding fiscal period. Precisely because they are incorporated as unquestioned assumptions rather than problems, actors in the budget and appropriations system will appear, at any given time, to be doing no more than what has been done before. And since these assumptions apply equally to major and minor programs, a higher level of support for an activity such as public aid, which may have been the object of a bitter political fight in one session, will be passed over quickly in succeeding sessions as something to be taken for granted, until sufficient pressure is generated by external actors to raise the issue of increasing the level of support once again. In this fashion incremental increases will typify most decisions made during any one session while major increases will occasionally occur, sometimes without question, and sometimes as an outcome of hard-fought political bargaining.

New activities will frequently be part of major appropriation increases—the interstate highway program or the new Chicago campus of the University of Illinois are examples. They may also result from gubernatorial decisions to implement different programs in less expensive areas, e.g., Governor Kerner's creation of a Board of Economic Development. But the Governor is severely limited in the new proposals he can offer in areas apart from the major state activities. Highways, Education, and Welfare continue to consume an increasing share of total state appropriations. To initiate a new activity in areas not related to the major state programs the Governor must find additional resources or he must literally take funds away from existing agencies. At best this is a difficult task, particularly since most existing agencies already are losing ground to the few agencies involved in the major state functions. Perhaps this difficulty explains why innovations in these less costly areas occur infrequently and, when they do occur, tend to take the form of new agencies closely related to existing agencies. Thus the relatively new Youth Commission and the new Department of Children and Family Services were both created from activities formerly conducted by the Department of Mental Health. Or again, the new Board of Economic Development was created by grafting some new activities and a new agency title onto several programs already in existence.

262

IS ANYBODY "GOVERNING"?

These considerations suggest a different perspective on the expenditure decisions made in 1963, a year in which there was neither a public outburst in favor of major new increases nor a gubernatorial commitment to promote such new directions. To be sure, several hundred million dollars in additional expenditures were approved in 1963, but these additions resulted more from past commitments than from present decisions. A one-shot decision made in 1957, coupled with statutory formulae governing gasoline taxes, made Illinois a partner of the federal government in a highway program which accounted for one-quarter of the 1963 budget. The increase which occurred in 1963 was something that the Governor, by his own admission, could do nothing about, since the state was already committed. Similar one-shot referenda approved in 1960 created long-term commitments which led to 1963 increases in mental health and higher education. Increases in these areas could be reduced slightly, but they could not be avoided. Existing statutes dictated a large school aid increase to accommodate greater numbers of pupils, again without requiring any new decisions in 1963. These were the areas in which major increases were recorded, but the commitments which produced the increases were made in other years, by other men, reacting to environmental pressures (school enrollments) or inducements (federal aid). Other agencies, playing the budget game, were able to achieve modest increases according to the more or less automatic patterns produced by the rules of that game. Over all, the state organization in 1963 appeared to be largely under the influence of environmental and organizational conditions which were at best dimly sensed, and thus beyond the conscious control of the actors involved.

But why, we may ask, were actors in 1963 willing to accept commitments without questioning them? As I pointed out earlier, contracts with the federal government can be reexamined, statutes can be changed, and procedures can be altered. Why, then, were none of these things done in 1963? Part of the answer, of course, is that attempts to achieve some reform were in fact attempted in 1963, but they were unsuccessful. The previous chapter has examined the failure of these attempts in some detail. Here I would like to offer two additional considerations, the first

of which has to do with widespread organizational reluctance to
see any virtue or effectiveness in reform. This attitude is particularly characteristic of the legislative and bureaucratic elite
and is composed of two parts. On the one hand the idea that
different techniques or organizational arrangements might improve the quality of expenditure decisions is dismissed as a
fanciful wish. Decisions to spend public money, in this view, are
bound to be imprecise and to some extent wasteful because they
are made by men whose prejudices cannot be made to coincide
neatly with the official purposes for which expenditures are made.
Other purposes, based upon political considerations, necessarily
creep in, regardless of the techniques used. "Sure, New York
may have 150 men working on their budget and California may
spend ten times more than we spend, but their decisions are
probably no better than ours" is a typical comment. Thus Governor Kerner's proposals for a program budget and for additions
to the staff of the Budget Division were generally regarded as
unnecessary. "What difference would it make?" was the response
of several officials. Another dismissed the program budget as
"something they want in Washington."

Associated with this attitude is a fatalistic acceptance of the
state's inability to fully control its financial affairs. With performance standards as well as total sums available determined by
federal officials in activities such as highway construction or
categorical aid to dependent persons, state actors frequently assert their inability to exert an independent influence over such
activities. Some, in fact, appear to have given up any attempt to
formulate and impose state judgments. As one official in a heavily
subsidized agency put it, "We can't tell how much we will get
from the federal government until the federal allotment comes in.
We spend whatever they give us, but it's impossible for us to
tell in advance how much it will be."

The second, and far more significant, consideration is the
absence of any well-developed conception of the purposes to be
served by actions of the state organization. Indeed, the entire
question of what "state government" is supposed to mean in
Illinois, and how this government is distinguished from local and
national governments is a subject scrupulously avoided by everyone involved in "state" action. State political parties do not
compete against one another on the basis of opposing ideologies,

or alternative programs of action; one slate of candidates competes against another slate of candidates for designated offices, with both slates exchanging charges of incompetence, inefficiency, or even corruption in the conduct of activities which are seldom mentioned. Assuming office, the victorious head of the ticket thus has no clear mandate for action and must, as Governor, formulate his own program and seek to impose it upon a situation in which there is neither a public nor an organizational definition of state—as opposed to agency or interest group—goals. Faced with this problem all recent governors have chosen the easy, and perhaps the only way out, financially, by retreating to the rhetoric of economy and efficiency practiced by their predecessors.[6] Symbolically useful, but ineffective in practice, the rhetoric of "fiscal integrity" has been repeatedly expressed by Democrat and Republican alike, in good times as well as bad, and has helped to obscure the question of what distinctive purposes, if any, are served or should be served by "state government" in Illinois.

This, of course, is the ultimate "political" question which confronts those who seek to control the state organization. Without an operative answer to this question the state organization must continue to be dominated by environmental pressures, reflected through the actions of other governments. Changing statutes and procedures, or reexamining federal contracts, are inherently political matters, involving changes in goals and changes in power relationships. In the absence of an articulated "state" purpose such adjustments can occur only when they are forced upon the organization by external pressure. Adjustments forced by external pressures have occurred with some regularity in the past, and in all probability will continue to occur in the future. So long as the state organization continues to lack recognized goals of its own, its influence over the course of such adjustments will be minimal. Buffeted by the push of federal funds and the pull of locally

---

[6] Summarizing gubernatorial orientations from 1933 to the present, Gilbert Y. Steiner and Samuel K. Gove write: "One of the most striking characteristics is the unchanging character of the major issues on which the governors focus. Of these, a point which comes home clearly is the continuing emphasis that has been placed on the need for economy in state government. Through depression, war, peace, and prosperity, Illinois governors have agreed on economy as a major theme." See "Governors, Issues, and Styles: 1933-1960," *op. cit.*, p. 34.

based educational needs, the state can only react to such pressures as they come, allowing others to set priorities in willy-nilly fashion. In such a context state decision-makers and their organization alike are caught in the middle, without a course of their own and without a compass to guide them.

Expenditure decisions made within this framework can allocate resources but they can seldom allocate values. It is entirely possible, of course, that nothing the state could do would permit it to impose its own values, if it had articulated such values, upon the decisions it must make every two years. Environmental pressures and the structure of relationships with other governments may well have developed to a point at which a politics of purpose is simply beyond the reach of the state. If so, the meaning of the concept "government," as applied to the Illinois state organization, may require considerable reevaluation. Financially speaking, many of the actions taken by the state are beyond its ability to control, while those areas which are susceptible to state direction are normally left to go their own way, unattended by anyone operating from a "state" point of view. The trappings of Constitutional sovereignty exist, but the expenditure decisions made under this protective umbrella are not the decisions of a sovereign; they are the decisions of an organizational system grown tired with age and enervated by a willingness to let others determine the direction in which the lifeblood of the organization shall flow. At best, the politics of expenditure in Illinois is a politics of games. At worst, it is a politics of futility.

DECISIONAL HISTORY OF AGENCY APPROPRIATIONS FOR 73rd BIENNIUM
(GENERAL REVENUE FUND)

	72nd Appropriation	72nd Expenditure	72nd Lapse	73rd Request	Total 73rd Request	Budgetary Commission[a]	Governor[a]	Budget Book	General Assembly[a]	Approved
Legislative Agencies	8,274,805	6,133,909	2,140,896	6,816,157	6,816,157	8,778		6,807,379	953,631	7,761,010
Judicial Agencies	11,814,656	10,925,515	899,141	24,585,836	24,585,836	417,545	723,347	23,444,944	426,411	23,871,355
Governor	596,316	562,348	33,968	605,220	605,220			605,220	1,200	604,020
Lt. Governor	114,800	95,097	19,703	112,300	112,300			112,300		112,300
Secretary of State	12,220,980	11,295,752	925,228	11,203,402 / 1,393,613[b]	12,597,015	50,000	832,846[b]	11,714,769	1,051,156	12,765,925
State Treasurer	4,663,150	4,207,008	456,142	3,962,150	3,962,150			3,962,150		3,962,150
Auditor of P.A.										
Operations	3,050,910	2,569,314	481,596	2,715,950	2,715,950	100,000		2,615,950	700	2,615,250
Common Sch. Fund[c]	393,396,000	398,392,873	3,127							433,090,000
Super. Pub. Inst.										
Oper. & Dist. Grants	51,810,149	51,340,910	469,239	77,948,344	612,198,344	20,988,110	6,750,000	63,710,234	4,141,700	67,851,934
Common Sch. Fund[c]				534,250,000		85,160,000	16,000,000	433,090,000		
Attorney General	3,162,600	3,116,796	45,804	3,162,600	3,162,600			3,162,600	300,000	3,462,600
University of Illinois	133,741,170	133,571,925	169,245	160,494,000 / 33,893,740[b]	194,387,740	4,427,819 / 14,925,200[b]	18,968,540[b]	156,066,681	4,414,840	160,481,521

Southern Ill. Univ.	41,986,941	41,852,130	134,811	61,072,998 / 41,472,446[b]	102,545,444	6,878,475 / 23,960,000[b]	54,761,163	3,689,154	58,450,317
Tea. College Bd.	47,475,140	47,331,656	143,484	63,646,047 / 7,442,982[b]	71,089,029	863,766 / 16,965,806[b]	64,164,186 / 6,071,087[b]	879,765	65,043,951
Dept. of Aeronautics	6,290,635	5,417,797	872,838	8,325,157	8,325,157	868,042 / 3,000,000	4,967,115	22,059	4,989,174
Dept. of Agriculture	12,347,240	10,125,794	2,221,446	12,320,159 / 185,000[b]	12,505,159	476,220 / 250,000 / 185,000[b]	11,593,939	1,002,690	12,596,629
Dept. of Audits	685,802	655,003	30,799	1,077,929	1,077,929	397,929	680,000	5,825	685,825
Dept. of Conservation	9,757,920	5,903,218	3,854,702	6,241,628 / 6,443,525[b]	12,685,153	47,893 / 6,098,786[b]	6,598,474	1,984,635	8,583,109
Dept. of Finance, Oper.	6,095,336	5,167,378	927,958	6,336,264	6,336,264		6,336,264	258,520	6,594,784
Dept. of Finance Ins.	4,804,565	4,082,918	721,647	4,836,081	4,836,081	504,536	4,331,545	496,000	4,827,545
Dept. of Insurance	2,471,544	2,297,881	173,663	2,797,940	2,797,940	321,280	2,476,660	494,145	2,970,805
Dept. of Labor	2,329,330	1,972,601	356,729	7,206,740	7,206,740	4,915,120	2,291,620	130,685	2,422,305
Dept. of Mental Health	206,136,237	187,128,991	19,007,246	255,519,210 / 2,538,200[b]	258,057,410	17,625,000 / 2,538,200[b]	237,894,210	9,808,715	247,702,925
Military & Naval Dept. (armories)	6,256,000 / 232,020	5,322,795 / 231,308	933,205 / 712	5,631,710 / 340,000[b]	5,971,710	340,860 / 340,000 / 263,000[b]	5,553,850	292,940	5,846,790
Dept. of Mines & Min.	1,409,061	1,396,246	12,815	1,477,567	1,477,567	37,040 / 18,720	1,459,247	29,570	1,488,817
Dept. of Personnel	1,787,930	1,615,200	172,730	1,680,020	1,680,020		1,680,020	52,230	1,732,250
Dept. of Public Health	19,853,579	18,862,913	990,666	24,980,521 / 1,359,400[b]	26,339,921	5,318,695 / 26,240 / 1,359,400[b]	19,688,066	1,211,813	20,899,879
Dept. of Public Safety	42,286,782	29,480,278	12,806,504	32,949,735 / 30,308,648[b]	63,258,383	800,000 / 660,000 / 21,638,587[b]	40,774,796	4,080,484	36,744,312
Dept. of Public Works & Bldgs. (no hwys.)	14,939,056	9,866,569	5,072,487	6,091,590 / 8,054,800[b]	14,146,390	328,320 / 1,586,500[b]	12,232,070	5,991,046	18,223,116

DECISIONAL HISTORY OF AGENCY APPROPRIATIONS FOR 73rd BIENNIUM (GENERAL REVENUE FUND)

	72nd Appropriation	72nd Expenditure	72nd Lapse	73rd Request	Total 73rd Request	Budgetary Commission[a]	Governor[a]	Budget Book	General Assembly[a]	Approved
Dept. of Reg. & Ed.	8,778,154	7,648,009	1,130,145	10,389,606 / 698,519[b]	11,088,125	1,633,972	698,519[b]	8,755,634	988,895	9,754,529
Dept. of Revenue	16,762,650	15,826,843	935,807	19,370,765	19,370,765	260,000	602,160	18,508,605	545,260	19,053,865
Dept. of Public Aid Federal Funds State Funds	615,707,478 280,586,446 335,121,032	604,556,192	11,151,286	701,556,483 302,721,06 398,835,415	701,556,483	254,716 63,178,621		638,123,146 302,466,352 335,656,794	1,881,255	640,004,401
Youth Commission	19,799,531	17,614,321	2,185,210	20,863,200 / 3,197,600[b]	24,060,800	1,940,769	8,197,600[b]	18,922,431	3,499,575	22,422,006
Athletic Commission	159,460	136,867	22,593	141,262	141,262			141,262	4,530	145,792
Bd. of Ed. for Blind & Deaf	160,000	147,187	12,813	200,000	200,000	20,000		180,000		180,000
Bldg. Bond Board	300,000	205,959	94,041							
Civil Defense Agency	267,760	258,064	9,696	607,990	607,990	145,830		462,160	22,905	485,065
Civil Service Comm.	186,030	159,425	26,605	193,690	193,690	12,960		180,730	5,610	186,340
Commerce Comm.	2,524,084	2,062,146	461,938	2,524,084	2,524,084			2,524,084	2,009,093	514,991
Bd. of Econ. Development	536,767	498,650	38,117	854,192	854,192	343,275	343,275	854,192	214,200	1,068,392
Fair Emp. Prac. Comm.	100,000	96,206	3,794	170,420	170,420	45,420	25,000	150,000		150,000
Great Lakes Comm.	22,500	18,520	3,980	22,500	22,500			22,500		22,500

Comm. for Handicapped Children	123,055	112,173	10,882	198,625	198,625	*75,570*		123,055	*23,055*d	100,000
Harness Racing Comm.	155,085	148,394	6,691	316,590	316,590	*48,880*		267,710	50,750	318,460
Bd. of Higher Ed.	150,000	98,624	51,376	150,000	150,000			150,000		150,000
Historical Library	513,332	506,991	6,341	541,212	541,212	*20,540*	13,040	533,712	14,085	547,797
Housing Board	383,460	316,565	66,895	296,188	296,188	*23,288*		272,900	33,548	306,448
Comm. on Human Rel.	103,970	86,903	17,067	167,400	167,400	*167,400*	167,400	167,400	*61,160*	106,250
Industrial Comm.	1,536,716	1,429,706	107,010	1,826,761	1,826,761	*279,040*		1,547,721	59,370	1,607,091
Ind. Dev. Authority	100,000	26,914	73,086							
Joliet Reg. Port Dist.	50,000	27,845	22,155	30,000	30,000	*15,000*		30,000		30,000
Liquor Cont. Comm.	746,792	703,036	43,756	873,988	873,988			858,988	30,655	889,643
Med. Center Comm.	1,624,636	1,406,162	218,474	223,336 / 2,699,421b	2,922,757		2,699,421b	223,336	1,309,075	1,532,411
N.E. Metro. Pl. Area	100,000	100,000		200,000	200,000	*100,000*		100,000		100,000
Racing Board	665,895	619,961	45,934	747,120	747,120			747,120	99,667	846,787
Scholarship Comm.	4,971,240	4,095,035	876,205	5,025,364	5,025,364	*105,840*		4,919,524	257,095	5,176,619
Sch. Bldg. Comm.	10,552,201	5,145,536	5,406,665	12,067,280	12,067,280	*1,515,079*b	4,000,000b	6,552,201		6,552,201
Sp.-Am. War Vets.	12,000	11,864	136	12,000	12,000			12,000	*9,000*	3,000
St. Emp. Ret. System	10,819,104	10,706,553	112,551	37,202,828	37,202,828	*23,677,081*		13,625,747	66,945	13,692,692
Tea. Ret. System	4,970,000	4,970,000		4,060,000	4,060,000			4,060,000		4,060,000
Tri-City Reg. Port Dist.	158,193	157,040	1,153	141,080	141,080			141,080		141,080
Univ. Civil Ser. Mer. Bd.	181,437	169,498	11,939	209,148	209,148	*27,711*		181,437		181,437
Univ. Ret. System	-15,500	15,500		4,960,300	4,960,300	*4,912,600*		47,700		47,700
Vets. Comm.	2,452,470	2,369,022	83,448	2,326,099	2,326,099	*96,360*		2,289,739	237,900	2,527,639

DECISIONAL HISTORY OF AGENCY APPROPRIATIONS FOR 73rd BIENNIUM (GENERAL REVENUE FUND)

	72nd Appropriation	72nd Expenditure	72nd Lapse	73rd Request	Total 73rd Request	Budgetary Commission[a]	Governor[a]	Budget Book	General Assembly[a]	Approved
Bd. of Voc. Ed.	9,517,899	9,503,486	14,413	9,191,385	9,191,385	*8,785,081*		6,406,304	643,781	7,050,085
Wab. Val. Int. Comm.	30,000	30,000		46,815	46,815			46,815	*16,815*	30,000
Waukegan Port Dist.	278,000	180,112	97,888	278,000	278,000	*50,000*		228,000	162,750	390,750
Voc. Rehab.	3,950,776	3,948,471	2,305	5,688,103	5,688,103	*640,814*	50,000	5,097,289	25,005	5,122,294
Court of Claims	138,431	100,854	37,577	117,431	117,431			117,431	36	117,467
Ill. Bldg. Authority								150,000		150,000
S.W. Metro. Area									37,500	37,500

[a] Reductions are italicized.

[b] Capital item.

[c] Budgeted to Superintendent of Public Instruction but appropriated to Auditor of Public Accounts.

[d] A statute enacted in 1963 replaced this commission with the Commission on Children and reduced the appropriation by this sum.

Source: Compiled from figures made available by the Department of Finance and from the following sources: State of Illinois, Department of Finance, *Forty-Sixth Annual Report* (Springfield, 1963); State of Illinois, Department of Finance, *Appropriations, Regular Session, 73rd General Assembly* (Springfield, 1963); State of Illinois, Department of Finance, *Financial Program for Illinois for 73rd Biennium* (Springfield, 1963); State of Illinois, Department of Finance, *The Illinois State Budget for the Biennium July 1, 1963 to June 30, 1965* (Springfield, 1963); State of Illinois, Department of Finance, *Appropriations, Regular Session, 72nd General Assembly* (Springfield, 1961).

INDEX

Abstract norms: absent from system, 192-193

Accounting: for line-item appropriation, 34; relationship to budgetary system, 35-36; and expenditure control, 46; juggling of accounts, 46; sophistication in larger agencies, 46-47; and agency budget roles, 52; and strategies, 69-70; and 73rd budget, 133-134; and decision-making, 203-204; effect of inaccuracy, 204; system expanded by functional appropriations, 228, 232

Accuracy: in decision-making, 179-180

Aeronautics, Department of: elimination recommended, 210

Agencies: influence on budget hearings, 40-41; submission of budget requests, 40-41; multiple appropriation bills, 151; Budgetary Commission expectations of, 185; Governor's expectations of, 187; advantages of budget game, 205; definition of "functional" categories, 230; effect of functional budget on, 235

Agency officials: uniformity of financial orientation, 44-53; length of state employment, 45; divorced from policy-making, 45-56; view of term "budget," 45-56; view of budget review, 47; prediction of budget decisions, 48-49; sensitivity to legislative scrutiny, 63; use of object accounts, 70; proprietary interest in basic budget, 70-71; and organizational change, 75; interest in appropriation bills, 181-182; expectations of other actors, 183; view of functional budgeting, 228; power summarized, 247

Aggressiveness: in budget hearings, 60

Amendments: by appropriations committees, 1963, 160

An Act in Relation to State Finance, 15

Appropriation: for judicial salaries, 91

Appropriation bills: relationship to budget, 147-148; lack of supporting information, 148; drafted by different agencies, 149; variation in authority to spend money, 149-150; lack of standard format, 151; relationship to budget, summarized, 153; Budgetary Commission review assumed, 154-155; House votes, 173-175; Senate votes, 174-175; as focus of legislator expectations, 186

Appropriations: legal characteristics, 9; increase between 1909 and 1913, 11n; must balance with revenues, 11n; "objects and purposes" format required, 14; formal relationship to requests, 18; increases since 1949, summarized, 19-20; relationship to accounting categories, 28-29; and basic-supplemental budgeting, 34-35, 71; agency view of relationship to

46, 49; early submission of, 77; as understood by Budgetary Commission, 91, 95; date of presentation, 147; as viewed by legislators, 153-154; use of "functional" categories, 230; effects of late presentation, 238-239. *See also* Budgeting; Decision-making; Review

Budget Advisory Committee: plans activities, 130; purposes explained by Kerner, 130; access to detailed budget forms gained, 131; activities analyzed, 131-132; proposes format change, 132-133

Budget comparisons: contents, 98

Budget Department: discussed by Kerner, 130

Budget Division: powers and duties specified, 13; orientation described, 39

Budget examiners: four employed by Finance Department, 38; responsibilities described, 38; clerk orientation, 38-39; distribution of responsibilities, 39; attend budget hearings, 40

Budget instructions: prepared by Finance Department, 28; distributed in Mental Health Department, 58

Budget message: 1961, 122-123; 1963, 139

Budget Superintendent: and existing informational categories, 36; watchdog orientation, 36; definition of Budget Division responsibilities, 39; orientation, 43, 189-190; power summarized, 248. *See also* Leth, T. R.

Budgetary Commission: established by law, 17, 77; powers and duties, 17, 78, 82-83, 85, 110-111; reputation, 37, 47-49, 76, 104, 106n, 109, 110, 154-155, 183, 186; role orientation,

48, 81, 85, 91-98 *passim,* 103-108 *passim,* 184, 212-215; use of information, 48, 97-99, 102; support for present appropriation levels, 51; and Governor, 79-80, 83-85, 104, 110-111, 137, 188; occasional reports issued, 79n, 161n; criticized, 81, 82, 211; approves Hodge's supplemental request, 82; appropriation enlarged, 1959, 83; membership, 86-90 *passim;* hearings, 90, 95, 212-215; and special funds, 92; reductions claimed, 93, 95, 121, 137; disagreement over Mines and Minerals budget, 107-108; power analyzed, 110, 246-247; rejects proposals of Economy Subcommittee, 212-215

Budgeting: and Governor, 18-19, 109-110, 113, 116, 123-124, 134-139, 140; as seen by Budget Superintendent, 25-28, 40, 41; and information, 29-33, 35-36, 52, 203-204; rules of the game, 36-38, 49, 51; and governmental "management," 46; as filling out forms, 46, 52n-53n; as translation of accounts, 47; and policy determination, 49, 56-57, 63, 71, 74-75; by Constitutional officers, 113-114; and businessmen, 129-134; and decentralization, 205; as model, compared to Illinois system, 251-252. *See also* Budget

Building Authority: Kerner administration use announced, 137; use explained, 141-142; S.B. 1177, 142-144; S.B. 1161, 144; S.B. 1233 passed, 144. *See also* Capital expenditures

Bureau of the Budget: compared to proposed state budget department, 130

Burkhead, Jesse, 252n

278

mission, 68; and accounting ambiguity, 69-70; and federal funds, 72; of Economy Bloc, 217-219

Stratton, William G. (former Governor): selection of Director of Finance, 24n; relationship to Leth, 27n; and Mental Health appropriations, 53; and Budgetary Commission, 81; vetoes expanded Budgetary Commission appropriation, 83; view of gubernatorial transitions, 120n; and centralization, 242n

Subcommittee on Economy Measures: report issued, September, 1962, 210

Superintendent of Budgets. See Budget Superintendent; Leth, T. R.

Superintendent of Public Instruction: S.B. 823 (1963) compared to budget, 151-153

Supplemental appropriations: number enacted, 179n; effect on decision-making, 179-180

Supplemental budget request: defined, 34-35; agencies expect elimination, 47, 184; submission to Budgetary Commission desirable, 51-52; as focus of Budgetary Commission questioning, 99; reduced by Budgetary Commission, 100, 104

Sweeney, Edmund (Senator): Budgetary Commission member, 89

Symbolism: of budget cuts, 201

System: as ratifier of major adjustments, 199-200; symbolic justification, 201; as holding operation, 202; distinguished from organization, 206-207; in Illinois, compared to "budgeting," 251-252; in Illinois, compared to "incrementalism," 253-255; and value allocation, 265

Task force: on revenue, 1961, 121

Task Force on Budget. See Budget Advisory Committee

Tax opposition: as symbol, exploited by Governor, 188-189

Taxpayers' Federation of Illinois: assists House Appropriations Committee, 1951, 161n; provides information to Economy Subcommittee, 213; provides staff assistance to Economy Bloc, 217

Teachers College Board: in Department of Registration and Education, 21; Governor's financial controls, 114

Transfers: consent of Governor required, 113

Truman campaign, 1948: managed by Powell in southern Illinois, 86

Uncertainty: and budget estimates, 65

Universities: retention of endowment funds, gifts, trust funds, and federal aid funds, 16; reductions by Higher Education Board listed, 94; capital expenditures influenced by Governor, 114n; appropriations, 1945-63, 259-260

University of Illinois: and Everett R. Peters, 87; Governor's financial controls, 114; functional budget categories, 230

University Retirement System: budget reduced, 95

Values: of system, 196-199; and decision-making, 248-249; and Illinois framework, 264-265

Veterans Bureau Fund: use by Mental Health Department, 72

Veterans' Commission: abolishment recommended, 210; ap-